ECONOMICS AND FOREIGN INVESTMENT IN CHINA

ECONOMICS AND FOREIGN INVESTMENT IN CHINA

J. I. CHENG
EDITOR

Nova Science Publishers, Inc.
New York

For permission to use material from this book please contact us:
Telephone 631-231-7269; Fax 631-231-8175
Web Site: http://www.novapublishers.com

NOTICE TO THE READER

The Publisher has taken reasonable care in the preparation of this book, but makes no expressed or implied warranty of any kind and assumes no responsibility for any errors or omissions. No liability is assumed for incidental or consequential damages in connection with or arising out of information contained in this book. The Publisher shall not be liable for any special, consequential, or exemplary damages resulting, in whole or in part, from the readers' use of, or reliance upon, this material.

This publication is designed to provide accurate and authoritative information with regard to the subject matter covered herein. It is sold with the clear understanding that the Publisher is not engaged in rendering legal or any other professional services. If legal or any other expert assistance is required, the services of a competent person should be sought. FROM A DECLARATION OF PARTICIPANTS JOINTLY ADOPTED BY A COMMITTEE OF THE AMERICAN BAR ASSOCIATION AND A COMMITTEE OF PUBLISHERS.

LIBRARY OF CONGRESS CATALOGING-IN-PUBLICATION DATA
Available upon request.

ISBN 13 1-60021-238-7
ISBN 10 1-60021-238-7

Published by Nova Science Publishers, Inc. ✦ New York

CONTENTS

PREFACE

This book includes in its scope the entire spectrum of contemporary politics and economics of China. The coverage is intended to deal with China, its political dynamics, economic policies, institutions and its future.

Topics include: foreign policy; domestic policy; treaties; monetary and fiscal policies; foreign economic aid; military policies; inflation news; security affairs; government; environment; elections; political parties and their activities; trade balance reports; energy policies; aging; pensions and insurance; interactions with international political and economic organizations; industrial policies; saving rates.

Concern has grown in Congress and elsewhere about China's military modernization. The topic is an increasing factor in discussions over future required U.S. Navy capabilities. As discussed in chapter 1, the issue for Congress addressed in this report is: How should China's military modernization be factored into decisions about U.S. Navy programs?

Several elements of China's military modernization have potential implications for future required U.S. Navy capabilities. These include theater-range ballistic missiles (TBMs), land-attack cruise missiles (LACMs), anti-ship cruise missiles (ASCMs), surface-to-air missiles (SAMs), land-based aircraft, submarines, surface combatants, amphibious ships, naval mines, nuclear weapons, and possibly high-power microwave (HPM) devices. China's naval limitations or weaknesses include capabilities for operating in waters more distant from China, joint operations, C4ISR (command, control, communications, computers, intelligence, surveillance, and reconnaissance), long-range surveillance and targeting systems, anti-air warfare (AAW), antisubmarine warfare (ASW), mine countermeasures (MCM), and logistics.

Observers believe a near-term focus of China's military modernization is to field a force that can succeed in a short-duration conflict with Taiwan and act as an anti-access force to deter U.S. intervention or delay the arrival of U.S. forces, particularly naval and air forces, in such a conflict. Some analysts speculate that China may attain (or believe that it has attained) a capable maritime anti-access force, or elements of it, by about 2010. Other observers believe this will happen later. Potential broader or longer-term goals of China's naval modernization include asserting China's regional military leadership and protecting China's maritime territorial, economic, and energy interests.

China's naval modernization has potential implications for required U.S. Navy capabilities in terms of preparing for a conflict in the Taiwan Strait area, maintaining U.S. Navy presence and military influence in the Western Pacific, and countering Chinese ballistic missile submarines. Preparing for a conflict in the Taiwan Strait area could place a premium on the following: on-station or early-arriving Navy forces, capabilities for defeating China's maritime anti-access forces, and capabilities for operating in an environment that could be characterized by information warfare and possibly electromagnetic pulse (EMP) and the use of nuclear weapons.

Certain options are available for improving U.S. Navy capabilities by 2010; additional options, particularly in shipbuilding, can improve U.S. Navy capabilities in subsequent years. China's naval modernization raises potential issues for Congress concerning the role of China in Department of Defense (DOD) and Navy planning; the size of the Navy; the Pacific Fleet's share of the Navy; forward homeporting of Navy ships in the Western Pacific; the number of aircraft carriers, submarines, and ASW-capable platforms; Navy missile defense, air-warfare, AAW, ASW, and mine warfare programs; Navy computer network security; and EMP hardening of Navy systems. This report will be updated as events warrant.

Jingwai juezhan, roughly translated as decisive battle offshore, offshore full-scale engagement, winning of the war off the Taiwanese coast, or outside of Taiwan or offshore engagement with the enemy, is one of the new jargons/slogans put forward by the Chen Shui-bian administration in Taiwan in June 2000 and is discussed in chapter 2.

Different interpretations and insights could emerge, if we were to associate this military jargon with another concept, geographic feature, and so on. If we pair it with the political jargon, Republic of China (ROC), we would have noticed that Chen is thinking himself in terms of the president of the ROC on Taiwan, which is at least politically different from national titles like the ROC; the Republic of Taiwan (ROT); Taiwan State (*guo*), the ROC; and so on. This should be a somewhat relief to the Beijing leaders, because the usage *jingwai*, implies that the Chen administration still legally takes the ROC's territory on mainland China into consideration.

Juezhan jingwai and *jingwai juezhan* are discussed and they are quite different. The former gives one the notion that the Taiwan armed forces may fire the first shot, whereas the latter gives us the impression that the Taiwan armed forces would react to an attack first launched by the Chinese People's Liberation Army (CPLA).

On the whole, the jargon *jingwai juezhan* is barely acceptable, because it can be applied to cyber war, which has to involve computers on the mainland. It is a form of deterrence, however controversial. The main reason for controversy is because tension flared up between both sides of the Taiwan Strait since July 1995, especially Lee's pronouncement of the "special state to state relationship" policy in July 1999. But, Taipei's (potential) enemy should fully understand this newest jargon, *jingwai juezhan*. As mentioned earlier, the purpose of deterrence is to avoid war. If a war broke out between both sides of the Taiwan Strait, it simply means that the jargon has failed to do its intended job. The ROC's survival cannot be based on this jargon alone. In other words, there should be other concepts and so on at work, which may strengthen, complement, detract, etc. *jingwai juezhan*.

How does inward foreign direct investment (FDI) affect a transitional economy? This study in chapter 3 attempts to analyze the role of FDI in China's income growth and market-oriented transition. We first identify possible channels through which FDI may have positive or negative effects on the Chinese economy. Using a reasonable growth model and cross-section and panel data in the period of 1984-98, we provide an empirical assessment, which suggests that FDI seems to help China's transition and promote income growth, and that this positive growth-effect seems to rise over time and to be stronger in the coastal than the inland regions.

Since economic reform began in 1978, the People's Republic of China (PRC) has sought the benefits of capitalism without surrendering government control of the commanding heights of the PRC's economy. The PRC has largely adhered to openness to international trade and investment, one of the characteristics of successful market economies. Not surprisingly, the PRC's greatest strength is its integration with the global economy.

As discussed in chapter 4, although the PRC has made some progress toward achieving other characteristics of successful market economies, the PRC retains many of the detrimental characteristics of command economies. In particular, the PRC's four major state-owned banks and other depository institutions have extended too many questionable loans to the state-owned enterprises and the state-influenced enterprises based on industrial policy, *guanxi* (i.e., connections) with government officials, or outright corruption. Along with below-market interest rates and distorted prices, non-market lending has sustained the PRC's unusually high rate of investment in capital assets (i.e., equipment, software, and structures) of 43.6 percent of GDP in 2004. In turn, this high investment rate has boosted the PRC's real GDP growth rate to 9.5 percent in 2004.

However, many state-owned enterprises and state-influenced enterprises are unprofitable. Protected through *guanxi* from bankruptcy and foreclosure, many state-owned enterprises and state-influenced enterprises are either unable or unwilling to service their debts. Consequently, non-market lending has saddled the PRC's four major state-owned banks and other depository institutions with enormous portfoliosof non-performing loans. Private economists estimate that the cost of resolving the PRC's bad loan problem would be about 40 percent of the PRC's GDP.

Non-market lending encouraged the state-owned enterprises and the state-influenced enterprises to invest in too many capital assets and the wrong types of capital assets to produce goods and services to satisfy market demand. The eventual liquidation of the resulting overinvestment or malinvestment poses a significant long-term risk to the continuation of the PRC's economic growth. Given the PRC's integration with the global economy, a significant slowdown or recession in the PRC could diminish the prospects for economic growth in the United States and other countries around the world.

In recent years, the United States and other countries have expressed considerable concern that China's national currency (the yuan or renminbi) is seriously undervalued. Some analysts say the yuan needs to rise by as much as 40% in order to reflect its equilibrium value. Critics say that China's undervalued currency provides it with an unfair trade advantage that has seriously injured the manufacturing sector in the United States. Chinese officials counter that they have not pegged the yuan to the dollar in order to gain trade advantages. Rather, they say the fixed rate promotes economic stability that is vital for the functioning of its domestic economy.

On July 21, 2005, China announced a new foreign exchange system which is intended to allow more flexibility and to permit the international value of the yuan to be established by market forces. The yuan was increased in value by 2% and a "managed float" was introduced. However, the value of the yuan has changed little since then. Despite the publication of many studies, scholars do not agree whether or by what percent the yuan is undervalued. The wide range of estimates suggests that there is no reason to believe that any particular figure is correct. It is not clear that the U.S. trade deficit would be lower or U.S. manufacturers would benefit if China raised the value of the yuan. In the short run, U.S. producers might be able to sell higher-priced products to U.S. consumers if the inflow of Chinese goods were reduced. In the long run, though, as long as the United States is a net importer of capital, it will have a trade deficit and other countries will ultimately replace China as suppliers of low-cost goods to the U.S. market.

The Treasury Department has strongly urged China in recent years to adopt procedures that would allow the yuan to rise in value. Congress is considering legislation that would penalize China if its currency is not revalued. The United States has pursued the yuan-dollar exchange rate issue as a bilateral U.S.-China issue. Other countries are also affected by the presumably undervalued yuan — some more than the U.S. — but they have allowed the United States to take the lead.

As discussed in chapter 5, there are at least five ways the United States could deal with the yuan exchange rate issue. Some of these would involve other countries more explicitly in the process. First, the United States could continue pressing China publicly to raise the value of the yuan on the assumption that change will not occur without foreign pressure. Second, it could stop pressing China publicly, on the expectation that China might move more rapidly towards reform if it is not pressured. Third, the United States could restrict imports from China pending action to revalue the yuan. Fourth, the U.S. could ask the IMF to declare that China is manipulating its currency in violation of IMF rules. Fifth, the United States could refer the issue to the World Trade Organization (WTO), asserting that the United States has been injured by unfair trade practices linked to the undervaluation of China's currency. The WTO, in turn, could authorize trade remedies (tariffs on Chinese goods, for example) aimed at correcting this abuse. This report will be updated as new developments arise.

The recent success of transnational advertising campaigns starring Chinese NBA star Yao Ming—spokesman for Citibank and Apple--underscores the robust potential for international collaboration in advertising. Yet, aside from a few notable exceptions, American advertisers have yet to penetrate the Chinese consumer veneer in China. Observers suggest that difficulties in reaching the Chinese market stem from Westerners' poor understanding of how to engage consumers in a venerable Eastern culture. In chapter 6, the present study content analyzed television commercials aired during prime time in these two countries to contrast the differential uses of advertising appeals and images conveyed in these commercials and to explicate these differences from a cultural perspective.

Chapter 7 presents a picture of administrative barriers to foreign direct investment (FDI) in China –its current situation, manifestations, causes, damaging effect and related measures to curb it. China is in a transition from a closed economy to an open market economy. Administrative barriers to FDI in China is reflected largely in investment restriction, non-transparent and inaccessible FDI rule and regulation, as well as bureaucratic interference in terms of the distortion of FDI operation behavior and the preclusion of market competition. They have become a pressing issue facing foreign investors in making decision to invest in china. China has made great effort to develop a regulation framework on incentive FDI, but this framework currently appears weak and powerless in the face of the administrative barriers. However, the construction of a complete legal framework for FDI and rebuild the government administrative system will be undoubtedly helpful in removing excessive administrative barriers.

Highlights of GAO-06-231, a report to congressional committees, are outlined in chapter 8.

In: Economics and Foreign Investment in China
Editor: J.I. Cheng, pp. 1-66

ISBN 1-60021-238-7

Chapter 1

CHINA NAVAL MODERNIZATION: IMPLICATIONS FOR U.S.NAVY CAPABILITIES - BACKGROUND AND ISSUES FOR CONGRESS[*]

Ronald O'Rourke

ABSTRACT

Concern has grown in Congress and elsewhere about China's military modernization. The topic is an increasing factor in discussions over future required U.S. Navy capabilities. The issue for Congress addressed in this report is: How should China's military modernization be factored into decisions about U.S. Navy programs?

Several elements of China's military modernization have potential implications for future required U.S. Navy capabilities. These include theater-range ballistic missiles (TBMs), land-attack cruise missiles (LACMs), anti-ship cruise missiles (ASCMs), surface-to-air missiles (SAMs), land-based aircraft, submarines, surface combatants, amphibious ships, naval mines, nuclear weapons, and possibly high-power microwave (HPM) devices. China's naval limitations or weaknesses include capabilities for operating in waters more distant from China, joint operations, C4ISR (command, control, communications, computers, intelligence, surveillance, and reconnaissance), long-range surveillance and targeting systems, anti-air warfare (AAW), antisubmarine warfare (ASW), mine countermeasures (MCM), and logistics.

Observers believe a near-term focus of China's military modernization is to field a force that can succeed in a short-duration conflict with Taiwan and act as an anti-access force to deter U.S. intervention or delay the arrival of U.S. forces, particularly naval and air forces, in such a conflict. Some analysts speculate that China may attain (or believe that it has attained) a capable maritime anti-access force, or elements of it, by about 2010. Other observers believe this will happen later. Potential broader or longer-term goals of China's naval modernization include asserting China's regional military leadership and protecting China's maritime territorial, economic, and energy interests.

China's naval modernization has potential implications for required U.S. Navy capabilities in terms of preparing for a conflict in the Taiwan Strait area, maintaining U.S. Navy presence and military influence in the Western Pacific, and countering Chinese ballistic missile submarines. Preparing for a conflict in the Taiwan Strait area

---

[*] Excerpted from CRS Report RL33153 dated November 18, 2005.

could place a premium on the following: on-station or early-arriving Navy forces, capabilities for defeating China's maritime anti-access forces, and capabilities for operating in an environment that could be characterized by information warfare and possibly electromagnetic pulse (EMP) and the use of nuclear weapons.

Certain options are available for improving U.S. Navy capabilities by 2010; additional options, particularly in shipbuilding, can improve U.S. Navy capabilities in subsequent years. China's naval modernization raises potential issues for Congress concerning the role of China in Department of Defense (DOD) and Navy planning; the size of the Navy; the Pacific Fleet's share of the Navy; forward homeporting of Navy ships in the Western Pacific; the number of aircraft carriers, submarines, and ASW-capable platforms; Navy missile defense, air-warfare, AAW, ASW, and mine warfare programs; Navy computer network security; and EMP hardening of Navy systems. This report will be updated as events warrant.

INTRODUCTION

Congressional Concern

Concern has grown in Congress and elsewhere since the 1990s about China's military modernization and its potential implications for required U.S. military capabilities. China's military modernization is an increasing element in discussions of future U.S. Navy requirements. Department of Defense (DOD) officials such as Secretary of Defense Donald Rumsfeld, uniformed U.S. military leaders, Members of Congress, and defense industry representatives have all expressed concern. A May 2005 press report, for example, states that

> China is one of the central issues, along with terrorism and weapons of mass destruction, in the U.S. military's 2005 Quadrennial Defense Review, a congressionally directed study of military plans.... [W]hen the chief of naval operations, Adm. Vern Clark, held a classified briefing for congressional defense committees earlier this month about threats, his focus was "mainly" on China, about which he is "gravely concerned," recalled John W. Warner, the Virginia Republican who chairs the Senate Armed Services Committee....

China has come up repeatedly in congressional debate over the size of the Navy. The 288-ship fleet of today is half the size it was three decades ago. "You never want to broadcast to the world that something's insufficient," Warner says, "but clearly China poses a challenge to the sizing of the U.S. Navy."[1]

---

[1] John M. Donnelly, "China On Course To Be Pentagon's Next Worry," *CQ Weekly,* May 2, 2005, p. 1126. See also Anne Plummer, "Republican Senators Concerned About Timing Of Nay Force Reduction Plans," *CQ Today,* March 9, 2005. The American Shipbuilding Association, which represents the six U.S. shipyards that build the Navy's larger warships, states that a very ominous potential threat is building on the horizon. China has been officially modernizing its military for two-and-a-half decades. By 2010, China's submarine force will be nearly double the size of the U.S. submarine fleet. The entire Chinese naval fleet is projected to surpass the size of the U.S. fleet *by 2015.* In short, the Chinese military is specifically being configured to rival America's Sea Power. (Web page of the American Shipbuilding Association, located at [http://www.americanshipbuilding.com/]. Underlining as in the original.) See also Statement of Ms. Cynthia L. Brown, President, American Shipbuilding Association, Presented by Ms. Amy Praeger, Director of Legislative Affairs, Before the U.S.-China Economic and Security Review Commission On U.S.-China Trade Impacts on the Defense Industrial Base, June 23, 2005.

ISSUE FOR CONGRESS

The issue for Congress addressed in this report is: How should China's military modernization be factored into decisions about U.S. Navy programs? Congress' decisions on this issue could significantly affect future U.S. Navy capabilities, U.S. Navy funding requirements, and the U.S. defense industrial base, including the shipbuilding industry.

Scope of Report

This report focuses on the implications that certain elements of China's military modernization may have for future required U.S. Navy capabilities. It does not discuss the following:

- other elements of China's military modernization that may be less relevant to future required U.S. Navy capabilities;
- the potential implications of China's military modernization for parts of DOD other than the Navy, such as the Air Force and the Missile Defense Agency, federal agencies other than DOD, such as the Department of State, and — countries other than the United States, such as Taiwan, Russia, Japan, South Korea, the Philippines, the countries of Southeast Asia, Australia, India, and (through issues such as arms sales) countries such as Israel and U.S. allies in Europe; and
- China's foreign or economic policy, U.S. defense policy toward Taiwan, or the political likelihood of a military conflict involving China and the United States over Taiwan or some other issue.

Other CRS reports address some of these issues.[2]

TERMINOLOGY

For convenience, this report uses the term China's naval modernization, even though some of the military modernization efforts that could affect required U.S. Navy capabilities are occurring in other parts of China's military, such as the air force or the missile force.

---

[2] See, for example, CRS Report RL3 1555, *China and Proliferation of Weapons of Mass Destruction and Missiles: Policy Issues,* by Shirley A. Kan; CRS Report 98-485, *China: Possible Missile Technology Transfers Under U.S. Satellite Export Policy — Actions and Chronology,* by Shirley A. Kan; CRS Report RL33001, *U.S.-China Counter-Terrorism Cooperation: Issues for U.S. Policy,* by Shirley Kan; CRS Report RL32496, *U.S.-China Military Contacts: Issues for Congress,* by Shirley Kan; CRS Report RL3 0427, *Missile Survey: Ballistic and Cruise Missiles of Selected Foreign Countries,* by Andrew Feickert; CRS Report RL32870, *European Union 's Arms Embargo on China: Implications and Options for U.S. Policy,* by Kristin Archick, Richard F. Grimmett, and Shirley Kan; CRS Report RL30341, *China/Taiwan: Evolution of the 'One China ' Policy — Key Statements from Washington, Beijing, and Taipei,* by Shirley A. Kan; CRS Report RL32804, *China-U.S. Relations: Current Issues and Implications for U.S. Policy,* by Kerry Dumbaugh; CRS Report RL30957, *Taiwan: Major U.S. Arms Sales Since 1990,* by Shirley A. Kan; CRS Issue Brief IB9 1121, *China-U.S. Trade Issues,* by Wayne W. Morrison; CRS Report RL32882, *The Rise of China and Its Effect on Taiwan, Japan, and South*

China's military is formally called the People's Liberation Army, or PLA. Its navy is called the PLA Navy, or PLAN, and its air force is called the PLA Air Force, or PLAAF. The PLA Navy includes an air component that is called the PLA Naval Air Force, or PLANAF. China refers to its ballistic missile force as the Second Artillery.

Sources

Sources of information for this report, all of which are unclassified, include the following:

- the 2005 edition of DOD's annual report to Congress on China's military power;[3]
- the 2004 edition of *Worldwide Maritime Challenges,* a publication of the U.S. Navy's Office of Naval Intelligence (ONI);[4]
- China's 2004 defense white paper;[5]
- the prepared statements and transcript of a July 27, 2005, hearing on China grand strategy and military modernization before the House Armed Services Committee;[6]
- the prepared statements for a September 15, 2005, hearing on China's military modernization and the cross-strait balance before the U.S.-China Economic and Security Review Commission, an advisory body created by the FY2001 defense authorization act (P.L. 106-398) and subsequent legislation,[7] and the prepared statements and published transcript of a similar hearing before the commission on February 6, 2004;[8]
- a 2003 report on China's military power by an independent task force sponsored by the Council on Foreign Relations;[9]
- open-source military reference sources such as the Jane's Information Group; and
- news articles, including articles from the defense trade press.

Korea: U.S. Policy Choices, by Dick K. Nanto and Emma Chanlett-Avery; CRS Report RL32688, *China-Southeast Asia Relations: Trends, Issues, and Implications for the United States,* by Bruce Vaughn.

[3] U.S. Department of Defense, *Annual Report To Congress [on] The Military Power of the People's Republic of China, 2005.* Washington, Office of the Secretary of Defense, released July 2005. (Hereafter cited as *2005 DOD CMP.)*

[4] U.S. Department of the Navy, *Worldwide Maritime Challenges 2004,* Washington, prepared by the Office of Naval Intelligence. (Hereafter cited as *2004 ONI WMC.)*

[5] The white paper is entitled *China 's National Defense in 2004.* (Hereafter cited as *2004 China White Paper.)* The English-language text of the white paper can be found on the Internet at [http://www.fas.org/nuke/guide/china/doctrine/natdef2004.html].

[6] Transcript hereafter cited as *7/27/05 HASC hearing.*

[7] Hereafter cited as *9/15/05 USCC hearing.* The Commission's website, which includes this and other past hearings, is at [http://www.uscc.gov].

[8] Hearing On Military Modernization and Cross-Strait Balance, Hearing Before the U.S.-China Economic and Security Review Commission, February 6, 2004. Washington, U.S. Govt. Print. Off., 2004. (Hereafter cited as 2/6/04 USCC hearing.)

[9] Chinese Military Power, Report of an Independent Task Force Sponsored by the Council on Foreign Relations Maurice R. Greenberg Center for Geoeconomic Studies. Washington, 2003. (Harold Brown, Chair, Joseph W.

BACKGROUND

China's Naval Modernization

Maritime-Relevant Elements of China's Military Modernization[10].

This section summarizes elements of China's military modernization that may have potential implications for required U.S. Navy capabilities. See **Appendix A** for additional details and commentary on several of these modernization activities.

Theater-Range Ballistic Missiles (TBMs)

One of the most prominent elements of China's military modernization has been the deployment of large numbers of theater-range ballistic missiles (TBMs)[11] capable of attacking targets in Taiwan or other regional locations, such as Japan.[12] Among these are CSS-6 and CSS-7 short-range ballistic missiles (SRBMs) deployed in locations across from Taiwan. DOD states that China as of 2005 has deployed 650 to 730 CSS-6 and CSS-7 TBMs, and that this total is increasing at a rate of about 100 missiles per year.[13]

Although ballistic missiles in the past have traditionally been used to attack fixed targets on land, observers believe China may now be developing TBMs equipped with maneuverable reentry vehicles (MaRVs). Observers have expressed strong concern about this potential development, because such missiles, in combination with a broad-area maritime surveillance and targeting system,[14] would permit China to attack moving U.S. Navy ships at sea. The U.S. Navy has not previously faced a threat from highly accurate ballistic missiles capable of hitting moving ships at sea. Due to their ability to change course, MaRVs would be more difficult to intercept than non-maneuvering ballistic missile reentry vehicles. According to one press report, "navy officials project [that such missiles] could be capable of targeting US warships from sometime around 2015."[15]

Land-Attack Cruise Missiles (LACMs)

China is developing land-attack cruise missiles (LACMs) that can be fired from land bases, land-based aircraft, or Navy platforms such as submarines to attack targets, including

---

Prueher, Vice Chair, Adam Segal, Project Director) (Hereafter cited as 2003 CFR task force report.)

[10] Unless otherwise indicated, shipbuilding program information in this section is taken from *Jane's Fighting Ships 2005-2006*. Other sources of information on these shipbuilding programs may disagree regarding projected ship commissioning dates or other details, but sources present similar overall pictures regarding PLA Navy shipbuilding.

[11] Depending on their ranges, TBMs can be divided into short-, medium-, and intermediate-range ballistic missiles (SRBMs, MRBMs, and IRBMs, respectively).

[12] ONI states that "China is developing TBM systems with sufficient range to threaten U.S. forces throughout the region, to include [those] in Japan." *(2004 ONI WMC, p. 20.)*

[13] *2005 DOD CMP*, p. 4. See also China's Military Power: An Assessment From Open Sources, Testimony of Richard D. Fisher, Jr., International Assessment and Strategy Center, Before the House Armed Services Committee, July 27, 2005, p. 9. (Hereafter cited as *Fisher 7/27/05 testimony.)*

[14] DOD stated in 2002: "China's procurement of new space systems, airborne early warning aircraft and long-range UAV, and over-the-horizon radar will enhance its ability to detect, monitor, and target naval activity in the Western Pacific Ocean. China may have as many as three over-the-horizon (OTH) sky-wave radar systems, which China aspires to use against aircraft carriers." (Department of Defense, *Annual Report On The Military Power of the People's Republic Of China, 2002.* Washington, 2002, released July 2002. pp. 4-5. See also pp. 28-29.)

[15] Yihong Chang and Andrew Koch, "Is China Building A Carrier?" *Jane's Defence Weekly,* August 17, 2005.

air and naval bases, in Taiwan or other regional locations, such as Japan or Guam. The U.S. Defense Intelligence Agency (DIA) states: "We judge that by 2015, [China] will have hundreds of highly accurate air- and ground-launched LACMs."[16]

Anti-Ship Cruise Missiles (ASCMs)

China is modernizing its extensive inventory of anti-ship cruise missiles (ASCMs), which can be launched from land-based strike fighters and bombers, surface combatants, submarines and possibly shore-based launchers. Among the most capable of the new ASCMs being acquired by the PLA Navy is the Russian-made SS-N-27 Sizzler, a highly dangerous ASCM that is to be carried by eight new Kilo-class submarines that China has purchased from Russia (see section below on submarines).

Surface-to-Air Missiles (SAMs)

China is deploying modern surface-to-air missile (SAM) systems across from Taiwan, including long-range and high-altitude systems that have an advertised range sufficient to cover the entire Taiwan Strait, which is roughly 100 nautical miles (185 kilometers) wide. Advanced SAMs may have some effectiveness against stealthy aircraft. Longer- and shorter-range SAM systems deployed along China's coast opposite Taiwan would in combination give
China a multilayer defense against enemy aircraft seeking to operate over the Strait or approach that portion of China's coast.[17]

Land-Based Aircraft

China is introducing increasing numbers of modern and capable (so-called fourth-generation) fighters and strike fighters into the PLA Air Force and PLA Naval Air Force. These include Russian-made Su-27s and Su-30s and indigenously produced FB-7s, F-10s, and F-11s. At least some of the strike fighters will be armed with modern ASCMs. China is also upgrading the ASCMs carried by its land-based maritime bombers. The effectiveness of China's combat aircraft could be enhanced by new support aircraft, including tankers and airborne warning and control system (AWACS) aircraft.

Submarines

China's submarine modernization effort has attracted substantial attention and concern.[18] The effort currently involves the simultaneous acquisition of at least five classes of submarines, making it, in terms of number of designs involved, one of the more ambitious submarine-acquisition efforts on record by any country. China is taking delivery on eight

---

[16] Current and Projected National Security Threats to the United States, Vice Admiral Lowell E. Jacoby, U.S. Navy, Director, Defense Intelligence Agency, Statement for the Record [before the] Senate Select Committee on Intelligence, 16 February 2005, p. 13. See also Current and Projected National Security Threats to the United States, Vice Admiral Lowell E. Jacoby, U.S. Navy, Director, Defense Intelligence Agency, Statement For the Record [before the] Senate Armed Services Committee, 17 March 2005, p. 13.

[17] See the map entitled "SAM Area Coverage Circles," in 2004 ONI WMC, p. 29.

[18] For a detailed discussion of China's submarine modernization program and a strong expression of concern regarding the implications of this effort for Taiwan and the United States, see the statement of Lyle J. Goldstein as printed in 2/6/04 USCC hearing, pp. 129-156. Goldstein's written statement was also published as a journal article; see Lyle Goldstein and William Murray, "Undersea Dragons, China's Maturing Submarine Force," International Security, spring 2004, pp. 161-196.

Russian-made Kilo-class nonnuclear-powered attack submarines (SSs) that are in addition to four Kilos that China purchased from Russia in the 1990s,[19] and is building four other classes of submarines, including the following:

- a new nuclear-powered ballistic missile submarine (SSBN) design called the Type 094;
- a new nuclear powered attack submarine (S SN) design called the Shang class or Type 093;
- a new SS design called the Yuan class or Type 041; and
- another (and also fairly new) SS design called the Song class or Type 03 9/03 9G.

These five classes of submarines are expected to be much more modern and capable than China's aging older-generation submarines.

As shown in *Table 1,* China commissioned one to three new submarines per year between 1995 and 2003. Observers project that 11 new submarines (including six Kilos) will be commissioned in 2005, and five or more new submarines (including two Kilos) will be commissioned in 2006. The projected total of 11 new submarines in 2004 appears to be a spike produced in part by the projected delivery that year of the six Russian-made Kilos.[20]

PLA Navy submarines are armed with one or more of the following: ASCMs, wire-guided and wake-homing torpedoes, and mines.[21] Although ASCMs are often highlighted as sources of concern, wake-homing torpedoes can also be very difficult for surface ships to counter. In addition to some combination of ASCMs, torpedoes, and mines, Type 094 SSBNs will carry a new type of submarine-launched ballistic missile (SLBM), and Shang-class SSNs may carry LACMs.

China's submarine modernization effort is producing a substantially more modern and capable submarine force. As shown in *Table 1*, observers expect China to have a total of 28 Shang, Kilo, Yuan, and Song class submarines in commission by the end of 2006.

Although China's aging Ming- and Romeo-class submarines are based on old technology and are much less capable than the PLA Navy's newer-design submarines, China may decide that these older boats have continued value as minelayers or as bait or decoy submarines that can be used to draw out enemy submarines (such as U.S. SSNs) that can then be attacked by more modern PLA Navy submarines.[22]

---

[19] A previous CRS report discussed these four Kilo-class boats at length. See CRS Report RL3 0700, *China 's Foreign Conventional Arms Acquisitions: Background and Analysis,* by Shirley Kan (Coordinator), Christopher Bolkcom, and Ronald O'Rourke.

[20] ONI states that all eight Kilo-class boats are scheduled for delivery by 2005. *(2004 ONI WMC,* p. 12.) Some other sources project that the final boat or boats will be delivered by 2007.

[21] There are also reports that the Kilos might also be armed with the Shkval, a Russian-made, supercavitating, high-speed torpedo, and that China might be building its own supercavitating torpedoes. (Statement of Lyle J. Goldstein as printed in *2/6/04 USCC hearing,* p. 139.) A supercavitating torpedo surrounds itself with an envelope of gas bubbles, which dramatically reduces its resistance as it moves through the water, thereby permitting very high underwater speeds. The Shkval has a reported speed of 200 knots or more.

[22] One observer states that older and less sophisticated submarines will likely be employed to screen the higher-value assets. Chinese sources openly describe using certain submarines as "bait." Employing this tactic, it is conceivable that United States submarines could reveal their own presence to lurking Kilos by executing attacks against nuisance Mings and Romeos. No wonder China continues to operate the vessels, which are widely derided as obsolete by Western observers. The threat from these older submarines cannot be dismissed out of hand. Informal United States Navy testimony suggests that the PLAN can operate the older classes of diesel

Table 1. PLA Navy Submarine Commissionings Actual (1995-2004) and Projected (2005-2010)

	Type 094 SSBN	Shang (Type 093) SSN	Kilo SS (Russian-made)	Yuan (Type 041) SS	Song (Type 039) SS	Ming (Type 035) SSa	Total
1995			2			1	3
1996						1	1
1997						2	2
1998			1			2	3
1999			1		1		2
2000						1	1
2001					2	1	3
2002						1	1
2003					2		2
2004					3		3
2005		2b	6		3		11
2006		n/a	2	2	1		>5
2007		n/a		n/a	n/a		n/a
2008	1	n/a		n/a	n/a		n/a
2009		n/a		n/a	n/a		n/a
2010	1c	n/a		n/a	n/a		n/a

Source: Jane's Fighting Ships 2005-2006, and previous editions.

Figures for Ming-class boats are when the boats were launched (i.e., put into the water for final construction). Actual commissioning dates for these boats may have been later.

Construction of a third ship may have started.

Additional units are expected, perhaps at two-year intervals.

n/a = data not available.

ONI states that "Chinese diesel submarine force levels are stabilizing as quality replaces quantity," and has published a graph accompanying this statement suggesting that the figure may stabilize at a level between 25 and 50.[23]

Another observer states that by 2010, the PLA Navy could take delivery of over 20 new domestic SONG A and YUAN-class conventional submarines, 12 Russian KILO-877/636/636M conventional submarines, and five or more new indigenous Type 093 nuclear attack submarines (SSNs) — the third Type 093 is now under construction. In addition, the PLAN could retain up to 20 older Type 035 MING-class conventional [attack submarines] and about 4 older Type 091 HAN-class SSNs. This raises the prospect by 2010 of a Chinese fleet of over 50 modern-tomoderate [sic] attack submarines capable of engaging Taiwan, U.S. and Japanese naval forces.[24]

A Separate Observer States:

---

submarines with surprising tactical efficiency. (Statement of Lyle J. Goldstein as printed in *2/6/04 USCC hearing,* p. 153)

[23] *2004 ONI WMC,* p. 11. The range of 25 to 50 is based on visual inspection of the graph.

[24] *Fisher 7/27/05 testimony,* p. 11. On page 4, Fisher similarly states "It can be estimated that by 2010 the PLA Navy could have 50 to 60 nuclear and new conventional attack submarines...."

China has been investing heavily in submarines which it sees as the poisoned arrow (Shashou j ian) to the Achilles Heel of American naval might....

By my count, China will have a net gain of 35 submarines over the next 15 years, with no production slow-down in sight. It is reasonable to assume that at current production levels, China will likely out-produce our shipyards and its submarines could out-number our submarines in the next 15 years. By 2020, the Chinese submarine fleet could boast nearly 50 modern attack boats....

[The 2005 DOD report on China's military power] has catalogued a list of China's foreign weapons and military systems acquisitions, but in my mind none is as worrisome as the expansion of the PLA Navy's submarine fleet. China has identified America's strategic center as its maritime predominance, and its sub fleet is clearly designed to overcome U.S. supremacy at sea.[25]

One more observer states that:

the PLA Navy now has the capability to make the antisubmarine warfare (ASW) mission very difficult for U.S. forces. With a total of more than 50 operational submarines, and with a substantial number of them new and quiet, China, quite simply, can put to sea more submarines than the U.S. Navy can locate and counter. Its older Ming and Romeo submarines are not only still lethal if ignored but also serve to disperse and dilute the efforts of the ASW forces. In other words, some, or even many, of the already large and diverse, but still rapidly growing, fleet of very capable Shang SSNs, and Kilo, Song, and Yuan SSs can reasonably expect to remain undetected as they seek to interdict the U.S. carrier strike groups. If the "shooting has started," eventually U.S. ASW forces could take a big toll against the Chinese submarine force, but the delay in sanitizing the area before the entry of carrier strike groups is what the Chinese are counting on as adequate delay to present the world with the aforementioned *fait accompli* with respect to Taiwan.[26]

Yet one more observer states:

Evidence suggests that China is seeking to become a first-class submarine power. While the PLAN modernization shows impressive breadth with major new purchases of naval aircraft and surface combatants, submarines appear to be the centerpiece of China's strategic reorientation toward the sea. The May 2002 contract for eight additional Kilos, the likely continuation of the Song program, and nuclear force modernization, taken together with the evident new priority on training, technological research and doctrinal development all suggest that Beijing recognizes the value of submarines as a potent, asymmetric answer to United States maritime superiority. The recent ascendance of a submariner, Adm. Zhang Dingfa, to the position of commanding officer of the PLAN underlines these tendencies. Further investments in diesel submarines, particularly when enhanced by air independent propulsion, will afford Beijing increasing near-term leverage in the East Asian littoral, while methodical

---

[25] China's Military Power, Testimony of John J. Tkacik, Jr., Senior Research Fellow in Asian Studies, The Heritage Foundation, Before the Committee on Armed Services, United States House of Representatives, Washington, D.C., July 27, 2005. p. 8. (Hereafter cited as *Tkacik 7/27/05 testimony.*)

[26] [Statement of] Rear Admiral (U.S. Navy, Retired) Eric A. McVadon, Director of Asia-Pacific Studies, Institute for Foreign Policy Analysis, Consultant on East Asia Security Affairs, Before the U.S.-China Economic and Security Review Commission, [regarding] Recent Trends in China's Military Modernization, 15 September 2005, p. 5. (Hereafter cited as *McVadon 9/15/05 testimony.*) The *fait accompli* mentioned at the end of the quote is discussed later in this report.

nuclear modernization signifies a long-term commitment to global power projection. As one Chinese strategist recently observed, "The scale [of recent purchases] indicates that in the coming years, China will build an offshore defense system with submarines as the key point."[27]

Aircraft Carriers

ONI states that "China's interest in aircraft carriers has not led it to build or purchase one, except as museums. Near-term focus on contingencies in the vicinity of Taiwan has minimized the importance of aircraft carriers in China's acquisition plan, but research into the ships and associated aircraft likely continues."[28] Another observer states that "while China is not yet believed to [be] building an aircraft carrier, for many years, the PLA has been developing aircraft carrier technologies. In early May [2005] the PLA moved the former Ukrainian [i.e., former Soviet] carrier Varyag, in [China's] Dalian harbor since early 2002, into a drydock, suggesting it might soon serve a military role."[29]

Surface Combatants

China since the early 1990s has purchased four Sovremenny-class destroyers from Russia and deployed eight new classes of indigenously built destroyers and frigates that demonstrate a significant modernization of PLA Navy surface combatant technology. The introduction of eight new destroyer and frigate designs over a period of about 15 years is an undertaking with few parallels by any country in recent decades. China has also deployed a new kind of fast attack craft that uses a stealthy catamaran hull design.

Sovremenny-Class Destroyers. China in 2002 ordered two Sovremennyclass destroyers from Russia. The ships, which reportedly are to be delivered in 2005 and 2006, are in addition to two Sovremenny-class destroyers that China ordered from Russia in 1996 and which entered service in 1991 and 2001. Sovremenny-class destroyers are equipped with the SS-N-22 Sunburn ASCM, another dangerous ASCM.[30] The SS-N-22s on the two Sovremenny-class ships ordered in 2002 are expected to be an improved version with a longer range. China reportedly has an option for two more Sovremenny-class ships, which, if exercised, would make for an eventual total of six ships.[31]

FIVE NEW INDIGENOUSLY BUILT DESTROYER CLASSES

China since the early 1990s has built five new classes of destroyers. Compared to China's 16 older Luda (Type 051) class destroyers, which entered service between 1971 and 1991,

---

[27] Statement of Lyle J. Goldstein as printed in *2/6/04 USCC hearing,* pp. 155-156.

[28] *2004 ONI WMC,* p. 10.

[29] Fisher 7/27/05 testimony, p. 4.

[30] A previous CRS report discussed the PLA Navy's first two Sovremenny-class destroyers and their SS-N-22 ASCMs at length. See CRS Report RL30700, op cit.

[31] ONI puts the potential number of additional ships at two or three. *(2004 ONI WMC,* p. 10.)

these five new destroyer classes are substantially more modern in terms of their hull designs, propulsion systems, sensors, weapons, and electronics. A key area of improvement in the new destroyer designs is their anti-air warfare (AAW) technology,[32] which has been a significant PLA Navy shortcoming. Like the older Luda-class destroyers, these new destroyer classes are armed with ASCMs.

As shown in *Table 2,* China to date has commissioned only 1 or 2 ships in each of these five classes, suggesting that a key purpose of at least some of these classes may have been to serve as stepping stones in a plan to modernize the PLA Navy's surface combatant technology incrementally before committing to larger-scale series production. If one or more of these designs are put into larger-scale production, it would accelerate the modernization of China's surface combatant force.

Table 2. New PLA Navy Destroyer Classes

Class name	Type	Number built	Hull number(s)	In service (actual or projected)
Luhu	052	2	112, 113	1994, 1996
Luhai	051B	1	167	1999
Luyang I	052B	2	168, 169	2004
Luyang II	052C	2	170, 171	2004, 2005
n/a	051C	2	115, n/a	2006, 2007

Source: Jane's Fighting Ships 2005-2006.
n/a = data not available.

The *Luhu-class ships* reportedly were ordered in 1985 but had their construction delayed by a decision to give priority to the construction of six frigates that were ordered by Thailand. *The Luhai-class ship* is believed to have served as the basis for the Luyang-class designs. Compared to the Luhai, the *Luyang I-class ships* appear stealthier and are believed to feature an anti-air warfare (AAW) system with a longer-ranged SAM.

The *Luyang II-class ships* appear to feature an even more capable AAW system that includes a SAM called the HQ-9 that has an even longer range, a vertical launch system (VLS), and a phased-array radar that is outwardly somewhat similar to the SPY-1 radar used in the U.S.-made Aegis combat system. Indeed, the Luyang II-class design bears some resemblance to U.S. and Japanese Aegis destroyers, though they are probably not as modern or capable in some respects than the U.S. and Japanese ships.[33] The two *Type 051C-class ships* feature a VLS and a long-range SAM, but in other respects might be less advanced in their design than the Luyang II-class destroyers. They may have been designed earlier and had their construction delayed. Even so, they are still relatively modern ships.

---

[32] AAW is a term most frequently found in discussions of naval systems. Discussions of systems in other military services tend to use the term air defense.

[33] For a detailed article about the Luyang II class, see James C. Bussert, "China Debuts Aegis Destroyers," *Signal,* July 2005, pp. 59-62. See also *Fisher 7/27/05 testimony,* p. 12.

Three New Indigenously Built Frigate Classes

China since the early 1990s has built three new classes of frigates that are more modern than China's 31 older Jianghu (Type 053) class frigates, which entered service between the mid- 1970s and 1989. The three new frigate classes, like the new destroyer classes, feature improved AAW capabilities. Unlike the new destroyer designs, the new frigate designs have been put into larger-scale series production. **Table 3** summarizes the three new classes.

Table 3. New PLA Navy Frigate Classes

Class name	Type	Number built or building	Hull number(s)	In service (actual or projected)
Jiangwei I	053G H2G	4	539-542	1991-1994
Jiangwei II	053H3	10	between 521 and 567	1998-2005
Jiangkai	054	3	525, 526, n/a	2004-2006

Source: *Jane's Fighting Ships 2005-2006.* n/a = data not available.

Construction of *Jiangwei I-class ships* appears to have ceased but observers believe that construction of the *Jiangwei II- and Jiangkai-class ships* is continuing and additional units beyond those shown in *Table 3* are expected. The Jiangkai-class ships feature a stealthy design that somewhat resembles France's La Fayette-class frigate, which first entered service in 1 996.[34]

New Class of Fast Attack Craft

In addition to its 190 older fast attack craft (including 37 armed with ASCMs), China in 2004 introduced a new type of ASCM-armed fast attack craft built on a stealthy, wave-piercing, catamaran hull that is one of the more advanced hull designs used by any navy in the world today. Observers believe the hull design is based on a design developed by a firm in Australia, a country which is a world leader in high-speed catamaran designs. At least three of these new fast attack craft are now in service, and additional units are expected.[35]

---

[34] France sold a modified version of the La Fayette-class design to Taiwan; the six ships that Taiwan built to the design entered service in 1996-1998. See also *Fisher 7/27/05 testimony,* pp. 12-13. One observer views the Jiangwei II-class ships as roughly comparable to France's Georges Leygues-class destroyer design, which entered service in 1979, Italy's Maestrale-class frigate design, which entered service in 1982, and the UK's Type 21 frigates, which entered service in starting in 1975 and were transferred to Pakistan in 1993-1994. (Massimo Annati, "China's PLA Navy, The Revolution," *Naval Forces,* No. 6, 2004, pp. 66-67.)

[35] Reference books do not show a name for this new class of attack craft, so the craft are identified by their hull numbers. The first three ships carry numbers 2208-22 10. See also *Fisher 7/27/05 testimony,* p. 13; "PRC Appears Ready To Field New Trimaran Fast Missile Warship," *Defense and Foreign Afairs Daily,* October 5, 2004; Yihong Chang, "First Sight Of Chinese Catamaran," *Jane 's Defense Weekly,* May 26, 2004.

Amphibious Ships

China is currently building three new classes of amphibious ships and landing craft, all of which began construction in 2003. Each type is being built at three or four shipyards. Between these three classes, China built a total of 19 amphibious ships and 8 amphibious landing craft in 2003 and 2004.

Mine Countermeasures (Mcm) Ships

China is building a new class of mine countermeasures (MCM) ship, the first unit of which is expected to enter service in 2005.

Naval Mines

Regarding naval mines, ONI states:

China is developing and exporting numerous advanced mines of all types. One example is the wireless remote controlled EM57, a mine that offers many tactical options. For example, the mine can be turned off and on remotely to prolong its life, or it can be activated and deactivated to allow safe passage for friendly vessels. [36]

DOD stated in 2003 that the PLA's mines

include bottom and moored influence mines, mobile mines, remotely controlled mines, command-detonated mines, and propelled-warhead mines. Use of propelled-warhead mines in deep waters has the potential to deny enemy naval formations large operational areas.[37]

DOD stated in 2002 that China "likely has enough mine warfare assets to lay a good defensive and a modest offensive minefield using a wide variety of launch platforms."[38]
Another observer stated in a presentation that China has

a large inventory of mines. And we see a tremendous interest in some of the most modern deadly mines going. These deep water rising mines [on the projection screen] can be

---

[36] 2004 ONI WMC, p. 19.

[37] U.S. Department of Defense, *Annual Report On The Military Power of the People's Republic of China, 2003.* Washington, Office of the Secretary of Defense, released July 2003. p. 27.

[38] Department of Defense, *Annual Report On The Military Power of the People's Republic Of China, 2002.* Washington, 2002, released July 2002. p. 23. In 2000, DOD stated:

The PLAN's mine stockpiles include vintage Russian moored-contact and bottom influence mines, as well as an assortment of domestically built mines. China currently produces the EM11 bottom-influence mine; the EM3 1 moored mine; the EM32 moored influence mine; the EM52 rocket-propelled rising mine; and, the EM-53 ship-laid bottom influence mine which is remotely controlled by a shore station. China is believed to have available acoustically activated remote control technology for its EM53. This technology probably could be used with other Chinese ship-laid mines including the EM52. Application of this technology could allow entire mines to be laid in advance of hostilities in a dormant position and activated or deactivated when required. China reportedly has completed development of a mobile mine and may be producing improved variants of Russian bottom mines and moored-influence mines. Over the next decade, China likely will attempt to acquire advanced propelled-warhead mines, as well as submarine-launched mobile bottom mines. (Department of Defense,

purchased from Russia. They have tremendous ability to mine deeper waters where we would prefer to operate. So what we would consider to have been a haven [for U.S. Navy ships] may no longer be a haven.[39]

In Formation Warfare/Information Operations (IW/IO)

China open-source writings demonstrate an interest in information warfare (IW), also called information operations (IO), as an increasingly important element of warfare, particularly against a sophisticated opposing force such as the U.S. military. Concern about potential PLA IW/IO capabilities has been heightened by recent press reports about attacks on U.S. computer systems that in some cases appear to have originated in China.[40] One observer has stated that "China even now is planting viruses in U.S. computer systems that they will activate" in the event of a military conflict with the United States.[41]

Nuclear Weapons

Although China is not necessarily modernizing its nuclear weapon technology, it is worth noting that China, as a longstanding nuclear weapon state, could put nuclear warheads on weapons such as TBMs, LACMs, ASCMs, torpedoes, and naval mines. China could use nuclear-armed versions of these weapons (except the LACMs) to attack U.S. Navy ships at sea. China might do so in the belief that it could subsequently confuse the issue in the public arena of whose nuclear warhead had detonated,[42] or that the United States in any event would not escalate the conflict by retaliating with a nuclear attack on a land target in China. During the Cold War, analysts debated whether the use of a Soviet nuclear weapon against U.S. Navy ships during a conflict would lead to a U.S. nuclear response.

China could also use a nuclear-armed ballistic missile to detonate a nuclear warhead in the atmosphere to create a high-altitude electromagnetic pulse (EMP) intended to temporarily or permanently disable the electronic circuits of U.S. or other civilian and military electronic systems. Some observers have expressed concern in recent years over the potential vulnerability of U.S. military systems to EMP effects.[43]

Annual Report On The Military Power of the People's Republic Of China, 2000. Washington, 2000. See the subsection on subsurface warfare.)

[39] Statement of Lyle J. Goldstein as printed in *2/6/04 USCC hearing,* p. 133. See also p. 152.

[40] See *2005 DOD CMP,* p. 36; *2003 CFR task force report,* pp. 55-56; Peter Brookes, "The Art Of (Cyber) War, *New York Post,* August 29, 2005; Bradley Graham, "Hackers Attack Via Chinese websites," *Washington Post,* August 25, 2005: 1; Frank Tiboni, "The New Trojan War," *Federal Computer Week,* August 22, 2005: 60.

[41] Eric McVadon, as quoted in Dave Ahearn, "U.S. Can't Use Trade Imbalance To Avert China Invasion Of Taiwan," *Defense Today,* August 2, 2005, pp. 1-2.

[42] Following the April 1, 2001, collision in international airspace off China's coast of a U.S. Navy EP-3 electronic surveillance aircraft and a PLA F-8 fighter, which many observers believed was caused by reckless flying by the pilot of the F-8, China attempted to convince others that the collision was caused by poor flying by the pilot of the slower-flying and less maneuverable U.S. EP-3. For more on this event, see CRS Report RL30946, *China-U.S. Aircraft Collision Incident of April 2001: Assessments and Policy Implications,* by Shirley A. Kan, coordinator.

43 See CRS Report RL32544, High Altitude Electromagnetic Pulse (HEMP) and High Power Microwave (HPM) Devices: Threat Assessments, by Clay Wilson; (Hereafter cited as CRS Report RL32544.) and John S. Foster, Jr., et al., Report of the Commission to Assess the Threat to the United States from Electromagnetic Pulse

High-Power Micro wave (HPM) Weapons

Some observers are concerned that China might develop or already possess high-power microwave (HPM) weapons, also called radio frequency weapons (RFWs) or E-bombs, which are non-nuclear devices that can be used to generate damaging EMP effects over relatively short distances to disable the electronic circuits of nearby enemy civilian and military systems.[44] In theory, an HPM weapon could be placed on a TBM or ASCM and fired at a U.S. Navy ship. Although the effective EMP radius of such devices might be on the order of only a few hundred yards,[45] such devices could be used to attack.

A second source says HPM weapons might have effective radii "on the order of hundreds of meters, subject to weapon performance and target set electrical hardness." (Section 4.1 of Carlo Kopp, "The Electromagnetic Bomb — a Weapon of Electrical Mass Destruction,"available on the Internet at [http://www.globalsecurity.org/military/library/report /1996/apjemp.htm].

A third source states that "a small RF device might have a range measured in feet, while a relatively large RF device might produce upset or damage in electronics systems at range measured in hundreds of feet, and interference at a range of hundreds of miles." (Statement of William R. Graham, Ph.D., before the Military Research and Development Subcommittee of the House Armed Services Committee, October 7, 1999.) individual U.S. Navy ships without the political or escalatory risks of a high-altitude nuclear detonation.[46]

MILITARY DOCTRINE, EDUCATION, TRAINING, EXERCISES, AND LOGISTICS

Military capability is a product not simply of having weapons, but of having a doctrine for how to use them, well-educated and well-trained personnel, realistic exercises, and logistic support. In past years, the PLA was considered weak in some or all of these areas, and PLA military capability consequently was considered not as great as its inventory of weapons alone might suggest. The 2004 China defense white paper states an intention to improve in

---

(EMP) Attack, Volume 1: Executive Report 2004. Washington, 2004, 53 pp. (Hereafter cited as 2004 EMP commission report.) See also the transcripts and written statements of hearings on EMP held before the House Armed Services Committee on July 22, 2004, and before the Military Research and Development Subcommittee of the House Armed Services Committee on October 7, 1999, and July 16, 1997. (In 1997, the full committee was called the House National Security Committee.)

[44] For more on HPM weapons, see CRS Report RL32544

[45] One source states that "a 2,000-pound microwave munition will have a minimum radius [of effect] of approximately 200 meters," or roughly 650 feet. ("High-power microwave (HPM)/E-Bomb," available on the Internet at [http://www.globalsccurity.org/military/ systcms/munitions/hpm.htm].)

[46] One source states that:

An electromagnetic warhead detonated within lethal radius of a surface combatant will render its air defence system inoperable, as well as damaging other electronic equipment such as electronic countermeasures, electronic support measures and communications. This leaves the vessel undefended until these systems can be restored, which may or may not be possible on the high seas. Therefore launching an electromagnetic glidebomb on to a surface combatant, and then reducing it with laser or television guided weapons is an alternate strategy for dealing with such targets. (Section 10.4 of Carlo Kopp, "The Electromagnetic Bomb — a Weapon of Electrical Mass Destruction," op cit.)

these areas,[47] and observers believe the PLA is acting on these intentions. DOD says that "China has stated its intentions and allocated resources to pursue force-wide professionalization, improve training, conduct more robust, realistic joint exercises, and accelerate acquisition of modern weapons."[48] The PLA in recent years has developed a doctrine for joint operations involving multiple military services,[49] improved its military education and training and conducted more realistic exercises,[50] and reformed its logistics system.[51] Improvements in these areas might be considered as important as the weapon-modernization activities discussed above. Some of these improvements may require several years to fully implement.

China's Naval Limitations and Weaknesses

In spite of the concerns raised by the modernization effort described above, observers believe PLA military (including naval) forces continue to have limitations or weaknesses in the following areas, among others:

- sustained operations in waters and air space that are more distant from China;
- joint operations;
- C4ISR (command, control, communications, computers, intelligence, surveillance and reconnaissance) systems, including, for example, airborne warning and control system (AWACS) capabilities;
- long-range surveillance and targeting systems for detecting and tracking ships at sea — a capability needed to take full advantage of longer-ranged anti-ship weapons;
- anti-air warfare (AAW) capability for defending surface ships against air attack;
- antisubmarine warfare (ASW) capability for defending surface ships against submarine attack;
- mine countermeasures (MCM) capability; and
- logistics.

The paragraphs below elaborate on these items.

Weaknesses and Limitations in General

Regarding PLA Navy limitations and weaknesses in general, DIA states:

---

[47] See the sections entitled "Reducing the PLA by 200,000," "Implementing the Strategic Project for Talented People," "Intensifying Joint Training," and "Deepening Logistical Reforms," in Chapter II on national defense policy.

[48] *2005 DOD CMP*, p. 26.

[49] See, for example, *2005 DOD CMP*, pp. 5-6; the statement of David M. Finkelstein as printed in *2/6/04 USCC hearing*, p. 90-93; and *2003 CFR task force report*, pp. 38-39.

[50] See, for example, [Statement of] Dennis J. Blasko, Independent Consultant, September 15, 2005, Hearing on "Net Assessment of Cross-Strait Military Capabilities" Before the U.S.-China Economic and Security Review Commission; the statement by Lyle J. Goldstein as printed in *2/6/04 USCC hearing*, pp. 131-132, 143-145; and *2003 CFR task force report*, pp. 39-41, 45-46, 49.

[51] Regarding reformed logistics, see *2005 DOD CMP*, p. 34, and the statement of Lyle J. Goldstein as printed in *2/6/04 USCC hearing*, p. 145.

China continues to develop or import modern weapons.... The PLA must overcome significant integration challenges to turn these new, advanced and disparate weapon systems into improved capabilities. Beijing also faces technical and operational difficulties in numerous areas.[52]

Another set of observers states:

The PLAN is limited by a lack of integration in its command, control, and communication systems; targeting; air defense; and antisubmarine warfare capabilities. PLAN ships are vulnerable to attack by aircraft, torpedoes, and antiship missiles. The navies of the ASEAN nations could, if able to operate together, exclude the PLAN from the South China Sea....

New capabilities are limited by the lack of some critical supporting systems. The PLAN is deficient in antisubmarine warfare capabilities. PLAN ships are also vulnerable to air attack by both aircraft and antiship missiles.[53]

Regarding the submarine force, one observer states that by no means should the PLAN submarine force be considered ten feet tall. China's submarine force has some significant weaknesses: a reliance on diesel submarines that have to approach the surface to snorkel; especially in the wake of the Ming 361 accident,[54] it is evident that crew training and professionalism remain a fundamental problem; finally, there is little evidence of a robust, remote cueing capability, and probable weakness in the sphere of command and control.[55]

Sustained Operations in Distant Waters

Regarding sustained operations in more distant waters, DOD states: "We assess that China's ability to project conventional military power beyond its periphery remains limited," and that China does not appear to have broadened its concept of operations for anti-access and sea denial to encompass sea control in waters beyond Taiwan and its immediate periphery. If China were to shift to a broader "sea control" strategy, the primary indicators would include: development of an aircraft carrier, development of robust anti-submarine warfare capabilities, development of a true area anti-air warfare capability, acquisition of large numbers of nuclear attack submarines, development of effective maritime C4ISR, and increased open water training....

With its present force structure, according to the Intelligence Community, Chinese surface combatants would have difficulty projecting power into the Strait of Malacca, especially if it were conducting simultaneous blockade or invasion operations elsewhere. Similarly, although the PLA Navy occasionally patrols as far as the Spratly Islands, its

---

[52] Current and Projected National Security Threats to the United States, Vice Admiral Lowell E. Jacoby, U.S. Navy, Director, Defense Intelligence Agency, Statement for the Record [before the] Senate Select Committee on Intelligence, 16 February 2005, p. 16. See also Current and Projected National Security Threats to the United States, Vice Admiral Lowell E. Jacoby, U.S. Navy, Director, Defense Intelligence Agency, Statement For the Record [before the] Senate Armed Services Committee, 17 March 2005, p. 16.

[53] 2003 CFR task force report, pp. 28 and 47.

[54] This is a reference to an April 2003 fatal accident aboard a Ming-class boat with hull number 361. See Appendix A for additional details concerning this accident.

[55] Statement of Lyle J. Goldstein as printed in 2/6/04 USCC hearing, p. 156.

limited organic air defense capability leaves surface ships vulnerable to attack from hostile air and naval forces. The PLA Navy Air Force and PLA Air Force currently lack the operational range to support PLA Navy operations. In recent years, however, the PLA Navy's South Sea Fleet, which has operational responsibility over the South China Sea, has been assigned more capable surface combatants and submarines, including two destroyers (one LUDA IV class and one LUHAI class) that provide it with its first short-range area air-defense capability, the HHQ-7C surface-to-air missile systems.[56]

Joint Operations

Regarding joint operations, DOD states:

Although the PLA has devoted considerable effort to develop joint capabilities, it faces a persistent lack of inter-service cooperation and a lack of actual experience in joint operations.... The lack of experience in joint operations is a subset of the overall lack of operational experience in the Chinese force.[57]

Similarly, Regarding training for amphibious and other expeditionary operations, DOD states:

Combined training for all these units is seldom conducted in a maj or amphibious assault exercise. Units tend to train for their missions in garrisons, local areas and regional training facilities. China's ability to integrate individual unit actions — or simulate integration — to assess accurately operational capability, is not known.[58]

Another observer states:

There is no question that China has achieved a remarkable leap in modernization of the forces needed for these missions and that it is urgently continuing on that path. There *is* question about how China is now proceeding to exercise these new assets so as to make them truly operational in a combat environment. There is *considerable question* about China's capability to coordinate all these forces in two major simultaneous operations: (1) to bring Taiwan to its knees and (2) cause the U.S. to be tardy, indecisive, or ineffective in responding.[59]

Anti-Air Warfare (AA W)

Regarding AAW, one observer states that China's decision to "shed its strictly coastal defense force structure in favor of acquiring larger and more modern fighting vessels capable of blue-water operations" has

---

[56] *2005 DOD CMP,* Executive Summary And Pp. 33-34.
[57] *2005 DOD CMP,* P. 17.
[58] Ibid., p. 31.
[59] *McVadon 9/15/05 testimony,* p. 6. Italics as in the original.

exposed a significant vulnerability — the PLAN's inability to provide a sophisticated, layered air defense for these new forces. Fleet air defense is the Achilles' heel of the 21 st-century Chinese Navy....

As the PLAN's ships increased in size, capability and endurance, and with operational deployments taking them well beyond the navy's traditional mainland-based air defenses, a challenge not faced previously became apparent: having to defend these units from air attack in the event of hostilities. Response to this concern has been slow and inadequate at best, and serious consideration to providing the surface navy with the kind of air defense systems one normally associates with modern naval fleets has only begun. Not until the late 1990s was an effort made to outfit PLAN destroyers and frigates with an antiair "point defense" system, giving them some measure of self-defense.... The PLAN surface fleet, however, still lacks "modern air surveillance systems and data links required for area air defense missions. The combination of short-range weapons and lack of modern surveillance systems limits the PLAN to self-defense and point-defense [AAW] only. As a result, except in unusual circumstances, no PLAN ship is capable of conducting air defense of another ship."[60]

In a similar vein, today's PLAN naval aviation forces alone cannot provide fighter coverage for the entire Chinese coast or the fleet, so interceptor duties have ben distributed by region between naval aviation units and the PLA Air Force. This increases the number of assets available for the task, but questions remain about joint patrolling, separate chains of command, and air force over-water proficiency. When faced with training scenarios that incorporated factors likely found in a modern air combat environment, such as electronic countermeasures or even inclement weather, neither service was up to the task. In light of these facts, the potential effectiveness of the cooperation between the two services is doubtful.

Significant gaps exist in the present PLAN fleet air defense posture. Given the forces available today, China cannot adequately defend its fleet from air attack in the modern air threat environment.[61]

Antisubmarine Warfare (A SW)

Regarding ASW, one observer states:

The most serious deficiency of the PLAN is certainly in the area of Anti-Submarine Warfare. Good submarines, like the "Kilo" class and (possibly) the forthcoming Type-093, will play an important ASW role, but the lack of maritime patrol aircraft and of surface ships equipped with advanced acoustic sensors make the Chinese vessels vulnerable for [sic] any of the foreign high-capability submarines operating in the area.[62]

---

[60] The passage at this point is quoting from the 2003 edition of DOD's annual report on China's military power (2003 DOD CMP, p. 25).

[61] Dominic DeScisciolo, "Red Aegis," U.S. Naval Institute Proceedings, July 2004, pp. 56-58.

[62] Massimo Annati, "China's PLA Navy, The Revolution," Naval Forces, No. 6, 2004, p. 75.

Mine Countermeasures (MCM)

Regarding MCM, one observer writes that for the PLA Navy a serious operational deficiency involves the mine countermeasures vessels (MCMV). Though China has an intense shipping [sic] along its coasts, the PLAN has virtually no mine-sweeping or mine-hunting capabilities. This was due, perhaps, to the consideration that the U.S. Navy is usually more concerned to keep the sea lanes open, instead of laying mines, but nevertheless the lack of MCM is simply stunning. Any hostile organisation (including, but not limited to, state-sponsored terrorists and insurgents) could play havoc with the Chinese shipping simply by laying a few mines here and there.[63]

Logistics

Regarding logistics, DOD states:

Since 2000, China has improved the structure, material coordination, and efficiency of its joint logistics system. However, the command system is still not compatible with the support system, and organization and planning is incompatible with supply management. The first experimental joint logistics unit was created only in July 2004.[64]

Regarding logistic support of China's new destroyers, one observer states:

The ships' new sensors, missiles and combat systems are mainly of Russian and Western origin. However, China now is faced with the challenge of operating and maintaining these advanced systems to create a credible threat to foreign navies in Far Eastern waters....
Every piece of equipment [on China's Sovremenny-class destroyers] from hull, mechanical and electrical (HMandE) technologies to guns, sonar, communications, electronic countermeasures (ECM) and missiles are totally new to the PLAN.... [For these ships,] China is dependent on Russian advisers for training, operations and maintenance. These ships largely remain in the Russian support cocoon in Dinghai rather than at a fleet base....
Isolation from other ships and crews hurts fleet integration and coordinated operations.... It is no coincidence that the Sovremnyi and Kilo submarine home bases are in an enclave of Russian support in an isolated area near the Eastern Fleet headquarters at Ningbo.
It is unlikely that Russian advisers would be onboard during actual combat operations against Taiwan and U.S. Navy air, surface and subsurface threats. PLAN officers and crew are not expected to be able to handle operations when under fire, sustaining hits and suffering system degradation or loss. This could include problems in night or rough weather environment as well. Because all of the combat systems, except for three noted, are modern Russian equipments, China has minimal capability even to repair peacetime losses in port....

A comparison [of the AAW system on the Luyang II class destroyers] to [the] U.S. Navy Aegis [combat system] is inevitable, but Aegis was on [the U.S. Navy test ship] Norton Sound for nine years of development testing prior to the first installation on the USS

---

[63] Ibid., p. 73.
[64] *2005 DOD CMP,* pp. 34-35.

Ticonderoga (CG-47) 20 years ago. Developing the software for signal processing and tracking a hundred air, surface and submarine targets will take even longer for China. Integration to various indigenous ship guns and missiles and other sensors, as well as other ships' data management and weapons, will take longer. These Chinese "Aegis" ships may be limited to 1 940s era radar tasks of detecting and tracking air and surface targets for their own ship weapons. Further in the future will be an 8,000-ton DDG that is predicted to be a true area-control warship with additional Aegis capabilities. It is now in early construction stages in the new Dalian shipyard.

What kind of record is provided by prior Chinese built warships with imported Russian and Western technology? These include sensors, fire control, weapons and communications as well as HMandE. The Chinese new-construction DDGs are a mix of local designed and manufactured systems, foreign imports with production rights, illegally copied import equipment and illegal examples with no local production capability at all. The latter two represent serious training and maintenance problems. Unfortunately for the PLAN, some of them are in the highest mission-critical areas. For example, the DDGs being built have a rapid-fire Gatling gun close-in weapon system that looks like the Dutch Goalkeeper system. Signaal and the Dutch government deny exporting the equipment or production rights to China. This key weapon responsible for downing incoming cruise missiles is probably lacking documentation and training because it must be illegally obtained.[65]

GOALS OR SIGNIFICANCE OF CHINA'S NAVAL MODERNIZATION

PLA Navy as A Modernization Priority

The PLA Navy is one of three stated priorities within China's overall military modernization effort. China's 2004 defense white paper says three times that the effort will emphasize the navy, air force, and the ballistic missile force.[66] Consistent with this stated emphasis, the heads of the PLA Navy, Air Force, and missile force were added to the Central Military Commission in September 2004, and Navy and Air Force officers were appointed Deputy Chiefs of the General Staff.[67]

---

[65] James C. Bussert, "China Builds Destroyers Around Imported Technology," *Signal,* August 2004, p. 67.
[66] The white paper states:
The PLA will promote coordinated development of firepower, mobility and information capability, enhance the development of its operational strength with priority given to the Navy, Air Force and Second Artillery Force, and strengthen its comprehensive deterrence and warfighting capabilities....
The Army is streamlined by reducing the ordinary troops that are technologically backward while the Navy, Air Force and Second Artillery Force are strengthened....
While continuing to attach importance to the building of the Army, the PLA gives priority to the building of the Navy, Air Force and Second Artillery Force to seek balanced development of the combat force structure, in order to strengthen the capabilities for winning both command of the sea and command of the air, and conducting strategic counter-strikes. *(2004 China White Paper,* op cit, Chapter II national defense policy.)
[67] See, for example, *2005 DOD CMP,* p. 1.

Near-Term Focus: Taiwan Situation

DOD and other observers believe that the primary near-term focus of China's military modernization is to develop military options for addressing the situation with Taiwan.[6868] DOD lists China's potential military options regarding Taiwan as follows:

-   **persuasion and coercion,** which "combines the credible threat to use military force with the economic and cultural tools that China has at its disposal";
-   **limited force options** that could employ "information operations, special operations forces on Taiwan, and SRBM or air strikes at key military or political sites, to try to break the will of Taiwan's leadership and population";
-   **an air and missile campaign,** in which "Surprise SRBM attacks and precision air strikes could support a campaign designed to degrade Taiwan defenses, decapitate its military and political leadership, and break its will to fight rapidly before the United States and other nations could intervene";
-   **a blockade,** which "Beijing could threaten or deploy... either as a 'non-war' pressure tactic in the pre -hostility phase or as a transition to active conflict";[69] and
-   **amphibious invasion,** which "would be a complex and difficult operation relying upon timing and pre-conditions set by many subordinate campaigns."[70]

Anti-Access Force for Short-Duration Conflict

More specifically, observers believe that China's military modernization is aimed at fielding a force that can succeed in a short-duration conflict with Taiwan that finishes before the United States is able to intervene, so that China can present the United States and the rest of the world with a fait accompli. DOD states that China is "emphasizing preparations to fight and win short-duration, high-intensity conflicts along China's periphery."[71]

Regarding the potential time line for a short-duration conflict with Taiwan, one observer states:

> The U.S. (particularly the U.S. Pacific Command/PACOM) seems to want Taiwan to focus on [acquiring] systems and defensive operational capabilities that would lengthen the amount of time Taiwan could deny the PRC from gaining air superiority, sea control, and physical occupation of Taiwan's leadership core (namely Taipei). The idea is to permit sufficient time to bring U.S. forces to bear. The amount of time needed is understood to be at least 5 days,

---

[68] Ibid., executive summary.

[69] Analysts disagree regarding China's potential for mounting an effective blockade, particularly with its submarine force. For an analysis that casts a skeptical eye on the potential, see Michael A. Glosny, "Strangulation from the Sea? A PRC Submarine Blockade of Taiwan," *International Security,* spring 2004, pp. 125-160. For an analysis that expresses more concern about this potential, see the statement of Lyle J. Goldstein as printed in *2/6/04 USCC hearing,* pp. 132-133, 147-151.

[70] *2005 DOD CMP,* pp. 39-42. See also *2003 CFR task force report,* pp. 2, 3, and 53.

[71] *2005 DOD CMP,* executive summary. See also Eric A. McVadon, "Alarm Bells Ring as China Builds up its Armoury on a Massive Sale," *Jane's Defence Weekly,* March 16, 2005, p. 23; Edward Cody, "China Builds A Smaller, Stronger Military," *Washington Post,* April 12, 2005, p. 1; Bryan Bender, "China Bolsters Its Forces, US Says," *Boston Globe,* April 10, 2005, p. 1; Jim Yardley and Thom Shanker, "Chinese Navy Buildup Gives Pentagon New Worries," *New York Times,* April 8, 2005.

presumably after credible warning that hostilities either are imminent or are already underway.[72]

Consistent with the goal of a short-duration conflict and a *fait accompli,* observers believe, China wants its modernized military to be capable of acting as a so-called anti-access force — a force that can deter U.S. intervention, or failing that, delay the arrival or reduce the effectiveness of U.S. intervention forces, particularly U.S. Navy forces. DOD states that, in addition to preventing Taiwan independence or trying to compel Taiwan to negotiate a settlement on Beijing's terms, "A second set of objectives includes building counters to third-party, including potential U.S., intervention in cross-Strait crises."[73]

China's emerging maritime anti-access force can be viewed as broadly analogous to the sea-denial force that the Soviet Union developed during the Cold War to deny U.S. use of the sea or counter U.S. forces participating in a NATO-Warsaw Pact conflict. One potential difference between the Soviet sea-denial force and China's emerging maritime anti-access force is that China's force could include MaRV-equipped TBMs capable of hitting moving ships at sea.

Some analysts speculate that China may attain (or believe that is has attained) a capable maritime anti-access capability, or important elements of it, by about 201 0.[74] Other observers believe China will attain (or believe that it has attained) such a capability some time after 2010. DOD states that "The U.S. Intelligence Community estimates that China will require until the end of this decade or later for its military modernization program to produce a modern force, capable of defeating a moderate-size adversary."[75] The term "moderate-size

---

[72] Testimony of Fu S. Mei, Director, Taiwan Security Analysis Center (TAISAC), Before the U.S.-China Economic and Security Review Commission [regarding] "Taiwan Straits Issues and Chinese Military-Defense Budget," September 15, 2005, p. 3.

[73] *2005 DOD CMP,* executive summary. DOD also states that "China is developing capabilities to achieve local sea denial, including naval mines, submarines, cruise missiles, and special operations forces." (Ibid., p. 33.) Another observer states that

This mission, in essence, is to be able quickly to overwhelm Taiwan's military, cow the Taiwan government, and deter, delay, or complicate effective and timely U.S. intervention....

The concept is ... to be able very rapidly, in a matter of days, to cause Taiwan to capitulate, with such capitulation abetted by the failure of the U.S. to respond promptly and effectively. As has been said often, Beijing's concept is to be able to present to Washington and the world a *fait accompli* concerning Taiwan....

Beijing has ... developed a concept to use force, if it feels it must, to defeat Taiwan, deter or delay U.S. intervention, and at least cause Japan to think twice before introducing overt military assistance in a developing crisis....

There is, in my opinion, no question that this is Beijing's concept for overwhelming Taiwan and deterring or confronting U.S. forces. *(McVadon 9/15/05 testimony,* pp. 1, 2, 2-3, 6.)

[74] One observer, for example, states:

Because the Chinese submarine fleet will operate in nearby waters and in the mid-Pacific, China need not wait until 2020 to challenge the U.S. at sea. It will likely have a home-field advantage in any East Asian conflict contingency as early as 2010, while the U.S. fleet will still have operational demands in the Middle East, and in tracking Russian ballistic missile submarines elsewhere. *(Tkacik 7/27/05 testimony,* p. 8.)

See also *Fisher 7/27/05 testimony,* which cites the year 2010 on pages 3, 4, 7, 9 (twice), 11, and 16 in discussing China's military modernization and the resulting impact on the regional military balance, and Fisher's statement as printed in *2/6/04 USCC hearing,* p. 85, which states, "It is possible that before the end of the decade the PLA will have the capability to coordinate mass missile attacks on U.S. Naval Forces by submarines and Su-30s," and p. 88, which prints his table summarizing potential PLA anti-carrier forces by 2010.

[75] *2005 DOD CMP,* p. 26. Another observer states: "QDR [Quadrennial Defense Review] planners have recently moved forward (to 2012) their estimate of when key warfighting capabilities might be needed to fight China, and have postulated conflict scenarios lasting as long as seven years." (Loren B. Thompson, "Pentagon Fighter Study Raises Questions," August 22, 2005. Lexington Institute Issue Brief.) *2003 CFR task force report* discusses the difficulty of assessing the pace at which China's military modernization is occurring and presents a

adversary" would appear to apply to a country other than the United States. The issue of when China might attain (or believe that it has attained) a capable anti-access capability is significant because it can influence the kinds of options that are available to U.S. policymakers for addressing the situation.

Broader or Longer-Term Regional Goals

In addition to the near-term focus on developing military options for addressing the situation with Taiwan, DOD and some (but not necessarily all) other observers believe that broader or longer-term goals of China's military modernization, including naval modernization, include one or more of the following:

- *asserting China's regional military leadership*, displacing U.S. regional military influence, prevailing in regional rivalries, and encouraging eventual U.S. military withdrawal form the region;
- *defending China's claims in maritime territorial disputes*, some of which have implications for oil, gas, or mineral exploration rights;[76]
- *protecting China's sea lines of communication*, which China relies upon increasingly for oil and other imports.[77]

Some PLA Navy units have recently been deployed outside China's home waters. In November 2004, for example, a Han-class SSN was detected in Japanese territorial waters near Okinawa.[78] DIA states that, as part of the same deployment, this submarine traveled "far into the western Pacific Ocean...."[79] Press reports state that the submarine operated in the vicinity of Guam before moving toward Okinawa.[80] As another example, on September 9, 2005,

China deployed a fleet of five warships... near a gas field in the East China Sea, a potentially resource-rich area that is disputed by China and Japan. The ships, including a guided-missile destroyer, were spotted by a Japanese military patrol plane near the

series of indicators on pages 11-15 (and again on pages 64-68) that can be monitored to help gauge the pace and direction of China's military modernization.

[76] For more on this topic, see CRS Report RL3 1183, *China's Maritime Territorial Claims: Implications for U.S. Interests,* Kerry Dumbaugh, coordinator.

[77] See, for example, *2005 DOD CMP,* pp. 12-13 and 33; *Fisher 7/27/05 testimony,* p. 4; *McVadon 9/15/05 testimony,* p. 1; *2003 CFR task force report,* pp. 24-25, 3 1-32, 62-63; Edward Cody, "China Builds A Smaller, Stronger Military," April 12, 2005, p. 1; David Lague, "China's Growing Undersea Fleet Presents Challenge To Its Neighbors," *Wall Street Journal,* November 29, 2004.

[78] Mark Magnier, "China Regrets Sub Incident, Japan Says," *Los Angeles Times,* November 17, 2004; Martin Fackler, "Japanese Pursuit Of Chinese Sub Raises Tensions," *Wall Street Journal,* November 15, 2004: 20; Kenji Hall, "Japan: Unidentified sub is Chinese," *NavyTimes. com (Associated Press),* November 12, 2004.

[79] Current and Projected National Security Threats to the United States, Vice Admiral Lowell E. Jacoby, U.S. Navy, Director, Defense Intelligence Agency, Statement for the Record [before the] Senate Select Committee on Intelligence, 16 February 2005, p. 16-17. See also Current and Projected National Security Threats to the United States, Vice Admiral Lowell E. Jacoby, U.S. Navy, Director, Defense Intelligence Agency, Statement For the Record [before the] Senate Armed Services Committee, 17 March 2005, p. 17.

[80] Timothy Hu, "Ready, steady, go...," *Jane's Defence Weekly,* April 13, 2005: 27; "China Sub Tracked By U.S. Off Guam Before Japan Intrusion," *Japan Times,* November 17, 2004.

Chunxiao gas field, according to the [Japan] Maritime Self-Defense Forces. It is believed to be the first time that Chinese warships have been seen in that area.[81]

As a third example,

China said on Sept. 29 [of 2005 that] it has sent warships to the disputed East China Sea, a day ahead of talks with Japan over competing territorial claims in the gas-rich waters.

> "I can now confirm that in the East China Sea, a Chinese reserve vessel squadron has been established," foreign ministry spokesman Qin Gang told a regular briefing....

No details were given on the size of the squadron or the area it will patrol. The establishment of the squadron follows China's creation of two naval groups in the Bohai Sea and Yellow Sea off the northern China coast, the agency said.[82]

Regarding base access and support facilities to support more distant PLA Navy operations, one press report states:

> China is building up military forces and setting up bases along sea lanes from the Middle East to project its power overseas and protect its oil shipments, according to a previously undisclosed internal report prepared for Defense Secretary Donald H. Rumsfeld.
> "China is building strategic relationships along the sea lanes from the Middle East to the South China Sea in ways that suggest defensive and offensive positioning to protect China's energy interests, but also to serve broad security objectives," said the report sponsored by the director, Net Assessment, who heads Mr. Rumsfeld's office on future-oriented strategies.

The Washington Times obtained a copy of the report, titled "Energy Futures in Asia," which was produced by defense contractor Booz Allen Hamilton.

The internal report stated that China is adopting a "string of pearls" strategy of bases and diplomatic ties stretching from the Middle East to southern China....[83]

---

[81] Norimitsu Onishi and Howard W. French, "Japan's Rivalry With China Is Stirring A Crowded Sea," *New York Times,* September 11, 2005. See also "Japan Upset Over Chinese Warships Near Disputed Area," *DefenseNews.com,* October 3, 2005.

[82] "China Sends Warships to East China Sea," *DefenseNews.com,* September 29, 2005.

[83] Bill Gertz, "China Builds Up Strategic Sea Lanes," *Washington Times,* January 18, 2005, p. 1. The report stated that China is:

operating an eavesdropping post and building a naval base at Gwadar, Pakistan, near the Persian Gulf;

building a container port facility at Chittagong, Bangladesh, and seeking "much more extensive naval and commercial access" in Bangladesh;

building naval bases in Burma, which is near the Strait of Malacca; operating electronic intelligence-gathering facilities on islands in the Bay of Bengal and near the Strait of Malacca;

building a railway line from China through Cambodia to the sea;

improving its ability to project air and sea power into the South China Sea from mainland China and Hainan Island;

considering funding a $20-billion canal that would cross the Kra Isthmus of Thailand, which would allow ships to bypass the Strait of Malacca and permit China to establish port facilities there.

According to the article,

The Pentagon report said China, by militarily controlling oil shipping sea lanes, could threaten ships, "thereby creating a climate of uncertainty about the safety of all ships on the high seas."

The report noted that the vast amount of oil shipments through the sea lanes, along with growing piracy and maritime terrorism, prompted China, as well as India, to build up naval power at "chokepoints" along the sea routes from the Persian Gulf to the South China Sea.

POTENTIAL IMPLICATIONS FOR REQUIRED U.S. NAVY CAPABILITIES

Potential implications of China's naval modernization for required U.S. Navy capabilities can be organized into three groups:

- capabilities for a crisis or conflict in the Taiwan Strait area;
- capabilities for maintaining U.S. Navy presence and military influence in the Western Pacific; and
- capabilities for detecting, tracking, and if necessary countering PLA Navy SSBNs equipped with long-range SLBMs.

Each of these is discussed below.

Capabilities for Taiwan Strait Crisis or Conflict

U.S. military operations in a potential crisis or conflict in the Taiwan Strait area would likely feature a strong reliance on U.S. Navy forces and land-based U.S. Air Force aircraft.[84] If air bases in Japan and South Korea are, for political reasons, not available to the United States for use in the operation, or if air bases in Japan, South Korea, or Guam are rendered less useful by PLA attacks using TBMs, LACMs, or special operations forces, then the reliance on U.S. Navy forces could become greater.

For the U.S. Navy, a crisis or conflict in the Taiwan Strait could place a premium on the following:

- on-station or early-arriving forces;
- forces with a capability to defeat PLA anti-access weapons and platforms;
- forces with an ability to operate in an environment that could be characterized by IW/IO and possibly EMP or the use of nuclear weapons directly against Navy ships; and
- forces that can be ready to conduct operations by about 2010, or by some later date.

"China ... is looking not only to build a blue-water navy to control the sea lanes, but also to develop undersea mines and missile capabilities to deter the potential disruption of its energy supplies from potential threats, including the U.S. Navy, especially in the case of a conflict with Taiwan," the report said....

"The Iraq war, in particular, revived concerns over the impact of a disturbance in Middle Eastern supplies or a U.S. naval blockade," the report said, noting that Chinese military leaders want an ocean-going navy and "undersea retaliatory capability to protect the sea lanes."
China believes the U.S. military will disrupt China's energy imports in any conflict over Taiwan, and sees the United States as an unpredictable country that violates others' sovereignty and wants to "encircle" China, the report said. See also Edward Cody, "China Builds A Smaller, Stronger Military," *Washington Post,* April 12, 2005, p. 1.

[84] For discussions relating to Taiwan's potential military capabilities in such a scenario, see CRS Report RL30957, *Taiwan: Major U.S. Arms Sales Since 1990;* and CRS Report RL3 0341, *China/Taiwan: Evolution of the 'One China' Policy — Key Statements from Washington, Beijing, and Taipei,* both by Shirley A. Kan.

On-Station and Early-Arriving Forces

In the scenario of a short-duration conflict, on-station and early-arriving U.S. Navy forces could be of particular value, while later-arriving U.S. Navy forces might be of less value, at least in preventing initial success by PLA forces.

On-Station Forces. Given the difficulty of knowing with certainty when a Taiwan Strait crisis or conflict might occur, having forces on-station at the start of the crisis or conflict is a goal that would most reliably be met by maintaining a standing forward deployment of U.S. Navy forces in the area. Maintaining a standing forward deployment of U.S. Navy forces in the area while also maintaining U.S. Navy forward deployments in other regions, such as the Persian Gulf/Indian Ocean region and the Mediterranean Sea, would require a Navy with a certain minimum number of ships.

Although it is sometimes said that it takes three U.S. Navy ships to keep one ship forward deployed in an overseas location, the actual ratio traditionally has been higher. For example, if U.S. Navy ships are operated in the traditional manner — with a single crew for each ship and deployments lasting six months — then maintaining one U.S. Navy cruiser or destroyer continuously forward-deployed to the Western Pacific might require a total of about five San Diego-based cruisers or destroyers.[85]

Stationkeeping multipliers like these can be reduced by homeporting U.S. Navy ships at locations closer to Taiwan (such as Japan, Guam, Hawaii, or perhaps Singapore) or by deploying ships for longer periods of time and operating them with multiple crews that are rotated out to each ship. The Navy has an aircraft carrier strike group and other ships[86] homeported in Japan, and three attack submarines homeported in Guam.[87] The Navy reportedly may transfer an additional aircraft carrier from the continental United States to Hawaii or Guam, and is studying options for transferring perhaps a few additional SSNs to Hawaii or Guam. The Navy is also experimenting with the concept of deploying certain Navy ships (particularly surface combatants) for 12, 18, or 24 months and rotating multiple crews out to each ship.[88]

Early-Arriving Forces

Having early-arriving U.S. Navy forces could mean having forces based in locations Western Pacific locations such as Japan, Guam, Singapore, or perhaps Hawaii, rather than on the U.S. West Coast.[89] *Table 4* shows potential ship travel times to the Taiwan Strait area

---

[85] For a discussion, see archived CRS Report 92-803, *Naval Forward Deploym ents and the Size of the Navy,* by Ronald O'Rourke. See *Table 1.* (Out of print and available directly from the author.)

[86] The other ships include amphibious ships and mine countermeasures ships.

[87] One of these SSNs, the San Francisco, was significantly damaged in a collision with an undersea mountain near Guam in January 2005. The ship was transferred to the Puget Sound Naval Shipyard at Bremerton, WA, for repairs. The San Francisco reportedly will be replaced at Guam by another SSN, the Buffalo, in September 2006. (David V. Crisostomo, "Guam To Receive Third Home-Ported Submarine In 2006," *Pacific Daily News (Guam),* November 1, 2005.)

[88] For a discussion see CRS Report RS2 1338, *Navy Ship Deployments: New Approaches — Background and Issues for Congress,* by Ronald O'Rourke.

[89] Other potential Western Pacific locations, at least in theory, include South Korea (where other U.S. forces have been based for years), the Philippines (where the U.S. Navy ships used as a major repair port until the early 1990s), and Australia.

from various ports in the Pacific, based on average ship travel speeds. All the ports shown in the table except Singapore are current U.S. Navy home ports.[90] U.S. Navy submarines, aircraft carriers, cruisers, and destroyers have maximum sustained speeds of more than 30 knots, but their average speeds over longer transits in some cases might be closer to 25 knots or less due rough sea conditions or, in the case of the cruisers or destroyers, which are conventionally powered, the need slow down for at-sea refueling.[91] The Navy's planned Littoral Combat Ship (LCS) is to have a maximum sustained speed of about 45 knots, but its average speed over long transits would likely be less than that.

Table 4. Potential Ship Travel Times to Taiwan Strait Area

Port	Straight-line distance to Taiwan Strait area[a] (nautical miles)	Minimum travel time in days, based on average speeds below[b]		
		20 knots	25 knots	30 knots
Yokosuka, Japan[c]	1,076	2.2	1.8	1.5
Guam	1,336	2.8	2.2	1.9
Singapore[d]	1,794	3.7	3.0	2.5
Pearl Harbor[e]	4,283	8.9	7.1	5.9
Everett, WA	5,223	10.9	8.7	7.3
San Diego	5,933	12.3	9.9	8.2

Source: Table prepared by CRS using straight-line distances calculated by the "how far is it" calculator, available at [http://www.indo.com/distance/].

Defined as a position in the sea at 24°N, 124°E, which is roughly 130 nautical miles *east* of Taiwan, i.e., on the other side of Taiwan from the Taiwan Strait.

Actual travel times may be greater due to the possible need for ships to depart from a straight-line course so as to avoid land barriers, remain within port-area shipping channels, etc.

Distance calculated from Tokyo, which is about 25 nautical miles north of Yokosuka.

No U.S. Navy ships are currently homeported at Singapore.

Distance calculated from Honolulu, which is about 6 nautical miles southeast of Pearl Harbor.

As can be seen in the table, Yokosuka, Guam, and Singapore are less than half as far from the Taiwan Strait area as are Pearl Harbor, Everett, WA,[92] and San Diego. Depending on their average travel speeds, ships homeported in Yokosuka, Guam, and Singapore could arrive in the Taiwan Strait area roughly two to four days after leaving port, ships homeported in Pearl Harbor might arrive about six to nine days after leaving port, and ships homeported on the U.S. West Coast might arrive about seven to twelve days after leaving port. The time needed to get a ship and its crew ready to leave port would add to their total response times. Depending on a ship's status at the moment it was ordered to the Taiwan Strait area, preparing it for rapid departure might require anywhere from less than one day to a few days.

Regarding the possible transfer of a carrier from the continental United States to Hawaii or Guam, one observer states:

---

[90] U.S. Navy ships visit Singapore, and there is a U.S. Navy logistic group there, but no U.S. Navy ships are currently homeported at Singapore.

[91] One version of the LCS has a sprint (i.e., high-speed) range of roughly 1,150 miles, while the other has a sprint range of about 1,940 miles.

[92] Everett is located on the Puget Sound, about 23 nautical miles north of Seattle.

Currently the United States maintains one aircraft carrier full-time in the Western Pacific. In the event of a conflict with China over Taiwan, however, particularly given the various [PLA] threats to land-based air outlined above, having more aircraft carriers on the scene will be extremely valuable. Other than any carriers that might be transiting through the region, however, currently the closest additional carriers would be those based on the west coast of the United States. Given that a conflict with China could begin with little warning, this means that as much as two weeks could elapse before additional aircraft carriers reached the area of combat operations. The Department of Defense has already recommended forward-deploying an additional aircraft carrier in the Pacific, but it is important to note that precisely where this carrier is forward-deployed is significant. In particular, an aircraft carrier based in Hawaii would still take at least a week to reach waters near Taiwan. An aircraft carrier based in Guam, Singapore, or elsewhere in the Western Pacific, by contrast, could arrive on the scene in about three days.[93]

Basing additional forces in Japan, Guam, Singapore, or Hawaii could increase the importance of taking actions to defend these locations against potential attack by TBMs, LACMs, or special operations forces.[94]

Defeating Pla Anti-Access Forces

Defeating PLA maritime anti-access forces would require capabilities for countering:

- large numbers of TBMs, including some possibly equipped with MaRVs;
- large numbers of LACMs and ASCMs, including some advanced ASCMs such as the SS-N-27 and SS-N-22;
- substantial numbers of land-based fighters, strike fighters, maritime bombers, and SAMs, including some built to modern designs;
- a substantial number of submarines, including a few that are nuclear-powered and a significant portion that are built to modern designs;
- a substantial number of destroyers, frigates, and fast attack craft, including some built to modern designs; and
- potentially large numbers of mines of different types, including some advanced models.

Countering TBMS

Countering large numbers of TBMs, including some possibly equipped with MaRVs, could entail some or all of the following:

---

[93] China's Military Modernization and the Cross-Strait Balance, [Statement of] Roger Cliff, September 2005, Testimony presented before the U.S.-China Economic and Security Review Commission on September 15, 2005, pp. 9-10. (Hereafter cited as *Clif 9/15/05 testimony.*)

[94] For a list of recommended actions for improving the ability of bases in the Western Pacific to defend themselves from PLA attack, see *Clif 9/15/05 testimony.*

- operating, if possible, in a way that reduces the likelihood of being detected and tracked by PLA maritime surveillance systems;
- attacking the surveillance systems that detect and track U.S. Navy ships operating at sea, and the network that transmits this targeting data to the TBMs;
- attacking TBMs at their launch sites;
- intercepting TBMs in flight, which in some cases could require firing two or perhaps even three interceptor missiles at individual TBMs to ensure their destruction;
- decoying MaRVs away from U.S. Navy ships.

Potential implications of the above points for Navy missile-defense programs are discussed in this next section of this report.

Countering Submarines

Countering a substantial number of submarines would likely require a coordinated effort by an ASW network consisting of some or all of the following: distributed sensors, unmanned vehicles, submarines, surface ships, helicopters, and maritime patrol aircraft. Defeating torpedoes fired by PLA submarines would require U.S. submarines and surface ships to have systems for detecting, decoying, and perhaps destroying those torpedoes.

ASW operations against well-maintained and well-operated submarines traditionally have often been time-consuming. Acoustic conditions in waters around Taiwan are reportedly poor for ASW, which could make the task of countering PLA submarines in these areas more difficult.[95] Success in an ASW operation is highly dependent on the proficiency of the people operating the ASW equipment. ASW operational proficiency can take time to develop and can atrophy significantly if not regularly exercised.

In December 2004, the Navy approved a new concept of operations (CONOPS) a new general approach — to ASW. As described in one article,

> The Navy's new concept of operations for anti-submarine warfare calls for the use of standoff weapons, networked sensor fields and unmanned vehicles to detect and attack diesel submarines in littoral waters, rather than a reliance on "force on force" engagements.

Chief of Naval Operations Adm. Vern Clark approved the CONOPS Dec. 20, according to a Navy spokesman. The five-page document will guide the development of a comprehensive ASW master plan that is expected to be classified, though it might have an unclassified version.

The CONOPS envisions hundreds or thousands of small sensors that would "permeate the operating environment, yielding unprecedented situational awareness and highly detailed pictures of the battlespace." Attack submarines that today carry sensors and weapons could in the future provide logistical support to and serve as command and control bases for off-board sensors and "kill vehicles," the CONOPS states. The

---

[95] See, for example, the statement of Lyle J. Goldstein in *2/6/04 USCC hearing,* pp. 148, 150, and 152.

networking of autonomous sensor fields with manned and unmanned vehicles will change ASW from a "platform-intensive" to a "sensor-rich" operation, it adds.[96]

At a June 20, 2005, conference on the future of the Navy organized by the American Enterprise Institute (AEI), Admiral Vernon Clark, who was the Chief of Naval Operations until July 22, 2005, stated:

> [The Chinese are] building submarines at a rapid rate. They're buying them from other countries. They're building their own capabilities. And let me just to make a long story short, I published a new ASW concept [of operations] a couple of months ago. I fundamentally don't believe that the old attrition warfare[,] force on force anti-submarine warfare[,] construct is the right way to go in the 21st century. [The questioner] mentioned that I had spent part of my past life in the submarine warfare business. I have. I trailed the Soviets around.
>
> I know what that's about. And what I really believe is going to happen in the future is that when we apply the netted force construct in anti-submarine warfare, it will change the calculus in that area of warfighting forever. And it will be a courageous commander who decides that he's going to come waltzing into our network.[97]

Implementing this new ASW concept of operations reportedly will require overcoming some technical challenges, particularly with regard to linking together large numbers of distributed sensors, some of which might be sonobuoys as small as soda cans.[98]

---

[96] Jason Ma, "ASW Concept Of Operations Sees 'Sensor Rich Way Of Fighting Subs," *Inside the Navy,* February 7, 2005. A January 2005 article stated:

The Navy cannot fight diesel subs with "force on force," such as sending one sub to defeat another sub, because that is not cost effective, [Rear Admiral John Waickwicz, chief of Fleet Anti-Submarine Warfare Command] told *Inside the Navy.* For example, the new Virginia-class subs cost about $2 billion each, while advanced diesel subs cost hundreds of millions of dollars each.

Instead of force on force, ASW tactics will emphasize using networked sensors and communications to allow one platform — like a sub, Littoral Combat Ship, or aircraft — to defeat multiple diesel subs, he said. "You have to be able to destroy them at a very large rate, because potential enemies may have a large number" of subs, he explained.

"We don't have that luxury to go one against one anymore," he added, noting that individual ASW platforms will rely on their greater capability to take on multiple subs. (Jason Ma, "Admiral: Navy's ASW Tactics To Be Aggressive And Offense-Minded," *Inside the Navy,* January 17, 2005.)

[97] Transcript of conference, as posted on the Internet by AEI at [http://www.aei.org/events/ filter.all,eventID. 105 1/transcript.asp]. An October 2004 article stated:

more than just improving antisubmarine operations, Clark's goal is to "fundamentally change" ASW operations away from individual platforms — ship, submarine or aircraft — to a system with the attributes of "pervasive awareness, persistence and speed, all enabled by technological agility."

To meet this goal, "we think we're going to have to go offboard of our platforms," using unmanned aerial, surface and underwater vehicles, and a network of distributed sensors to provide the identification and localization that would allow quick transition to the attack, [Rear Admiral Mark W. Kenny, the flag officer in charge of Task Force ASW] said. "That's what we're focused on: (finding) a high number of quiet contacts in a demanding environment with a timeline that requires us to gain access quickly."

The task force has tested those concepts in at-sea experiments focused on distributive systems, which could be an array of easily deployed underwater sensors, passive and active, networked together and linked to manned platforms, he explained.

Among them is the Advanced Deployable System, which the Program Executive Office for Integrated Warfare Systems currently is studying, along with such other AS W-related concepts as a multisensor Torpedo Recognition and Alertment Function Segment (previously known as Torpedo Recognition and Alertment Function Processor) and the Multifunction Towed Array to improve detection and tracking capability. (Otto Kreisher, "As Underwater Threat Re-Emerges, Navy Renews Emphasis On ASW," *Seapower,* October 2004, p. 15.)

[98] Jason Ma, "Autonomous ASW Sensor Field Seen As High-Risk Technical Hurdle," *Inside the Navy,* June 6, 2005. See also Jason Ma, "Navy's Surface Warfare Chief Cites Progress In ASW Development," *Inside the Navy,* January 17, 2005.

Countering Mines

Countering naval mines is a notoriously time-consuming task that can require meticulous operations by participating surface ships, submarines, and helicopters. The Navy's mine countermeasures (MCM) capabilities have been an area of concern in Congress and elsewhere for a number of years.[99] The Navy for the last several years has been developing several new MCM systems that are scheduled to enter service over the next few years.[100100] Unmanned surface vehicles (USVs) and unmanned underwater vehicles (UUVs) are playing an increasing role in MCM operations.

Operating Amidst IW/IO, EMP, and Nuclear Weapons

Operating effectively in an environment that could be characterized by IW/IO and possibly EMP or the use of nuclear weapons directly against Navy ships could require, among other things:

- measures to achieve and maintain strong computer network security;
- hardening of ships, aircraft, and their various systems against EMP; and
- hardening of ships against the overpres sure, thermal, and radiation effects of a nuclear weapon that is detonated somewhat close to the ship, but not close enough to destroy the ship outright.

Forces Ready by About 2010, or by a Later Date

As mentioned earlier, some analysts speculate that China may attain (or believe that is has attained) a capable maritime anti-access capability, or important elements of it, by about 2010, while other observers believe this will happen some time after 2010. The issue of whether or when China might attain such a capability can influence the kinds of options that are available to U.S. policymakers for addressing the situation.

Options for a Con flict Between Now and 2010. Options that could enhance U.S. Navy capabilities for a crisis or conflict in the Taiwan Strait area between now and 2010 include, among others, the following:

---

[99] See, for example, General Accounting Office, *Navy Acquisitions[:] Improved Littoral War-Fighting Capabilities Needed,* GAO-01-493, May 2001; and General Accounting Office, *Navy Mine Warfare[:] Plans to Improve Countermeasures Capabilities Unclear,* GAO/NSIAD-98-135, June 1998.

[100] The Navy's mine warfare plan is available on the Internet at [http://www.exwar.org/ Htm/4000.htm]. For additional discussions of the Navy's mine warfare programs, see Department of the Navy, *Highlights of the Department of the Navy FY2006/FY2007 Budget,* Washington, 2005. (Office of Budget, February 2005) pp. 5-9; Richard R. Burgess, "New Mine Countermeasure System Designs Are Hitting the Water," *Seapower,* August 2005, p. 46, 48; Jason Ma, "Fielding Of Organic Mine Warfare Systems Slips At Least Two Years," *Inside the Navy,* March 21, 2005; William E. Landay III and Hunter C. Keeter, "Breaking the Mold," *Seapower,* March 2005, pp. 42, 44, 46; Scott C. Truver, "Mine Countermeasures And Destruction," *Naval Forces,* No. 3, 2004, pp. 63-64, 66-71; Glenn W. Goodman, Jr., "Organic Mine Countermeasures To Clear Path For Navy," *Armed Forces Journal,* January 2004, p. 36.

- increasing currently planned activities for physically surveying the physical environment around Taiwan, so as to more quickly update older data that might unreliable, and to fill in any gaps in understanding regarding how local atmospheric and water conditions might affect the performance of radars and sonars;
- increasing currently planned levels of monitoring and surveillance of PLA forces that are likely to participate in a crisis or conflict in the Taiwan Strait area;
- increasing currently planned levels of contact between the U.S. Navy and Taiwan military forces, so as to maintain a fully up-to-date U.S. understanding of Taiwan military capabilities, plans, and doctrine (and vice versa);
- increasing currently planned military exercises that are tailored to the potential requirements of a crisis or conflict in the Taiwan Strait area;
- increasing the number of ships that are assigned to the Pacific Fleet, or the number that are forward-homeported at locations such as Japan, Guam, Hawaii, and perhaps Singapore, or the numbers of both;
- deferring current plans for retiring existing ships or aircraft before 2010, particularly ships and aircraft whose nominal service lives would otherwise extend to 2010 or beyond;
- modernizing ships and aircraft now in service;
- reactivating recently retired ships and aircraft;[101] and
- procuring new items that can be completed between now and 2010, such as weapons, aircraft, and Littoral Combat Ships (LCSs).

Options for a Conflict After 2010

Options that could enhance U.S. Navy capabilities for a crisis or conflict in the Taiwan Strait area some time after 2010 include items from the above list, plus the procurement of larger ships that take several years to build (e.g., SSNs, aircraft carriers, destroyers, and cruisers), and the development and procurement of aircraft and weapons that are not currently ready for procurement.

Capabilities for Maintaining Regional Presence and Influence

For the U.S. Navy, maintaining regional presence and military influence in the Western Pacific could place a premium on the following, among other things:

- maintaining a substantial U.S. Navy ship presence throughout the region;
- making frequent port calls in the region;
- conducting frequent exercises with other navies in the region;
- taking actions to ensure system compatibility between U.S. Navy ships and ships of allied and friendly nations in the region; and

---

[101] Potential candidates include, among others, Spruance (DD-963) class destroyers, which could be reactivated as ASW platforms or missile shooters, Oliver Hazard Perry (FFG-7) class frigates and TAGOS-type ocean surveillance (i.e., towed-array sonar) ships, both of which could be reactivated as ASW platforms, and ASW-capable aircraft such as S-3 carrier-based airplanes and P-3 land-based maritime patrol aircraft.

- conducting frequent exchanges between U.S. Navy personnel and military and political leaders of other countries in the region.

Factors influencing the Navy's ability to maintain a substantial U.S. Navy ship presence throughout the region include the total number of ships in the Navy's Pacific Fleet, the number of Navy ships forward-homeported at locations such as Japan, Guam, Hawaii, and perhaps Singapore, and ship-crewing and -deployment approaches (e.g., six-month deployments and single crews vs. longer deployments with crew rotation).

Capabilities for Tracking and Countering PLA SSBN

Detecting, tracking, and if necessary countering PLA Navy SSBNs equipped with long-range SLBMs could require some or all of the following:

- a seabed-based sensor network analogous to the Sound Surveillance System (SOSUS) that the U.S. Navy used during the Cold War to detect and track Soviet nuclear-powered submarines;
- ocean surveillance ships with additional sonars, which would be similar to the TAGOS-type ocean-surveillance ships that the Navy also used during the Cold War to help detect and track Soviet nuclear-powered submarines; and
- enough SSNs so that some can be assigned to tracking and if necessary attacking PLA SSBNs.[102]

POTENTIAL OVERSIGHT ISSUES FOR CONGRESS

Potential oversight questions for Congress arising from China's military modernization and its potential implications for required U.S. Navy capabilities can be organized into three groups:

- questions relating to China's military modernization as a defense-planning priority;
- questions relating to U.S. Navy force structure and basing arrangements; and
- questions relating to Navy warfare areas and programs. Each of these is discussed below.

CHINA AS A DEFENSE-PLANNING PRIORITY

DOD Planning

Is DOD giving adequate weight in the 2005 Quadrennial Defense Review (QDR) and other planning activities to China 's military modernization as opposed to other concerns, such as current operations in Iraq and Afghanistan and the global war on terrorism (GWOT)

---

[102] Additional measures that could assist in tracking PLA SSBNs include satellite surveillance (particularly when the SSBNs are in port or if they surface during their deployments) and human intelligence.

generally? Is DOD giving adequate weight in its planning to the funding needs of the Navy as opposed to those of the other services, such as the Army?

Operations in Iraq and Afghanistan have led to increased focus on the funding needs of the Army and Marine Corps, since these two services are heavily committed to those operations. Placing increasing emphasis on China in DOD planning, on the other hand, would likely lead to increased focus on the funding needs of the Navy and Air Force, since these two services are generally viewed as the ones most likely to be of the most importance for a crisis or conflict in the Taiwan Strait area. In a situation of finite DOD resources, striking the correct planning balance between operations in Iraq and Afghanistan and the GWOT generally, and China's military modernization is viewed by some observers as a key DOD planning challenge.

Navy Planning

Is the Navy is giving adequate weight in its planning to China 's military modernization as opposed to other concerns, such as the GWOT?

Required Navy capabilities for participating in the GWOT overlap with, but are not identical to, required Navy capabilities for responding to China's naval modernization. In a situation of finite Navy resources, striking the correct balance between investments for participating in the GWOT and those for responding to China's naval modernization is viewed by some observers as a key Navy planning challenge.

The Navy in recent months has taken some actions that reflect an interest in increasing the Navy's role in the GWOT. In June 2005, for example, Admiral Vernon Clark, who was the Chief of Naval Operations until July 22, 2005, directed the Navy to take nine "actions to expand the Navy's capabilities to prosecute the GWOT..." Among these are the establishment of a Navy riverine force, the establishment of a reserve civil affairs battalion, the establishment of a Foreign Area Office (FAO) community in the Navy, and concept development work for a potential Navy expeditionary combat battalion composed of sailors rather than Marines. "To the extent possible," the Navy wants to implement these actions without increasing Navy active and reserve end strength.[103] In October 2005, Admiral Clark's successor as CNO, Admiral Michael Mullen, issued a guidance statement for the Navy for 2006 that contained follow-on initiatives intended to strengthen the Navy's role in the GWOT.[104] The Navy has also commissioned a study from the Naval Studies Board (an arm of the National Academy of Sciences) on the adequacy of the role of naval forces in the GWOT and options for enhancing that role.[105]

---

[103] See July 12, 2005 memorandum for distribution from Director, Navy Staff on implementation of Chief of Naval Operations (CNO) guidance — global war on terrorism (GWOT) capabilities, posted in the "Defense Plus" section of [http://www.insidedefense.com]. See also, Andrew Scutro, "Navy To Establish Expeditionary And Riverine Forces," *NavyTimes.com,* July 7, 2005; Jason Sherman, "Navy To Establish Ground Combat Units, River Force For Terror War," *Inside the Navy,* July 11, 2005; Jason Ma, "For War On Terror, Navy Could Field New 'SOF-Lite Ground Troops," July 18, 2005; Christian Lowe, "U.S. Navy Considers New Combat Battalion," *Defense News,* July 25, 2005; "Navy Creates Riverines, Landing Unit To Lighten Marine, Army Force Load," *Seapower,* August 2005, pp. 6-7.

[104] M. G. Mullen, *CNO Guidance for 2006, Meeting the Challenge of a New Era.* Washington, 2005. 9 pp.

[105] Christopher J. Castelli, "Navy Commissions Study On 'Adequacy' Of Naval Role In War On Terror," *Inside the Navy,* July 11, 2005.

At the same time, the Navy has affirmed the importance of China's military modernization in its budget planning. At a June 20, 2005 conference on the future of the Navy organized by the American Enterprise Institute (AEI), for example, Admiral Clark was asked to comment on China. He stated in part:

> Well, I think that, you know, we're always quick to point out that China's not our enemy, but China is building a very capable maritime capability, and so we should not be blind to that.
> So what does it mean? Well, here's what I believe that it means. I believe that if you study the Chinese, you see that there's been some change in their thinking over the course of the last number of years. Here's this mammoth land, continent; here's — you know, it would be easy to think about this country as being land-centric in terms of its national security focus, but what we're seeing is that that really isn't where they're putting their money. They're putting their investments in, and what it looks like, if you interpret their actions, is that their primary concerns are in the area of aviation and maritime capability that other nations would bring to bear in their area, in their region of the world. And so they're trying to build a capability to make sure that they're not pushed into a corner in their own part of the world.
> I understand that this morning there was conjecture about their ability to build missile systems that will threaten long-range land bases and moving targets in the future, like ships at sea. And I will tell you that whether they're going to do that or not, I guarantee you that I believe that it is my duty and responsibility to expect that, based on what I understand about what they're doing, to expect that they're trying to do that. And I will tell you that the budget submit that's on the Hill is providing the kind of capability to make sure that the United States
> Navy can fight in that theater or exist in that theater, understanding the kind of capability that they're trying to bring to bear.[106]

NAVY FORCE STRUCTURE AND BASING ARRANGEMENTS

Size of the Fleet

Is the Navy planning a fleet with enough ships to address potential challenges posed by China 's naval modernization while also meeting other responsibilities?

As of November 2005, the Navy included a total of about 280 ships of various kinds. In early 2005, the Navy stated that it wanted the fleet in the future to include a total of 260 to 325 ships.[107] The Navy has stated that it will announce a successor ship force structure plan by early 2006. A key potential issue for Congress in assessing the adequacy of the Navy's ship force structure plan is whether it includes enough ships to address potential challenges posed by China's naval modernization while also meeting other responsibilities, including maintaining forward deployments of Navy ships in the Persian Gulf/Indian Ocean region and the Mediterranean Sea and conducting less-frequent operations in other parts of the world, such as the Caribbean, the waters around South America, and the waters off West Africa. If increased numbers of Navy ships are needed to address potential challenges posed by China's naval modernization, fewer ships might be available for meeting other responsibilities.

---

[106] Transcript of conference, as posted on the Internet by AEI at [http://www.aei.org/events/ filter.all,eventID. 105 1/transcript.asp].

[107] For a discussion, see CRS Report RL32665, *Potential Navy Force Structure and Shipbuilding Plans: Background and Issues for Congress,* by Ronald O'Rourke.

Some Members of Congress have expressed concern in recent years that the declining total number of ships in the Navy may make it difficult for the Navy to perform all if its various missions, at least not without putting undue stress on Navy personnel and equipment. In response, Navy officials in recent years have argued that the total number of ships in the Navy is no longer, by itself, a very good measure of total Navy capability over time, because of the significant increase in individual Navy ship and aircraft capabilities in recent years and the effect that computer networking technology has on further increasing the collective capability of Navy ships and aircraft. Navy officials acknowledge, however, that ship numbers are one factor in understanding Navy capabilities, particularly for conducting simultaneous operations of different kinds in multiple locations around the world.

Division of Fleet Between Atlantic and Pacific

Should a greater percentage of the Navy be assigned to the Pacific Fleet?

Forward Homeporting in the Western Pacific

Is the Navy moving quickly enough to forward-homeport additional ships in the Western Pacific? Should the Navy expand the number of additional ships it is thinking of homeporting in the area?

Increasing the number of ships forward homeported in the Western Pacific can increase both the number of ships that the Navy can maintain forward-deployed to that area on a day to day basis, and the number that can arrive in the early stages of a conflict in the Western Pacific, including the Taiwan Strait area. As mentioned earlier, the Navy may transfer an additional aircraft carrier from the continental United States to Hawaii or Guam, and is studying options for transferring perhaps a few additional SSNs to Hawaii or Guam. Observers who are concerned about deterring or responding to a conflict in the Taiwan Strait area by 2010 might emphasize the importance of implementing these actions as quickly as possible.

In addition, observers concerned about China's military modernization might argue in favor of expanding the number of ships to be transferred to Western Pacific home ports. These additional ships could include SSNs, converted Trident cruise missile submarines (SSGNs), surface combatants, and perhaps one more aircraft carrier. The final report of the 2001 Quadrennial Defense Review (QDR) stated that "The Secretary of the Navy will increase aircraft carrier battlegroup presence in the Western Pacific and will explore options for homeporting an additional three to four surface combatants, and guided missile submarines (SSGNs), in that area.[108] A 2002 Congressional Budget Office (CBO) report discussed the option of homeporting a total of up to 11 SSNs at Guam.[109] Expanding the number of ships to be homeported in the Western Pacific could require construction of additional homeporting facilities, particularly in locations such as Guam. Transferring ships

---

[108] U.S. Department of Defense, *Quadrennial Defense Review Report,* Washington, 2001(September 30, 2001) p. 27.

[109] U.S. Congressional Budget Office, *Increasing the Mission Capability of the Attack Submarine Force,* Washington, CBO, 2002. (A CBO Study, March 2002), 41 pp.

from the U.S. West Coast to the Western Pacific can also have implications for crew training and ship maintenance for those ships.

Number of Aircraft Carriers

Should the Navy maintain a force of 12 carriers, or a smaller number?

As part of its FY2006 budget submission, the Navy proposed accelerating the retirement of the aircraft carrier John F. Kennedy (CV-67) to FY2006 and reducing the size of the carrier force from 12 ships to 11. The issue is discussed at some length in another CRS report.[110] Advocates of maintaining a force of not less than 12 carriers could argue that, in light of China's naval modernization, including the introduction of new land-based fighters and strike fighters and the possibility that the PLA might, as part of a conflict in the Taiwan Strait area, use TBMs, LACMs, or special operations forces to attack U.S. land bases in the Western Pacific, a force of at least 12 carriers is needed to deter or prevail in such a conflict. Those supporting a reduction in the carrier force to 11 or fewer ships could argue that such a reduction is acceptable in light of the increasing capabilities of individual Navy carrier air wings, the Navy's plan to transfer an additional carrier to the Western Pacific, and options for improving the defenses of U.S. bases in the Western Pacific against attack from TBMs, LACMs, and special operations forces.

Number of Attack Submarines (SSNS)

Should the number of nuclear-powered attack submarines be about 40, about 55, or some other number?

The Navy at the end of FY2005 operated a total of 54 SSNs. The Navy's early-2005 plan for a fleet of 260 to 325 ships includes a total of 37 to 41 SSNs plus four converted Trident cruise missile submarines, or SSGNs. The number of SSNs that will be included in the new force structure plan that the Navy is expected to announce by early 2006 is not clear. Supporters of SSNs argue that the Navy needs to maintain a force of at least 55 boats, if not more. The issue of the SSN force-level goal is discussed at length in another CRS report.[111]

Supporters of SSNs have argued in recent months that China's naval modernization, and in particular China's submarine modernization, is a significant reason for supporting a force of 55 or more SSNs rather than a lower number such as 40. The argument was an element of the successful campaign in 2005 by supporters of the New London, CT, submarine base to convince the Base Realignment and Closure (BRAC) to reject DOD's recommendation to close the base.[112]

---

[110] CRS Report RL32731, *Navy Aircraft Carriers: Proposed Retirement of USS John F. Kennedy — Issues and Options for Congress,* by Ronald O'Rourke.

[111] CRS Report RL324 18, *Navy Attack Submarine Force-Level Goal and Procurement Rate: Background and Issues for Congress,* by Ronald O'Rourke.

[112] See, for example, Chris Johnson, "Lawmaker Points To China Buildup In Effort To Protect Sub Base," *Inside the Navy,* August 1, 2005; Anthony Cronin, "Hunter Says China Bolsters Case To Keep Sub Base Open," *New London (CT) Day,* June 28, 2005; William Yardley, "If Bases Aren't Needed, Some Fear Fleet Is Next," *New York Times,* August 22, 2005.

Although the discussion is sometimes cast in terms of U.S. SSNs fighting PLA Navy submarines, this captures only a part of how U.S. SSNs would fit into potential U.S. Navy operations against PLA forces. On the one hand, ASW is conducted by platforms other than SSNs, and an SSN is not always the best platform for countering an enemy submarine. On the other hand, SSNs perform a number of potentially significant missions other than ASW.

Supporters of maintaining a larger number of SSNs in light of China's naval modernization could argue that, in addition to participating in operations against PLA Navy submarines, U.S. SSNs could do the following:

- Conduct pre-crisis covert intelligence, surveillance, and reconnaissance (ISR) of PLA Navy forces and bases. Such operations could improve U.S. understanding PLA capabilities and weaknesses.
- Covertly lay mines around China's naval bases. In light of the PLA Navy's limited mine countermeasures capabilities, the presence of mines around PLA Navy bases could significantly delay the deployment of PLA Navy forces at the outset of a crisis or conflict.
- Attack or threaten PLA Navy surface ships. In light of the PLA Navy's limitations in ASW, a threat from U.S. SSNs could substantially complicate PLA military planning, particularly for an intended short-duration conflict.
- Fire Tomahawk cruise missiles from unexpected locations. Tomahawks could be used to attack on PLA command and control nodes, air bases, and TBM, LACM, ASCM, and SAM launch sites.
- *Covertly insert and recover special operations forces (SOF).* SOF can be used to attack PLA Navy bases or other PLA coastal facilities.

Supporters of maintaining a larger number of SSNs could also argue that submerged U.S. SSNs cannot be attacked by conventionally armed TBMs and ASCMs and are less vulnerable than are U.S. Navy surface ships to EMP effects and to certain other nuclear weapon effects.

Supporters of maintaining a smaller number of SSNs could argue that U.S. SSNs, though very capable in certain respects, are less capable in others. U.S. SSNs, they can argue, cannot shoot down enemy missiles or aircraft, nor can they act as platforms for operating manned aircraft. U.S. cruisers and destroyers, they could argue, carry substantial numbers of Tomahawks. In light of the complementary capabilities of Navy platforms and the need for an array of U.S. Navy capabilities in operations against PLA forces, they could argue, the need for SSNs needs to be balanced against the need for aircraft carriers and surface combatants.

ASW-Capable Ships and Aircraft

Will the Navy have enough ASW-capable ships and aircraft between now and 2010? Should recently deactivated ASW-capable ships and aircraft be returned to service?

The Navy in recent years has deactivated a substantial number of ASW-capable ships and aircraft, including Spruance (DD-963) class destroyers, Oliver Hazard Perry (FFG-7) class frigates, TAGOS-type ocean surveillance ships, carrier-based S-3 airplanes, and land-based P-3 maritime patrol aircraft. Since ASW traditionally has been a platform-intensive undertaking — meaning that a significant number of platforms (e.g., ships and aircraft) traditionally has been required to conduct an effective ASW operation against a small number of enemy submarines, or even a single submarine — some observers have expressed concern about the resulting decline in numbers of U.S. Navy ASW-capable platforms.[113113]

As discussed earlier, the Navy plans to shift to a new, less platform-intensive ASW concept of operations. The Navy also plans to introduce new ASW-capable platforms in coming years, including a substantial number of Littoral Combat Ships (LCSs). Fully realizing the new ASW concept of operations, however, may take some time, particularly in light of the technical challenges involved, and LCSs will not be available in large numbers until after 2010. This raises a potential question of whether the Navy will have enough ASW-capable ships and aircraft between now and 2010, and whether the Navy should reactivate recently retired ASW-capable platforms and keep them in service until the new ASW concept is substantially implemented and larger numbers of LCSs and other new ASW-capable platforms join the fleet.

Advocates of this option could argue that the recent retirements of ASW-capable platforms occurred before the dimensions of the PLA Navy submarine modernization effort were fully understood. Opponents could argue that even with these recent retirements, the Navy retains a substantial number of such platforms, including SSNs, Aegis cruisers and destroyers, remaining Oliver Hazard Perry (FFG-7) class frigates, carrier- and surface combatant-based SH-60 helicopters, and remaining P-3s. They could also argue that there are more cost-effective ways to improve the Navy's ASW capabilities between now and 2010, such as increased ASW training and exercises (see discussion below).

NAVY WARFARE AREAS AND PROGRAMS

Missile Defense

Replacement for NAD Pro gram[114]

Should the canceled Navy Area Defense (NAD) program be replaced with a new sea-based terminal missile defense program?

In December 2001, DOD announced that it had canceled the Navy Area Defense (NAD) program, the program that was being pursued as the Sea-Based Terminal portion of the Administration's overall missile-defense effort. (The NAD program was also sometimes called the Navy Lower Tier program.) In announcing its decision, DOD cited poor performance, significant cost overruns, and substantial development delays.

The NAD system was to have been deployed on Navy Aegis cruisers and destroyers. It was designed to intercept short- and medium-range theater ballistic missiles in the final, or descent, phase of flight, so as to provide local-area defense of U.S. ships and friendly forces, ports, airfields, and other critical assets ashore. The program involved modifying both the Aegis ships' radar capabilities and the Standard SM-2 Block IV air-defense missile fired by Aegis ships. The missile, as modified, was called the Block IVA version. The system was

---

[113] See, for example, John R. Benedict, "The Unraveling And Revitalization Of U.S. Navy Antisubmarine Warfare," *Naval War College Review,* spring 2005, pp. 93-120, particularly pp. 104-106; and the statement by Lyle J. Goldstein in *2/6/04 USCC hearing,* pp. 149-150.

[114] This section includes material adapted from the discussion of the NAD program in CRS Report RL3 1111, *Missile Defense: The Current Debate,* coordinated by Steven A. Hildreth

designed to intercept descending missiles within the Earth's atmosphere (endoatmospheric intercept) and destroy them with the Block IVA missile's blast-fragmentation warhead.

Following cancellation of the program, DOD officials stated that the requirement for a sea-based terminal system remained intact. This led some observers to believe that a replacement for the NAD program might be initiated. In May 2002, however, DOD announced that instead of starting a replacement program, MDA had instead decided on a two-part strategy to (1) modify the Standard SM-3 missile — the missile to be used in the sea-based midcourse (i.e., Upper Tier) program — to intercept ballistic missiles at somewhat lower altitudes, and (2) modify the SM-2 Block four air defense missile (i.e., a missile designed to shoot down aircraft and cruise missiles) to cover some of the remaining portion of the sea-based terminal defense requirement. DOD officials said the two modified missiles could together provide much (but not all) of the capability that was to have been provided by the NAD program. One aim of the modification strategy, DOD officials suggested, was to avoid the added costs to the missile defense program of starting a replacement sea-based terminal defense program.

In October 2002, it was reported that

> Senior navy officials, however, continue to speak of the need for a sea-based terminal BMD capability "sooner rather than later" and have proposed a path to get there. "The cancellation of the Navy Area missile defence programme left a huge hole in our developing basket of missile-defence capabilities," said Adm. [Michael] Mullen. "Cancelling the programme didn't eliminate the warfighting requirement."
>
> "The nation, not just the navy, needs a sea-based area missile defence capability, not to protect our ships as much as to protect our forces ashore, airports and seaports of debarkation" and critical overseas infrastructure including protection of friends and allies.[115]

The above-quoted Admiral Mullen became the Chief of Naval Operations (CNO) on July 22, 2005.

In light of PLA TBM modernization efforts, including the possibility of TBMs equipped with MaRVs capable of hitting moving ships at sea, one issue is whether a new sea-based terminal-defense procurement program should be started to replace all (not just most) of the capability that was to have been provided by the NAD program, and perhaps even improve on the NAD's planned capability. In July 2004 it was reported that

> The Navy's senior leadership is rebuilding the case for a sea-based terminal missile defense requirement that would protect U.S. forces flowing through foreign ports and Navy ships from short-range missiles, according to Vice Adm. John Nathman, the Navy's top requirements advocate.
>
> The new requirement, Nathman said, would fill the gap left when the Pentagon terminated the Navy Area missile defense program in December 2001. ... However, he emphasized the Navy is not looking to reinstate the old [NAD] system. "That's exactly what we are not talking about," he said March 24....

The need to bring back a terminal missile defense program was made clear after reviewing the "analytic case" for the requirement, he said. Though Nathman could only talk in general terms about the analysis, due to its classified nature, he said its primary focus was "pacing the threat" issues. Such issues involve threats that are not a concern today, but could be in the future, he said. Part of the purpose of the study was to look at the potential time line for those threats and the regions where they could emerge.[116]

Reported options for a NAD-replacement program include a system using a modified version of the Army's Patriot Advanced Capability-3 (PAC-3) interceptor or a system using a modified version of the Navy's new Standard Missile 6 Extended Range Active Missile (SM-6 ERAM) air defense missile.[117]

Aegis Radar Upgrades

Should the adar capabilities of the Navy 's Aegis cruisers and destroyers be upgraded more quickly or extensively than now planned?

Current plans for upgrading the radar capabilities of the Navy's Aegis cruisers and destroyers include the Aegis ballistic missile defense signal processor (BSP), which forms part of the planned Block 06 version of the Navy's Aegis ballistic missile defense capability. Installing the Aegis BSP improves the ballistic missile target-discrimination performance of the Aegis ship's SPY-1 phased array radar.

In light of PLA TBM modernization efforts, including the possibility of TBMs equipped with MaRVs capable of hitting moving ships at sea, one issue is whether current plans for developing and installing the Aegis BSP are adequate, and whether those plans are sufficiently funded. A second issue is whether there are other opportunities for improving the radar capabilities of the Navy's Aegis cruisers and destroyers that are not currently being pursued or are funded at limited levels, and if so, whether funding for these efforts should be increased.

Ships With DD(X)/CG(X) Radar Capabilities

Should planned annual procurement rates for ships with DD(X)/CG(X) radar capabilities be increased?

The Navy plans to procure a new kind of destroyer called the DD(X) and a new kind of cruiser called the CG(X). The Navy plans to begin DD(X) procurement in FY2007, and CG(X) procurement in FY20 11. The Navy had earlier planned to begin CG(X) procurement in FY2018, but accelerated the planned start of procurement to FY2011 as part of its FY2006-FY2011 Future Years Defense Plan (FYDP). DD(X)s and CG(X)s would take about five years to build, so the first DD(X), if procured in FY2007, might enter service in 2012, and the first CG(X), if procured in FY2011, might enter service in 2016.

---

[115] Michael Sirak, "Sea-Based Ballistic Missile Defence: The 'Standard' Response," *Jane's Defence Weekly,* October 30, 2002.

[116] Malina Brown, "Navy Rebuilding Case For Terminal Missile Defense Requirement," *Inside the Navy,* April 19, 2004.

[117] See, for example, Jason Ma and Christopher J. Castelli, "Adaptation Of PAC-3 For Sea-Based Terminal Missile Defense Examined," *Inside the Navy,* July 19, 2004; Malina Brown, "Navy Rebuilding Case For Terminal Missile Defense Requirement," *Inside the Navy,* April 19, 2004.

The Navy states that the DD(X)'s radar capabilities will be greater in certain respects than those of Navy Aegis ships. The radar capabilities of the CG(X) are to be greater still, and the CG(X) has been justified primarily in connection with future air and missile defense operations.

Estimated DD(X)/CG(X) procurement costs increased substantially between 2004 and 2005. Apparently as a consequence of these increased costs, the FY2006-FY2011 FYDP submitted to Congress in early 2005 reduced planned DD(X) procurement to one ship per year. The reduction in the planned DD(X) procurement rate suggests that, unless budget conditions change, the combined DD(X)/CG(X) procurement rate might remain at one ship per year beyond FY20 11.[118]

If improvements to Aegis radar capabilities are not sufficient to achieve the Navy's desired radar capability for countering modernized PLA TBMs, then DD(X)/CG(X) radar capabilities could become important to achieving this desired capability. If so, then a potential additional issue raised by PLA TBM modernization efforts is whether a combined DD(X)/CG(X) procurement rate of one ship per year would be sufficient to achieve this desired capability in a timely manner. If the Navy in the future maintains a total of 11 or 12 carrier strike groups (CSGs), and if DD(X)/CG(X) procurement proceeds at a rate of one ship per year, the Navy would not have 11 or 12 DD(X)s and CG(X)s — one DD(X) or CG(X) for each of 11 or 12 CSGs — until 2022 or 2023. If CG(X)s are considered preferable to DD(X)s for missile defense operations, then the earliest the Navy could have 11 or 12 CG(X)s would be 2026 or 2027.

DD(X)/CG(X) radar technologies could be introduced into the fleet more quickly by procuring DD(X)s and CG(X)s at a higher rate, such as two ships per year, which is the rate the Navy envisaged in a report the Navy provided to Congress in 2003. A DD(X)/CG(X) procurement rate of two ships per year, however, could make it more difficult for the Navy to procure other kinds of ships or meet other funding needs, particularly in light of the recent growth in estimated DD(X)/CG(X) procurement costs.

A potential alternative strategy would be to design a reduced-cost alternative to the DD(X)/CG(X) that preserves DD(X)/CG(X) radar capabilities while reducing other DD(X)/CG(X) payload elements. Such a ship could more easily be procured at a rate of two ships per year within available resources. The option of a reduced-cost alternative to the DD(X)/CG(X) that preserves certain DD(X)/CG(X) capabilities while reducing others is discussed in more detail in another CRS report.[119]

Block II/Block IIA Version of SM-3 Interceptor

If feasible, should the efort to develop the Block I/Block IA version of the Standard Missile 3 (SM-3) interceptor missile be accelerated?

The Navy plans to use the Standard Missile 3 (SM-3) interceptor for intercepting TBMs during the midcourse portion of their flight. As part of the Aegis ballistic missile defense block upgrade strategy, the United States and Japan are cooperating in developing

---

[118] For more on the DD(X) and CG(X), see CRS Report RS20159, *Navy DD(X) and CG(X) Programs: Background and Issues for Congress,* by Ronald O'Rourke; and CRS Report RL32 109, *Navy DD(X), CG(X), and LCS Ship Acquisition Programs: Oversight Issues and Options for Congress,* by Ronald O'Rourke.

[119] See the "Options For Congress" section of CRS Report RL32109, op cit.

technologies for a more-capable version of the SM-3 missile called the SM-3 Block II/Block IIA. In contrast to the current version of the SM-3, which has a 21-inch-diameter booster stage but is 13.5 inches in diameter along the remainder of its length, the Block II/Block IIA version would have a 21-inch diameter along its entire length. The increase in diameter to a uniform 21 inches would give the missile a burnout velocity (a maximum velocity, reached at the time the propulsion stack burns out) that is 45% to 60% greater than that of the current 13.5-inch version of the SM-3.[120] The Block IIA version would also include a improved kinetic warhead.[121] The Missile Defense Agency (MDA) states that the Block II/Block IIA version of the missile could "engage many [ballistic missile] targets that would outpace, fly over, or be beyond the engagement range" of earlier versions of the SM-3, and that the net result, when coupled with enhanced discrimination capability, is more types and ranges of engageable [ballistic missile] targets; with greater probability of kill, and a large increase in defenses "footprint" or geography predicted.... The SM-3 Blk II/IIA missile with it[s] full 21-inch propulsion stack provides the necessary fly out acceleration to engage IRBM and certain ICBM threats.[122]

Regarding the status of the program, MDA states that "The Block II/IIA development plan is undergoing refinement. MDA plans to proceed with the development of the SM-3 Blk II/IIA missile variant if an agreeable cost share with Japan can be reached.... [The currently envisaged development plan] may have to be tempered by budget realities for the agency."[123]

In March 2005, the estimated total development cost for the Block II/Block IIA missile was reportedly $1.4 billion.[124] In September 2005, it was reported that this estimate had more than doubled, to about $3 billion.[125] MDA had estimated that the missile could enter service in 2013 or 2014,[126] but this date reportedly has now slipped to 2015.[127]

In light of PLA TBM modernization efforts, a potential question is whether, if feasible, the effort to develop the Block II/Block IIA missile should be accelerated, and if so, whether this should be done even if this requires the United States to assume a greater share of the development cost. A key factor in this issue could be assessments of potential PLA deployments of longer-ranged PLA TBMs.

---

[120] The 13.5-inch version has a reported burnout velocity of 3.0 to 3.5 kilometers per second (kps). See, for example, J. D. Marshall, *The Future Of Aegis Ballistic Missile Defense,* point paper dated October 15, 2004, available at [http://www.marshall.org/pdf/materials/259.pdf]; "STANDARD Missile-3 Destroyers a Ballistic Missile Target in Test of Sea-based Missile Defense System," Raytheon news release circa January 26, 2002, available on the Internet at [http://www.prnewswire.com/cgi-bin/micro_stories.pl?ACCT=683 1 94andTICK=RTN4and STORY=/www/story/0 1-26-2002/0001 655926andEDATE=Jan+26,+2002]; and Hans Mark, "A White Paper on the Defense Against Ballistic Missiles," *The Bridge,* summer 2001, pp. 17-26, available on the Internet at [http://www.nae.edu/nae/bridgecom.nsf/weblinks/ NAEW-63BM86/$FILE/BrSum01.pdf?OpenElement]. See also the section on "Sea-Based Midcourse" in CRS Report RL3 1111, *Missile Defense: The Current Debate,* coordinated by Steven A. Hildreth.

[121] Source for information on SM-3: Missile Defense Agency, "Aegis Ballistic Missile Defense SM-3 Block IIA (21-Inch) Missile Plan (U), August 2005," a 9-page point paper provided by MDA to CRS, August 24, 2005.

[122] "Aegis Ballistic Missile Defense SM-3 Block IIA (21-Inch) Missile Plan (U), August 2005," op cit, pp. 3-4.

[123] Ibid., p. 3.

[124] Aarti Shah, "U.S. Navy Working With Japanese On Billion-Dollar Missile Upgrade," *Inside the Navy,* March 14, 2005.

[125] "Cost Of Joint Japan-U.S. Interceptor System Triples," Yomiuri Shimbun (Japan), September 25, 2005.

[126] "Aegis Ballistic Missile Defense SM-3 Block IIA (21-Inch) Missile Plan (U), August 2005," op cit, p. 7.

[127] "Cost Of Joint Japan-U.S. Interceptor System Triples," Yomiuri Shimbun (Japan), September 25, 2005.

Kinetic Energy Interceptor (KEI)

Should funding for development of the Kinetic Energy Interceptor (KEI) be increased?

The Kinetic Energy Interceptor (KEI) is a proposed new ballistic missile interceptor that, if developed, would be used as a ground-based interceptor and perhaps subsequently as a sea-based interceptor. Compared to the SM-3, the KEI would be much larger (perhaps 40 inches in diameter and 36 feet in length) and would have a much higher burnout velocity. Basing the KEI on a ship would require the ship to have missile-launch tubes that are bigger than those currently installed on Navy cruisers, destroyers, and attack submarines. The Missile Defense Agency (MDA), which has been studying possibilities for basing the KEI at sea, plans to select a preferred platform in May 2006.[128] Because of its much higher burnout velocity, the KEI could be used to intercept longer-ranged ballistic missiles, including intercontinental ballistic missiles (ICBMs) during the boost and early ascent phases of their flights. Development funding for the KEI has been reduced in recent budgets, slowing the missile's development schedule. Under current plans, the missile could become available for Navy use in 2014-2015.[129]

Although the KEI is often discussed in connection with intercepting ICBMs, it might also be of value as a missile for intercepting TBMs, particularly longer-range TBMs, which are called Intermediate-Range Ballistic Missiles (IRBMs). If so, then in the context of this report, one potential question is whether the Navy should use the KEI as a complement to the SM-3 for countering PLA TBMs, and if so, whether development funding for the KEI should be increased so as to make the missile available for Navy use before 2014-2015.

Ships With Missile-Launch Tubes

Should the planned number of Navy missile-launch tubes be increased, and if so, how might this be done?

Missile-launch tubes on U.S. Navy surface combatants, which are installed in batteries called vertical launch systems (VLSs), are used for storing and firing various weapons, including Tomahawk cruise missiles, antisubmarine rockets, air defense missiles, and SM-3 ballistic missile defense interceptors. The potential need to counter hundreds of PLA TBMs raises a potential question of whether U.S. Navy forces involved in a conflict in the Taiwan Strait area would have enough missile launch tubes to store and fire required numbers of SM-3s while also meeting needs for storing adequate numbers of other types of weapons.

Options for increasing the planned number of missile-launch tubes in the fleet include reactivating VLS-equipped Spruance (DD-963) class destroyers (61 tubes per ship), building additional Arleigh Burke (DDG-5 1) class Aegis destroyers (96 tubes per ship), building additional DD(X)s (80 tubes per ship), building additional CG(X)s (more than 80 tubes per ship), or designing and procuring a new and perhaps low-cost missile-tube ship of some kind. Options for a new-design ship include, among other things,

---

[128] Marc Selinger, "MDA TO Pick Platform For Sea-Based KEI in May," *Aerospace Daily and Defense Report,"* August 19, 2005: 2.

[129] Government Accountability Office, *Defense Acquisitions[:] Assessments of Selected Major Weapon Programs,* GAO-05-301, March 2005, pp. 89-90. See also Thomas Duffy, "Northrop, MDA Working On KEI Changes Spurred By $800 Million Cut," *Inside Missile Defense,* March 30, 2005: p. 1.

-    a large ship equipped with hundreds of missile-launch tubes,[130]
-    an intermediate size ship with several dozen tubes,
-    a small and possibly fast ship equipped with a few dozen tubes, and
-    a submarine equipped with perhaps several dozen tubes.

AIR WARFARE

Mix of F/A-18E/Fs and F-35 Joint Strike Fighters (JSFs)

Should the Navy 's planned mix of carrier-based F/A-18E/F strike fighters and F-35 Joint Strike Fighters (JSFs) be changed to include more JSFs and fewer F/A-18E/Fs?

The Department of the Navy, which includes the Navy and the Marine Corps, currently plans to procure a total of 462 F/A-18E/F Super Hornet strike fighters and a total of 680 F-35 Joint Strike Fighters (JSFs). The F/A-18E/Fs would be operated by the Navy, and the JSFs would be operated by both services. The division of JSFs between the Navy and Marine Corps is under review, but earlier plans showed the Navy procuring a total of about 300 JSFs. Marine Corps JSFs could be operated from Navy carriers to perform Navy missions. The F/A-18E/F incorporates a few stealth features and is believed to be very capable in air-to-air combat. Compared to the F/A-18E/F, the JSF is much more stealthy and is believed to be more capable in air-to-air combat.

The growing number of fourth-generation fighters and strike-fighters in the PLA Air Force and the PLA Naval Air Force, and the growing number of modern PLA SAM systems, raises a potential question of whether the Navy should change its planned mix of carrier-based strike fighters to include more Navy JSFs and fewer F/A-18E/Fs. Such a change would produce a force with a better ability to avoid PLA SAM systems and more total air-to-air combat capability than the currently planned force.

The Department of the Navy's planned mix of F/A-18E/Fs and JSFs can be compared to the Air Force's strike fighter procurement plans. The Air Force plans to replace its current force of F-15 and F-16 fighters with a mix of 179 F/A-22 Raptor strike fighters and 1,763 JSFs. The F-22 is more stealthy and capable in air-to-air combat than the JSF. The Navy does not have an equivalent to the F-22. The Air Force argues that a mix of F/A-22s and JSFs will be needed in the future in part to counter fourth-generation fighters and strike fighters operated by other countries, including China. Supporters of the F/A-22 argue that the challenge posed by fourth-generation fighters in combination with modern integrated air defenses, is a key reason for procuring 381 or more F/A-22s, rather than 179.[131] Potential oversight questions include the following:

---

[130] Such a ship might be similar in some respects to the arsenal ship concept that the Navy pursued in 1996-1997. For more on the arsenal ship, see archived CRS Report 97-455, *Navy/DARPA Arsenal Ship Program: Issues and Options for Congress;* and archived CRS Report 97-1044, *Navy/DARPA Maritime Fire Support Demonstrator (Arsenal Ship) Program: Issues Arising From Its Termination,* both by Ronald O'Rourke. Both reports are out of print and are available directly from the author.

[131] For more on the F-22, JSF, and F/A-18E/F, see CRS Issue Brief IB921 15, *Tactical Aircraft Modernization: Issues for Congress;* CRS Report RL3 1673, *F/A-22 Raptor,* by Christopher Bolkcom; CRS Report RL30563, *F-35 Joint Strike Fighter (JSF) Program: Background, Status, and Issues ;* and CRS Report RL30624, *Military Aircraft, the F/A -1 8E/F Super Horn et Program: Background and Issues for Congress,* all by Christopher Bolkcom.

- If the Air Force is correct in its belief that a combination of F/A-22s and JSFs will be needed in part to counter fourth-generation fighters and modern SAM systems operated by other countries, including China, would the Department of the Navy's planned mix of JSFs and F/A-18E/Fs be sufficient to counter a PLA force of fighters and strike fighters that includes fourth-generation designs?
- If PLA attacks on U.S. air bases in the Western Pacific reduce the number of Air Force F/A-22s and JSFs that can participate in a conflict in the Taiwan Strait area, would the Department of the Navy's planned mix of F/A-18E/Fs and JSFs have sufficient air-to-air combat capability to counter the PLA's force of fighters and strike fighters?

Long-Range Air-to-Air Missile (Phoenix Successor)

Should the Navy acquire a long-range air-to-air missile analogous to the now-retired Phoenix missile?

During the Cold War, when the U.S. Navy prepared to confront a Soviet sea-denial force that included land-based aircraft armed with long-range ASCMs, Navy carrier air wings included F-14 Tomcat fighters armed with Phoenix long-range (60 nautical miles to 110 nautical miles) air-to-air missiles. A key purpose of the F - 14/Phoenix combination was to enable the Navy to shoot down approaching Soviet land-based aircraft flying toward U.S. Navy forces before they got close enough to launch their multiple long-range ASCMs. The strategy of shooting down the aircraft before they could launch their ASCMs was viewed as preferable because the aircraft were larger and less numerous than the ASCMs. This strategy of "shooting the archer rather than its arrows" formed part of a long-range air-to-air combat effort that was referred to as the Outer Air Battle.

Following the end of the Cold War 1989-1991, the need for waging an Outer Air Battle receded. Procurement of new Phoenixes ended in FY1990, and a planned successor to the Phoenix called the Advanced Air-To-Air Missile (AAAM) was canceled. The Phoenix was removed from service at the end of FY2004, and the F-14 is currently being phased out of service, with the last aircraft scheduled to be removed by mid-FY2007. Without the Phoenix, Navy strike fighters, like Air Force strike fighters, rely on a combination of medium- and short-range air-to-air missiles with ranges of roughly 10 nautical miles to 40 nautical miles.

In light of a potential need to counter PLA land-based strike fighters and maritime bombers protected by long-range SAMs, one question is whether a new program for acquiring a successor to the Phoenix should be initiated. The Air Force during the Cold War did not operate the Phoenix because it did not face a scenario equivalent to the Navy's scenario of shooting down a Soviet aircraft armed with multiple long-range ASCMs. In a conflict in the Taiwan Strait, however, the United States might benefit from having both Navy and Air Force strike fighters equipped with a long-range air-to-air missile for shooting down PLA strike fighters and maritime bombers equipped with ASCMs. If so, then the cost of developing a new long-range air-to-air missile could be amortized over a combined Navy-Air Force purchase of the missile.

ANTI-AIR WARFARE (AAW)

Surface Ship AAW Upgrades

Are current Navy plans for upgrading surface ship anti-air warfare (AAW) capabilities adequate?

The PLA's acquisition of advanced and highly capable ASCMs such as the SS-N-27 Sizzler and the SS-N-22 Sunburn raises the question of whether current plans for modernizing Navy surface ship AAW capabilities are adequate. The Government Accountability Office (GAO) in previous years has expressed concerns regarding the Navy's ability to counter ASCMs.[132] Potential areas for modernization include, among other things, the following:

- ship radars, such as the SPY-1 radar on Aegis ships or the radars now planned for the DD(X) destroyer and CG(X) cruiser;
- AAW-related computer networking capabilities, such as the Cooperative Engagement Capability (CEC);[133]
- air defense missiles such as the Standard Missile,[134] the Evolved Sea Sparrow Missile (ESSM), and the Rolling Airframe Missile (RAM);
- close-in weapon systems, such as the Phalanx radar-directed gun;
- potential directed-energy weapons, such as solid state or free-electron lasers;
- decoys, such as the U.S-Australian Nulka active electronic decoy; and
- aerial targets for AAW tests and exercises, particularly targets for emulating supersonic ASCMs.[135]

---

[132] General Accounting Office, *Navy Acquisitions[:] Improved Littoral War-Fighting Capabilities Needed,* GAO-01-493, May 2001; and General Accounting Office, *Defense Acquisitions[:] Comprehensive Strategy Needed to Improve Ship Cruise Missile Defense,* GAO/NSIAD-00-149, July 2000.

[133] For more on CEC, see CRS Report RS20557, *Navy Network-Centric Warfare Concept: Key Programs and Issues for Congress,* by Ronald O'Rourke.

[134] The Navy is currently developing a new version of the Standard Missile called the SM-6 Extended Range Active Missile (ERAM) that will have a considerably longer range than the current SM-2 air defense missile. The SM-6 will also have an active seeker that will permit the missile to home in on the target on its own, without being illuminated by a ship-based radar, as is the case with the SM-2.

[135] An October 2005 report from the Defense Science Board (DSB) highlights "The dire need for several types of supersonic targets to represent existing anti-ship cruise missile threats." (Page 1) The report states:

The Russians have produced and deployed a variety of supersonic, anti-ship cruise missiles. Some of these missiles are sea-skimming vehicles; others attack from high altitudes. At the time of the Task Force, the United States had zero capability to test its air defense systems such as AEGIS or Improved Sea Sparrow against supersonic targets, and the Task Force views this shortfall as the maj or deficiency in our overall aerial targets enterprise. Aggressive actions are needed to fix the problem. (Department of Defense, *Report of the Defense Science Board Task Force on Aerial Targets.* Washington, 2005. (October 2005, Office of the Under Secretary of Defense for Acquisition, Technology, and Logistics) pp. 2.)

A cover memorandum attached to the report from William P. Delaney and General Michael Williams, USMC (Ret.), the co-chairmen of the task force, states:

The area of greatest concern to the Task Force was our gap in supersonic anti-ship cruise missiles for testing. The Russians have deployed at least three such cruise missiles that involve either sea-skimming flight profiles or a high-altitude profile involving a power dive to the target. At this time, we have no test vehicles for either flight profile.

See also John Liang, "DSB Highlights 'Dire' Need For Supersonic Cruise Missile Targets," *Inside the Navy,* November 14, 2005. The lack of targets for fully emulating supersonic ASCMs has been an issue since the early 1 980s, when the Navy first deployed the Aegis AAW system. See CRS Report 84-180, *The Aegis Anti-Air Warfare System: Its Principal Components, Its Installation On The CG-47 And DDG-51 Class Ships, And Its*

Littoral Combat Ship (LCS) AAW Capability

Should the currently planned AAW capability of the Littoral Combat Ship (LCS) be increased?

The Navy's planned Littoral Combat Ship (LCS) is to be armed with a 21-round Rolling Airframe Missile (RAM) launcher. The ship will also be equipped with an AAW decoy launcher.[136]

The PLA's acquisition of ASCMs that can be fired from aircraft, surface ships, and submarines raises the possibility that LCSs participating in a conflict in the Taiwan Strait area could come under attack by substantial numbers of ASCMs. Other Navy ships, such as Aegis cruisers and destroyers and, in the future, DD(X) destroyers and CG(X)s cruisers, could help defend LCSs against attacking ASCMs, but such ships might not always be in the best position to do this, particularly if ASCMs are launched at LCSs from undetected submarines or if the supporting U.S. Navy ships were busy performing other duties. If LCSs were damaged or sunk by ASCMs, the Navy's ability to counter enemy mines, submarines, and small boats — the LCS's three primary missions — would be reduced.

The possibility that the LCS's AAW system might be overwhelmed or exhausted by attacks from multiple ASCMs raises the question of whether the AAW capability planned for the LCS should be increased. Options for increasing the LCS's planned AAW capability include, among other things, adding another 21-round RAM launcher or supplementing the currently planned RAM launcher with a battery of Evolved Sea Sparrow (ESSM) missiles. In assessing such options, one factor to consider would be whether installing additional RAMs or ESSMs would require an increase in the planned size and cost of the LCS.

Antisubmarine Warfare (ASW)

Technologies

Are current Navy eforts for improving antisubmarine warfare (ASW) technologies adequate?

In addition to the issue discussed earlier of whether the Navy between now and 2010 will have enough ASW-capable platforms, another potential issue raised by the PLA submarine modernization effort is whether current Navy plans for improving antisubmarine warfare (ASW) technologies are adequate. The Navy states that it intends to introduce several new ASW technologies, including distributed sensors, unmanned vehicles, and technologies for netcworking ASW systcms and platforms.[137] Admiral Michael Mullen, who became the Chief

---

Efectiveness, by Ronald O'Rourke. (October 24, 1984) pp. 16-17. (This report is out of print and is available directly from the author.)

[136] For more on the LCS, see CRS Report RS21305, *Navy Littoral Combat Ship (LCS): Background and Issues for Congress;* and CRS Report RL32 109, *Navy DD(X), CG(X), and LCS Ship Acquisition Programs: Oversight Issues and Options for Congress,* both by Ronald O'Rourke.

[137] For discussions of new ASW technologies, see Jennifer H. Svan, "Pacific Fleet Commander: Sub Threats Top Priority," *Pacific Stars and Stripes,* October 3, 2005; Jason ma, "Autonomous ASW Sensor Field Seen AS High-Risk Technical Hurdle," *Inside the Navy,* June 6, 2005; John R. Benedict, "The Unraveling And Revitalization Of U.S. Navy Antisubmarine Warfare," *Naval War College Review,* spring 2005, pp. 93-120, particularly pp. 109-110; Richard R. Burgess, "'Awfully Slow Warfare'," *Seapower,* April 2005, pp. 12-14; Jason Ma, "ASW Concept Of Operations Sees 'Sensor-Rich' Way Of Fighting Subs," *Inside the Navy,* February 7, 2005; Jason Ma, "Navy's Surface Warfare Chief Cites Progress In ASW Development," *Inside the Navy,*

of Naval Operations (CNO) on July 22, 2005, has issued a guidance statement for the Navy for 2006 which says that Navy tasks for FY2006 will include, among other things, "Rapidly prototyp[ing] ASW technologies that will: hold at risk adversary submarines; substantially degrade adversary weapons effectiveness; and, compress the ASW detect-to-engage sequences. Sensor development is key."[138]

Training and Exercises

Are current Navy plans for ASW training and exercises adequate?

As mentioned earlier, success in an ASW operation is highly dependent on the proficiency of the people operating the ASW equipment, and ASW operational proficiency can take time to develop and can atrophy significantly if not regularly exercised. At various times since the end of the Cold War, some observers have expressed concerns about whether the Navy was placing adequate emphasis on maintaining ASW proficiency. The Navy in April 2004 established a new Fleet ASW Command, based in San Diego, to provide more focus to its ASW efforts, and since then has taken steps to enhance its ASW training and exercises:

- In April 2004, it was reported that carrier strike groups deploying from the U.S. West Coast would now stop in Hawaiian waters for three- to five-day ASW exercises before proceeding to the Western Pacific.[139]
- In March 2005, the Navy reached an agreement to lease a Swedish non-nuclear-powered submarine and its crew for a 12-month period. The submarine, which is equipped with an air-independent propulsion (AIP) system, arrived in San Diego in June 2005, where it is being used to as a mock enemy submarine in Pacific Fleet ASW exercises.[140]
- The Navy in 2005 also reached an agreement with Colombia and Peru under which one non-nuclear-powered submarine from each country deployed to the Navy base at Mayport, FL, in April 2005 to support Atlantic Fleet ASW exercises for a period of two to five months. South American non-nuclear-powered submarines have been integrated into U.S. Navy exercises since 2002.[141]
- In October 2005, the commander of the Navy's Pacific Fleet said that, upon assuming command earlier in the year, he made ASW his highest priority and

---

January 17, 2005; Otto Kreisher, "As Underwater Threat Re-Emerges, Navy Renews Emphasis On ASW," *Seapower,* October 2004, p. 15; and David Wood, "U.S. Navy Confronts Growing New Submarine Threat," *Newhouse.com,* September 10, 2004.

[138] M. G. Mullen, CNO Guidance for 2006, Meeting the Challenge of a New Era, Washington, 2005, p. 5.

[139] Christopher Munsey, "Fleet Anti-Sub Command Stands Up," *Navy Times,* April 19, 2004, p. 29.

[140] Jose Higuera, "Sweden's Gotland Heads For A Year With US Navy," *Jane's Navy Intern ational,* July/August 2005; 8; S. C. Irwin, "Swedish Submarine Expected To Enhance Navy's Antisubmarine Warfare Primacy," *Navy Newsstand,* June 20, 2005; Gidget Fuentes, "Swedish Sub To Drill With U.S. Navy For A Year," *DefenseNews.com,* May 18, 2005; "U.S., Swedish Navies Sign Agreement To Bilaterally Train On State-Of-The-Art Sub," *Navy Newsstand,* March 23, 2005.

[141] Christopher Munsey, "Colombian, Peruvian Subs To Take Part In Exercise," *NavyTimes.com,* April 14, 2005; Mark O. Piggott, "South American Submarines Enhance U.S. Navy's Fleet Readiness," *Navy Newsstand,* April 14, 2005.

instituted a cyclic approach to ASW training that includes more frequent (quarterly) assessments, as well as training exercises with other navies.[142]

In light of these actions, the potential question is whether the Navy ASW training and exercises are now adequate, or whether they should be expanded further.

Active-Kill Torpedo Defense

If feasible, should Navy plans for acquiring an active-kill torpedo defense system be accelerated?

Navy surface ships and submarines are equipped with decoy systems for diverting enemy torpedoes away from their intended targets. Such decoys, however, might not always work, particularly against wake-homing torpedoes, which can be difficult to decoy. Under the Navy's surface ship torpedo defense (SSTD) development program, the U.S. Navy is developing an "active-kill" torpedo-defense capability for surface ships and also submarines that would use a small (6.75-inch diameter) anti-torpedo torpedo (ATT) to physically destroy incoming torpedoes. Current Navy plans call for the ATT to enter low-rate initial procurement (LRIP) in FY2009 and achieve initial operational capability on surface ships in FY20 11.[143143] In light of the modern torpedoes, including wake-homing torpedoes, that are expected to be carried by modern PLA submarines, a potential question is whether, if feasible, the current ATT acquisition schedule should be accelerated. Hitting an approaching torpedo with another torpedo poses technical challenges which could affect the potential for accelerating the ATT development schedule.

Mine Warfare

Are current Navy mine warfare plans adequate?

The PLA's interest in modern mines may underscore the importance of the Navy's efforts to develop and acquire new mine countermeasures (MCM) systems, and perhaps raise a question regarding whether they should be expanded or accelerated. The Navy's MCM capabilities have been a matter of concern among members of the congressional defense committees for several years.

Conversely, the PLA Navy's own reported vulnerability to mines (see section on PLA Navy limitations and weaknesses) can raise a question regarding the lessfrequently discussed topic of the U.S. Navy's offensive mine warfare capability. To what degree can minelaying complicate PLA plans for winning a conflict, particularly a short-duration conflict, in the Taiwan Strait area? Do U.S. Navy plans include sufficient mines and minelaying platforms to

---

[142] Jennifer H. Svan, "Pacific Fleet Commander: Sub Threats Top Priority," *Pacific Stars and Stripes,* October 3, 2005.

[143] Sources: Department of the Navy, Department of the Navy Fiscal Year (FY) 2006/FY2007 Budget Estimates, Justification of Estimates, February 2005, Research, Development, Test and Evaluation, Navy Budget Activity 4, entry on Surface Ship Torpedo Defense program, PE (Program Element) 0603 506N; and Pennsylvania State University Applied Research Laboratory web page on the torpedo defense programs office, available on the Internet at [http://www.arl.psu.edu/capabilities/td.html].

fully exploit the PLA Navy's vulnerability to mines? The Navy has various mines either in service or under development,[144] and is exploring the option of starting development of an additional new mine called the 2010 Mine.[145]

Computer Network Security

Are Navy eforts to ensure computer network security adequate?

The PLA's published interest in IW/IO, and concerns that recent attacks on U.S. computer networks have in some cases originated in China, underscore the importance of U.S. military computer network security. The Navy in July 2002 established the Naval Network Warfare Command in part to prevent and respond to attacks on Navy computer networks.[146] Another CRS report discusses computer network security at length.[147]

EMP Hardening

Are Navy eforts to harden its systems against electromagnetic pulse (EMP) adequate?

The possibility that the PLA might use nuclear weapons or high-power microwave (HPM) weapons to generate electromagnetic pulse (EMP) effects against the electronic systems on U.S. Navy ships and aircraft raises a potential question regarding the adequacy of the Navy's efforts to harden its systems against EMP effects. A 2004 commission studying the EMP issue expressed concerns about the potential vulnerability of U.S. tactical forces to EMP.[148]

---

[144] Current information on Navy mines and mine development programs is available on the Internet at [http://www.exwar.org/Htm/4000.htm].

[145] Andrew Koch, "USN May Launch Offensive Naval Mining Mission," *Jane's Defence Weekly,* December 1, 2004, p. 10.

[146] Harold Kennedy, "Navy Command Engages In Info Warfare Campaign," *National Defense,* November 2003. See also Frank Tiboni, "DOD's 'Manhattan Project'," *Federal Computer Week,* August 29, 2005.

[147] CRS Report RL321 14, *Computer Attack and Cyberterrorism: Vulnerabilities and Policy Issues for Congress,* by Clay Wilson.

[148] *2004 EMP commission report.* The report of the commission stated on page 1 that "The high-altitude nuclear weapon-generated electromagnetic pulse (EMP) is one of a small number of threats that has the potential to hold our society seriously at risk and might result in defeat of our military forces." The report stated later that

The end of the Cold War relaxed the discipline for achieving EMP survivability within the Department of Defense, and gave rise to the perception that an erosion of EMP survivability of military forces was an acceptable risk. EMP simulation and test facilities have been mothballed or dismantled, and research concerning EMP phenomena, hardening design, testing, and maintenance has been substantially decreased. However, the emerging threat environment, characterized by a wide spectrum of actors that include near-peers, established nuclear powers, rogue nations, sub-national groups, and terrorist organizations that either now have access to nuclear weapons and ballistic missiles or may have such access over the next 15 years have combined to place the risk of EMP attack and adverse consequences on the US to a level that is not acceptable.

Current policy is to continue to provide EMP protection to strategic [i.e., long-range nuclear] forces and their controls; however, the end of the Cold War has relaxed the discipline for achieving and maintaining that capability within these forces....

The situation for general-purpose forces (GPF) is more complex.... Our increasing dependence on advanced electronics systems results in the potential for an increased EMP vulnerability of our technologically advanced forces, and if unaddressed makes EMP employment by an adversary an attractive asymmetric option.

The United States must not permit an EMP attack to defeat its capability to prevail. The Commission believes it is not practical to protect all of the tactical forces of the US and its coalition partners from EMP in a regional conflict. A strategy of replacement and reinforcement will be necessary. However, there is a set of critical

The commission's report was received at a July 22, 2004, hearing before the House Armed Services Committee. At the hearing, Representative Steve Israel asked about the role of EMP in exercises simulating operations in the Taiwan Strait:

Representative Steve Israel: [Representative Roscoe] Bartlett and I just attended an NDU [National Defense University] tabletop [exercise] with respect to the Straits of the Taiwan just last week. To your knowledge, has there been any tabletop exercise, has there been any simulation, any war-game that anticipates an EMP attack, and, if there has not been, do you believe that that would, in fact, be a useful exercise for NDU, the Pentagon or any other relevant entity? Dr. Graham, do you want to answer that?

Dr. William R. Graham (Commission Chairman): Thank you. Let me poll the commission and see if they have any experience with that. General Lawson?

General Richard L. Lawson, USAF (Ret.) (Commissioner): No, sir. *Graham:* Dr. Wood?

Dr. Lowell L. Wood, Jr. (Commissioner): I don't believe there's been any formal exercise, certainly not to my knowledge. There's been extensive discussion of what the impact of Chinese EMP laydowns would be, not on Taiwan, which is, after all, considered by China to be part of its own territory, but on U.S. forces in the region which might be involved in the active defense of Taiwan. In particular, the consequences the EMP laydown on U.S. carrier task forces has been explored, and while, it's not appropriate to discuss the details in an open session like this, the assessed consequences of such an attack, a single-explosion attack, are very somber.

Since that is a circumstance in which the target might be considered a pure military one in which the loss of life might be relatively small, but the loss of military capability might be absolutely staggering, it poses a very attractive option, at least for consideration on the part of the Chinese military.

I would also remark that Chinese nuclear explosive workers at their very cloistered research center in northwestern China very recently published an authoritative digest and technical commentary on EMP in English, in a Chinese publication. It is very difficult to understand what the purpose of publishing a lengthy, authoritative article in English in a Chinese publication would be, if it was not to convey a very pointed message. This came not from military workers. It came from the people who would be fielding the weapon that would conduct the attack.

Graham: Dr. Pry on our staff has made a survey of foreign writings on EMP, and he noted that while U.S. exercises have not to our knowledge played that scenario, Chinese military writings have discussed that scenario. So it's certainly something they have thought of and it is within their mind. I have observed generally over the last 40 years that there's a tendency in the U.S. military not to introduce nuclear weapons in general and EMP in particular into exercise scenarios or game scenarios because it tends to end the game, and that's not a good sign. I think it would be a very interesting subject for the NDU group to take up and see and

---

capabilities that is essential to tactical regional conflicts that must be available to these reinforcements. This set includes satellite navigation systems, satellite and airborne intelligence and targeting systems, an adequate communications infrastructure, and missile defense.

The current capability to field a tactical force for regional conflict is inadequate in light of this requirement. Even though it has been US policy to create EMP-hardened tactical systems, the strategy for achieving this has been to use the DoD acquisition process. This has provided many equipment components that meet criteria for durability in an EMP environment, but this does not result in confidence that fielded forces, as a system, can reliably withstand EMP attack. Adherence to the equipment acquisition policy also has been spotty, and the huge challenge of organizing and fielding an EMP-durable tactical force has been a disincentive to applying the rigor and discipline needed to do so. (Pages 47-48.)

force them not to end the game. Time will not stop if such an event happens. Let them understand what the consequences will be.[149]

Later in the hearing, Representative Roscoe Bartlett returned to the topic of the potential effects of EMP on Navy ships:

Representative Bartlett: If China were to detonate a weapon high over our carrier task force, can we note in this [open] session what would the effects on the carrier task force be?
Graham: Mr. Bartlett, several years ago, the Navy dismantled the one simulator it had for exposing ships directly [to EMP]. It was the Empress simulator located in the Chesapeake Bay. So I don't believe any direct experimental work has been done for quite some time.
However, the general character of modern naval forces follows the other trends we've described, which is an increasing dependence upon sophisticated electronics for its functionality, and, therefore, I believe there's substantial reason to be concerned.
[Would] Any other commissioners [care to comment]? *Representative Bartlett:* Dr. Wood?
Wood: In open session, sir, I don't believe it's appropriate to go much further than the comment that I made to [Representative] Israel that the assessments that are made of such attacks and their impacts are very somber.
The Navy generally believes — that portion of the Navy that's at all cognizant of these matters — that because they operate in an extremely radar-intensive environment, [since] they have a great deal of electromagnetic gear on board, some of which radiates pulses — radar pulses, for instance — because they can operate in that type of environment, that they surely must be EMP robust. These free-floating beliefs on the part of some Navy officers are not — repeat not — well grounded technically.[150]

APPENDIX A: ADDITIONAL DETAILS ON CHINA'S NAVAL MODERNIZATION EFFORTS[151]

This appendix presents additional details and commentary on several of the elements of China's military modernization discussed in the Background section of this report.

Theater-Range Ballistic Missiles (TBMs)

Regarding the potential for using TBMs against moving U.S. Navy ships at sea, DOD states that "China is exploring the use of ballistic missiles for anti-access/sea-denial missions."[152] ONI states that "One of the newest innovations in TBM weapons developments

---

[149] Source: Transcript of hearing.
[150] Ibid.
[151] Unless otherwise indicated, shipbuilding program information in this section is taken from *Jane's Fighting Ships 2005-2006.* Other sources of information on these shipbuilding programs may disagree regarding projected ship commissioning dates or other details, but sources present similar overall pictures regarding PLA Navy shipbuilding.
[152] *2005 DOD CMP,* p. 4. Page 33 similarly states that China is "researching the possibility of using ballistic missiles and special operations forces to strike ships or their ashore support infrastructure."

involves the use of ballistic missiles to target ships at sea. This is assessed as being very difficult because it involves much more than just a missile."[153] ONI continues:

> The use of ballistic missiles against ships at sea has been discussed for years. Chinese writings state China intends to develop the capability to attack ships, including carrier strike groups, in the waters around Taiwan using conventional theater ballistic missiles (TBMs) as part of a combined-arms campaign. The current conventional TBM force in China consists of CSS-6 and CSS-7 short-range ballistic missiles (SRBMs) deployed in large numbers. The current TBM force would be modified by changing some of the current missiles' ballistic reentry vehicles (RVs) to maneuvering reentry vehicles (MaRVs) with radar or IR seekers to provide the accuracy needed to attack ships at sea. The TBMs with MaRVs would have good defense penetration capabilities because of their high reentry speed and maneuverability. Their lethality could be increased, especially with terminally guided submunitions.
>
> In order to attack a ship or a carrier battle group with TBMs, the target must be tracked, and its position, direction, and speed determined. This information would be relayed in near real time to the missile launchers. China may be planning ultimately to use over-the-horizon (OTH) radar, satellites, and unmanned aerial vehicles (UAVs) to monitor the target's position. Reconnaissance assets would be used to detect the ship or carrier strike group before it entered into the range of Chinese TBMs, facilitating early preparation for the engagement, and refining the target's position. Target information would be relayed through communication satellites or other channels to a command center, and then to the missile launchers. TBMs with MaRVs would then be launched at the target's projected position. The missiles would fly their preplanned trajectories until onboard seekers could acquire the ship and guide the missiles to impact.[154]

Another observer states:

> The PLA's historic penchant for secrecy and surprise, when combined with known programs to develop highly advanced technologies that will lead to new and advanced weapons, leads to the conclusion that the PLA is seeking [to] field new weapon systems that could shock an adversary and accelerate their defeat. In the mid-1990s former leader Jiang Zemin re-popularized an ancient Chinese term for such weapons, "Shashaoj ian," translated most frequently as "Assassin's Mace," or "silver bullet" weapons.
>
> One potential Shashoujian is identified by the [DOD's 2005 report on China military power]: a maneuvering ballistic missile design to target U.S. naval forces. In 1996 a Chinese technician revealed that a "terminal guidance system" that would confer very high accuracy was being developed for the DF-21 [intercontinental ballistic missile, or ICBM]. Such a system could employ a radar similar to the defunct U.S. Pershing-2 MRBM or could employ off-board sensors with rapid data-links to the missile tied to satellite-navigation systems. Nevertheless, should such missiles be realized they will pose a considerable threat as the U.S. Navy is not yet ready to deploy adequate missile defenses.[155]

A separate observer states:

---

[153] *2004 ONI WMC,* p. 21. On Page 3 (Overview), ONI notes, without reference to any specific country, that "antiship ballistic missiles could be fired at our ships at sea."

[154] *2004 ONI WMC,* p. 22. Page 20 states: "Maneuvering reentry vehicles serve two purposes: one to provide an unpredictable target to complicate missile defense efforts and the other, potentially, to adjust missile flight path to achieve greater accuracy."

[155] *Fisher 7/27/05 testimony,* p. 6.

Land-based conventional tipped ballistic missiles with maneuverable (MarV) warheads that can hit ships at sea.... would be a Chinese "assassin's mace" sort of capability — something impossible to deal with today, and very difficult under any circumstances if one is forced to defend by shooting down ballistic missiles. The capability is dependent on Beijing's ability to put together the appropriate space-based surveillance, command, and targeting architecture necessary to make this work.[156]

One more observer states:

There is yet another exceedingly important chapter being written in the [PLA] ballistic-missile saga. China is trying to move rapidly in developing ballistic missiles that could hit ships at sea at MRBM [medium-range ballistic missile] ranges — in other words, to threaten carriers beyond the range at which they could engage Chinese forces or strike China. Among its other advantages for China, this method of attack avoids altogether the daunting prospect of having to cope with the U.S. Navy submarine force — as anti-submarine warfare is a big Chinese weakness. Along with these efforts to develop ballistic missiles to hit ships, they are, of course, working diligently to perfect the means to locate and target our carrier strike groups (CSGs). In that regard, an imperfect or rudimentary (fishing boats with satellite phones) means of location and targeting might be employed even earlier than the delay of several more years likely needed to perfect more reliable and consistent targeting of ships. Chinese missile specialists are writing openly and convincingly of MaRV'd ballistic missiles (missiles with maneuverable reentry vehicles) that maneuver both to defeat defenses and to follow the commands of seekers that spot the target ships. There seems little doubt that our naval forces will face this threat long before the Taiwan issue is resolved.[157]

Land-Attack Cruise Missile (LACMs). Regarding LACMs, DOD states:

China is developing LACMs to achieve greater precision than historically available from ballistic missiles for hard target strikes, and increased standoff. A first- and second-generation LACM remain under development. There are no technological bars to placing on these systems a nuclear payload, once developed.[158]

ONI states:

Land-attack cruise missiles (LACMs) are available for sale from many countries, and are marketed at arms shows around the world. Land-attack cruise missiles are becoming a significant adjunct to theater ballistic missiles in strike and deterrent roles. The number of countries manufacturing and purchasing LACMs continues to grow. Some of the systems in development are derivatives of antiship missiles, and some are dedicated designs, and a few weaponized UAVs [unmanned aerial vehicles] complete the inventory....
Israel, China, Germany, and South Africa are among the countries with LACM development programs.[159]

---

[156] Presentation entitled "Beijing Eye View of Strategic Landscale" by Mike McDevitt at a June 20, 2005, conference on the future of the U.S. Navy held in Washington, DC, by the American Enterprise Institute. Quote taken from McDevitt's notes for the presentation, which he provided to CRS.
[157] *McVadon 9/15/05 testimony*, pp. 4-5.
[158] *2005 DOD CMP*, p. 29.
[159] *2004 ONI WMC*, pp. 25, 26

Another observer states:

Since the 1970s the PLA has placed a high priority on developing an indigenous strategic land attack cruise missile (LACM). This effort has been aided by the PLA's success in obtaining advanced cruise missile technology from Russia, Israel, the Ukraine and the United States. In early June an Internet-source photo appeared of anew Chinese cruise missile with unmistakable LACM characteristics. This would tend to support revelation from Taiwan earlier this year that by 2006 the PLA will deploy 200 new land-based LACMs. With their very high accuracy such cruise missiles allow strategic targets to be destroyed with non-nuclear warheads.[160]

Anti-Ship Cruise Missiles (ASCMs). Regarding ASCMs, DOD states:

The PLA Navy and Naval Air Force have or are acquiring nearly a dozen varieties of ASCMs, from the 1950s-era CSS-N-2/STYX to the modern Russian-made SS-N-22/SUNBURN and SS-N-27/SIZZLER. The pace of indigenous ASCM research, development, and production — and of foreign procurement — has accelerated over the past decade. Objectives for current and future ASCMs include improving closure speed (e.g., ramjet propulsion, such as with the SS-N-22), standoff distance (e.g., longer-range assets, such as the C-802), and stealthier launch platforms (e.g., submarines). SS-N-22 missiles may be fitted on smaller platforms in the future (e.g., the Russian Molniya patrol boat, which originated as a joint effort with China, or on the new stealth fast attack patrol boat).[161]

Regarding the SS-N-27s expected to be carried by the eight additional Kilo-class submarines China has ordered, ONI states:

Russia continues to develop supersonic ASCMs. The most interesting is the 3M-54E design which has a cruise vehicle that ejects a rocket-propelled terminal sprint vehicle approximately 10 nautical miles from its target. The sprint vehicle accelerates to speeds as high as Mach 3 and has the potential to perform very high-g defensive maneuvers.[162]
Another observer states that "the very dangerous and lethal SS-N-27Bs [are] said by experts to be part of the best family of ASCMs in the world...."[163]

Land-Based Surface-to-Air Missiles (SAMs). Regarding SAM systems, DOD states:

In August 2004, China received the final shipment from Russia of four S-300PMU-1/SA-20 surface-to-air missile (SAM) battalions. China has also agreed to purchase follow-on S-300PMU-2, the first battalion of which is expected to arrive in 2006. With an advertised intercept range of 200 km, the S-300PMU-2 provides increased lethality against tactical ballistic missiles and more effective electronic counter-counter measures.[164]

---

[160] *Fisher 7/27/05 testimony,* p. 9 Comments about LACMs also appear on pp. 3, 4, 5, andCRS-65
[161] *2005 DOD CMP,* p. 29.
[162] *2004 ONI WMC,* p. 23
[163] *McVadon 9/15/05 testimony,* p. 5.
[164] *2005 DOD CMP,* p. 4. See also p. 32.

Another observer states that "before 2010," China could deploy more than 300 S-3 00 SAM systems to locations covering the Taiwan Strait.[165]

Land-Based Aircraft

Regarding land-based aircraft, DOD states:

China has more than 700 aircraft within un-refueled operational range of Taiwan. Many of these are obsolescent or upgrades of older-generation aircraft. However, China's air forces continue to acquire advanced fighter aircraft from Russia, including the Su-30MKK multirole and Su-30MK2 maritime strike aircraft. New acquisitions augment previous deliveries of Su-27 fighter aircraft. China is also producing its own version of the Su-27SK, the F-11, under a licensed co-production agreement with Moscow. Last year, Beijing sought to renegotiate its agreement and produce the multirole Su-27SMK for the remainder of the production run. These later generations of aircraft make up a growing percentage of the PLA Air Force inventory.

China's indigenous 4th generation fighter, the F-10, completed development in 2004 and will begin fielding this year. Improvements to the FB-7 fighter program will enable this older aircraft to perform nighttime maritime strike operations. China has several programs underway to deploy new standoff escort jammers on bombers, transports, tactical aircraft, and unmanned aerial vehicle platforms.[166]

ONI states:

China operates a force of 1950s vintage B-6D Badger dedicated naval strike bombers. Today, these aircraft are armed with the C601, an air-launched derivative of the Styx ASCM, but a program to arm them with the modern C802K is underway....

China and Russia also are working on new tactical aircraft dedicated to the antiship mission. China's FB-7 Flounder has been in development since the 1970s; its production limited by engine difficulties. The C801K-armed FB-7 entered service with the Chinese Navy, and integration of the longer-range C802K on the FB-7 is underway.[167]

Another observer states that "By 2006, in my estimation, the PLA will have 400 Sukhoi [i.e., Su-27 and Su-30] fighters and fighter-bombers."[168]

Submarines

The paragraphs below discuss China's submarine modernization effort in more detail on a class-by-class basis.

Type 094 SSBN. China is building a new class of SSBN known as the Type 094 class. The first two Type 094 boats are expected to enter service in 2008 and 2010. The Type 094

---

[165] *Fisher 7/27/05 testimony,* p. 4. See also p. 10.
[166] *2005 DOD CMP,* p. 4. See also pp. 23-24, 25, 31-32.
[167] *2004 ONI WMC,* p. 27. *Fisher 7/27/05 testimony,* pp. 3-4, 9-10.
[168] Statement of Richard D. Fisher, Jr., as printed in *2/6/04 USCC hearing,* p. 72.

design may be derived from the Shang-class (Type 093) SSN design discussed below. ONI states that China "wishes to develop a credible, survivable, sea-based deterrent with the capability to reach the United States" and that the Type 094 design "benefits from substantial Russian technical assistance."[169]

The Type 094 SSBN is expected to be armed with 12 CSS-NX-5 nuclear-armed submarine-launched ballistic missiles, also known as JL-2s. Observers believe these missiles will have a range of about 8,000 kilometers to 12,000 kilometers (about 4,320 nautical miles to 6,480 nautical miles). The latter figure could permit Type 094 SSBNs to attack targets in most of the continental United States while operating in protected bastions close to China.[170]

Shang (Type 093) SSN

China is building a new class of SSN, called the Shang (or Type 093) class. The first two Shang-class boats are expected to enter service in 2005, and construction of a third may have begun.

Observers believe the Shang-class SSNs will likely represent a substantial improvement over China's five older and reportedly fairly noisy Han (Type 091) class SSNs, which entered service between 1974 and 1990. The first Han-class boat reportedly was decommissioned in 2003, and observers expect the others will be decommissioned as Shang-class boats enter service.

The Shang class reportedly was designed in conjunction with Russian experts and is derived from the Soviet Victor III-class SSN design that was first deployed by the Soviet Union around 1978. The Victor III was the first in a series of quieter Soviet SSN designs that, by the mid-1980s, led to substantial concern among U.S. Navy officials that the Soviet Union was closing the U.S. lead in SSN technology and creating what Navy officials described an antisubmarine warfare (ASW) "crisis" for the U.S. Navy.[171]

ONI states that the Shang-class "is intended primarily for antisurface warfare at greater ranges from the Chinese coast than the current diesel force. China looks at SSNs as a primary weapon against aircraft carrier battle groups and their associated logistics support."[172] Observers expect the Shang-class boats to be armed with a modern ASCM and also with a LACM broadly similar to the U.S. Tomahawk land-attack cruise missile. One observer states:

---

[169] *2004 ONI WMC*, p. 37.

[170] A map published by ONI suggests that the JL-2 range is 4,300 nautical miles to 6,500 nautical miles. The caption for the map states "JL-2 range assessments extend to over 5,000 nautical miles, potentially putting all of the continental United States at risk." The map shows that range of 4,300 nautical miles would be sufficient to reach Alaska, Hawaii, and northwest Canada, that a range of 5,400 nautical miles would be sufficient to reach much or most of the continental United States, and that a range of 6,500 nautical miles would be sufficient to reach all of the continental United States with the possible exception of southern Florida. *(2004 ONI WMC, p. 37.)*

China also operates a single Xia (Type 092) class SSBN that entered service in 1987, and a single Golf (Type 031) non-nuclear-powered ballistic missile submarine (SSB) that entered service in the late 1 960s. The Xia-class boat is armed with 12 CSS-N-3 (JL- 1) SLBMs that have a range of roughly 1,200 nautical miles. The Golf-class boat is used as an SLBM test platform.

[171] See, for example, Ronald O'Rourke, "Maintaining the Edge in US ASW," *Navy Intern ational,* July/August 1988, pp. 348-354.

[172] *2005 ONI WMC,* p. 14.

At first, [China's LACMs] will be launched by Second Artillery units, but soon after, they may also be used by PLA Air Force H-6 bombers and by the Navy's new Type 093 nuclear attack submarines. When used by the latter, the PLA will have its first platform capable of limited but politically useful non-nuclear power projection on a global scale....

Once there is a build-up of Type 093s it should be expected that the PLA Navy may undertake patrols near the U.S. in order to draw U.S. SSNs back to defensive patrols.[173]

Kilo-Class SS

China ordered four Kilo-class SSs from Russia in 1993; the ships entered service in 1995-1999. The first two were of the less capable (but still fairly capable) Project 877 variant, which Russia has exported to several countries; the other two were of the more capable Project 636 variant that Russia had previously reserved for its own use.

China in 2002 ordered eight additional Kilos from Russia, reportedly all of the Project 636 design. The ships reportedly are to be delivered in 2005 (six boats) and 2006 (two boats).[174] ONI states that the delivery of these eight boats "will provide the Chinese Navy with a significant qualitative increase in warfighting capability,"[175] while another observer states that the Kilo-class boats are "Among the most worrisome of China's foreign acquisitions...."[176]

The eight Kilos are expected to be armed with the Russian-made SS-N-27 Sizzler ASCM, also known as the Novator Alfa Klub 3M-54E — a highly dangerous ASCM that might as difficult to shoot down, or perhaps even more difficult to shoot down, than the SS-N-22 Sunburn ASCM on China's Russian-made Sovremennyclass destroyers (see discussion below on surface combatants). China's first four Kilos (or the two Project 636 boats, if not the two Project 877 boats) might also be refitted with the SS-N-27.

Yuan (Type 041) Class SS

China is building a new class of SS called the Yuan (or Type 041) class. The first Yuan-class boat, whose appearance reportedly came as a surprise to western observers,[177177] was launched (i.e., put into the water for final construction) in 2004. Observers expect the first two Yuan-class boats to enter service in 2006.

Some observers believe the Yuan class may incorporate technology from Russia's most recent SS design, known as the Lada or Amur class, including possibly an air-independent

---

[173] *Fisher 7/27/05 testimony,* pp. 9, 11.

[174] As mentioned earlier, ONI states that all eight Kilo-class boats are scheduled for delivery by 2005 *(2004 ONI WMC,* p. 12), while some other sources project that the final boat or boats will be delivered by 2007.

[175] *2004 ONI WMC,* p. 12.

[176] *Tkacik 7/27/05 testimony,* p. 8. See also *Fisher 7/27/05 testimony,* pp. 11-12.

[177] *Jane's Fighting Ships 2005-2006,* for example, states: "It is fair to say that the intelligence community was caught completely unawares by the emergence of the Yuan class...." *Jane's Fighting Ships 2005-2006,* p. 30 (Executive Overview). See also Bill Gertz, "Chinese Produce New Type Of Sub," *Washington Times,* July 16, 2004: 1.

propulsion (AIP) system.[178] One observer says the Yuan class strongly resembles both the Russian Amur 1650-class and French Agosta-class SS designs.[179]

Song (Type 039/039g) Class SS

China is also building a relatively new SS design called the Song (or Type 039/039G) class. The first Song-class boat entered service in 1999, and a total of 12 are expected to be in service by 2006. The first boat reportedly experienced problems, resulting in design changes that were incorporated into subsequent (Type 039G) boats. Some observers believe the Song-class design may have benefitted from PLA Navy experience with the Kilo class. One report states that one Song-class boat has been equipped with an AIP system.[180] Observers are uncertain whether Song-class production will end as a result of the start of Yuan-class production, or continue in parallel with the Yuan class.

Older Ming (Type 035) and Romeo (Type 033) Class SSs

China in 2005 also had about 20 older Ming (Type 035) class SSs and about 21 even older Romeo (Type 033) class SSs (with an additional 10 in reserve status).

The first Ming-class boat entered service in 1971 and the 20th was launched in 2002. Production may have ended in favor of Song- and Yuan-class production. In April 2003, a malfunction aboard one of the boats (hull number 361) killed its 70-man crew. Observers believe they were killed by carbon monoxide or chlorine poisoning. The boat was repaired and returned to service in 2004.

The Romeo-class boats entered service between the early 1 960s and the late 1 980s. A total of 84 were built. Of the 21 still in service, one is a modified boat that has been used as a cruise missile test ship. The 10 boats in reserve status may be of dubious operational condition. The total number of Romeos in service and reserve status has been declining over time.

If China decides that Ming- and Romeo-class boats have continued value as minelayers or as bait or decoy submarines that can be used to draw out enemy submarines (such as U.S. SSNs), it may elect to keep some of these older submarines in service even as new submarines enter service.

Aircraft carriers. An August 2005 press report states:

Chinese shipyard workers have been repairing a badly damaged ex-Russian aircraft carrier and have repainted it with the country's military markings, raising the question once again of whether China is pursuing longer-term plans to field its first carrier.

In the latest developments, images show that workers at the Chinese Dalian Shipyard have repainted the ex-Russian Kuznetsov-class aircraft carrier Varyag with the markings and colour

---

[178] An AIP system, such as a fuel cell system or a closed-cycle diesel engine, extends the stationary or low-speed submerged endurance of a non-nuclear-powered submarine from a few days to perhaps two or three weeks. AIP technology does not extend the high-speed submerged endurance of a non-nuclear-powered submarine, which remains limited, due to battery capacity, to about 1 to 3 hours of high-speed operations.

[179] *Fisher 7/27/05 testimony,* p. 11.

[180] "CHINA — Submarine Force Moving Forward," *Submarine Review,* April 2005: 106.

scheme of the People's Liberation Army (PLA) Navy (PLAN). Additional new photographs show that other work, the specifics of which could not be determined, appears to be continuing and that the condition of the vessel is being improved....

Still, China's ultimate intentions for the Varyag remain unclear. One possibility is that Beijing intends to eventually have it enter into some level of service. A military strategist from a Chinese military university has commented publicly that the Varyag "would be China's first aircraft carrier."

It is possible that the PLAN will modify the Varyag into a training aircraft carrier. A US intelligence official said the vessel could be made seaworthy again with enough time, effort and resources. However, US defence officials said that repairing the Varyag to become fully operational would be an extraordinarily large task. The carrier was about 70 per cent complete at the time of transfer and sensitive portions were destroyed, including damage to the core structure, before China was permitted to take possession. Given the difficulty and expense, it is questionable whether Beijing would pursue the effort only to use the Varyag as a training platform; such a move could, however, mark a transitional phase en route to a fully operational capability.

Another possibility is that China does, indeed, plan to repair the vessel to become its first seagoing aircraft carrier or use knowledge gained from it for an indigenously built carrier programme. The US intelligence official said such an outcome "is certainly a possibility" if China is seeking a blue- water navy capable of protecting long-range national interests far from its shores such as sea lanes in the Strait of Malacca. If this strategy were to be followed, China would have to reinstate the structural integrity degraded before delivery and study the structural design of the carrier's deck. These two activities, along with the blueprints and the ship itself, could be used to design an indigenous carrier. Such a plan would very likely be a long-term project preceded by the development of smaller vessels such as amphibious landing ships.[181]

Surface Combatants. One observer states that by 2010, China's surface combatant force could exceed 31 destroyers and 50 frigates, backed up by 30 ocean-capable stealthy fast attack craft. Such a force could then be used in conjunction with submarines and attack aircraft to impose a naval blockade around Taiwan. Surface ships could also defend the airspace around Taiwan from U.S. Naval forces, especially its P-3 anti-submarine warfare aircraft which would play a critical role in defeating a blockade.[182]

Regarding the HQ-9 SAM believed to be carried by the Luyang II-class destroyers, ONI states[183]:

The most challenging threat to aircraft and cruise missiles comes from high-performance, long-range [SAM] systems like the Russian SA-10/SA-20 family. The system combines very powerful three-dimensional radar and a high-performance missile with engagement ranges in excess of 100 nautical miles against a conventional target. The SA- 1 0/SA-20 has been marketed widely and has enjoyed some success in the export market, but its high cost has limited its proliferation. Technology from the SA- 10 is being incorporated into China's 50-

---

[181] Yihong Chang and Andrew Koch, "Is China Building A Carrier?," *Jane's Defence Weekly,* August 17, 2005. See also Ian Storey and You Ji, "China's Aircraft Carrier Ambitions, Seeking Truth from Rumors," *Naval War College Review,* winter 2004, pp. 77-93.

[182] *Fisher 7/27/05 testimony,* p. 12.

[183] *2004 ONI WMC,* p. 29.

nautical mile range HQ-9 SAM, which is intended for use on the new LUYANG destroyer. The HQ-9 will provide China's navy with its first true area air defense capability when the SAM becomes operational in the next few years.

Amphibious Ships

The three new classes of amphibious ships and craft now under construction in China, all of which began construction in 2003, are as follows:

- *Yuting II-class helicopter-capable tank landing ships (LSTs).* Three of these ships entered service in 2003 and another six in 2004. Each ship can transport 10 tanks and 250 soldiers, and has a helicopter landing platform for two medium-sized helicopters. The ships were built at three shipyards, and additional units are expected.
- *Yunshu-class landing ships (LSMs).* Ten of these ships entered service in 2004. Each ship can transport 6 tanks or 12 trucks or 250 tons of supplies. The ships were built at four shipyards, and additional units are expected.
- *Yubei-class utility landing craft (LCUs).* Eight of these landing
- craft entered service in 2004. Each craft can transport 10 tanks and
- 150 soldiers. The ships were built at four shipyards, and additional
- units arc cxpcctcd.

DOD states:

The PLA recently increased amphibious ship production to address its lift deficiencies — although the intelligence community believes these increases will be inadequate to meet requirements — and is organizing its civilian merchant fleet and militia, which, given adequate notification, could augment the PLA's organic lift in amphibious operations.[184]

Information Warfare/Information Operations (IW/IO)

Regarding IW/IO capabilities, ONI states, without reference to any specific country:

IO is the combination of computer network attack, electronic warfare, denial and deception (DandD), and psychological operations (PSYOP)....

Outside attack on Navy networks can take different forms depending on the attacker's goals and sophistication. Navy networks have been targeted for denial of service attacks from the Internet. More sophisticated operations, perhaps conducted by foreign military or intelligence services, might include covertly mapping Navy networks, installing backdoors to facilitate future intrusions, stealing data, and leaving behind destructive code packages to be activated in time of conflict. Malicious codes like the Melissa virus have appeared in classificd networks, demonstrating that an external attack on ostensibly protected networks could succeed. Attacks could selectively alter information in Navy databases and files, introducing errors into the system. When discovered or revealed, this corruption of trusted data could cause us to lose confidence in the integrity of the entire database.[185]

Nuclear Weapons

Regarding the potential use of nuclear weapons against U.S. Navy forces, one study states that

> there is some evidence the PLA considers nuclear weapons to be a useful element of an anti-access strategy. In addition to the nuclear-capable [ballistic] missiles... China has nuclear bombs and aircraft to carry them, and is reported to have nuclear mines for use at sea and nuclear anti-ship missiles. At the very least, China would expect the presence of these weapons and the threat to use them to be a significant deterrent to American action.[186]

Regarding the possibility of China using a high-altitude nuclear detonation to create an EMP effect, DOD states:

> Some PLA theorists are aware of the electromagnetic effects of using a high-altitude nuclear burst to generate high-altitude electromagnetic pulse (HEMP), and might consider using HEMP as an unconventional attack, believing the United States and other nations would not interpret it as a use of force and as crossing the nuclear threshold. This capability would most likely be used as part of a larger campaign to intimidate, if not decapitate, the Taiwan leadership. HEMP causes a substantial change in the ionization of the upper atmosphere, including the ionosphere and magnetosphere. These effects likely would result in the degradation of important war fighting capabilities, such as key communication links, radar transmissions, and the full spectrum of electro-optic sensors. Additional effects could include severe disruptions to civil electric/power and transportation. These effects cannot easily be localized to Taiwan and would likely affect the mainland, Japan, the Philippines, and commercial shipping and air routes in the region.[187]

Whether China would agree with the above view that EMP effects could not easily be localized to Taiwan and surrounding waters is not clear. The effective radius of a high-altitude EMP burst is dependent to a strong degree on the altitude atwhich the warhead is exploded (the higher the altitude, the greater the radius).[188] China might therefore believe that it could detonate a nuclear warhead somewhere east of Taiwan at a relatively low altitude, so that the resulting EMP radius would be sufficient to affect systems in Taiwan and on surface

---

[184] *2005 DOD CMP*, p. 31. See also *Fisher 7/27/05 testimony*, p. 13.

[185] *2004 ONI WMC*, p. 38.

[186] *The Chinese Military, An Emerging Maritime Challenge,* Washington, Lexington Institute, 2004, pp. 13-14.

[187] *2005 DOD CMP,* p. 40.

[188] A report by the Office of Technology Assessment (a congressional support agency that was closed in 1995), states: "The size of the area that could be affected by EMP is primarily determined by the height of burst and is only very weakly dependent on the yield." *(MX Missile Basing.* Washington, Office of Technology Assessment, 1981. (September 1981) p. 297. The document is available on the Internet at [http://www.wws.princeton.edu/ota/ ns20/year_f.html].

ships in surrounding waters, but not great enough to reach systems on China's mainland.[189] Following the detonation, China could attempt to confuse the issue in the public arena of whose nuclear warhead had detonated. Alternatively, China could claim that the missile launch was an accident, and that China command-detonated the warhead at altitude as a failsafe measure, to prevent it from detonating closer to the surface and destroying any nearby ships.[190]

High-Power Microwave (Hpm) Weapons

Regarding radio-frequency weapons, ONI states:

One observer states that a detonation height of 200 kilometers (108 nautical miles) would produce an EMP effect out to a radius of about 1,600 kilometers (864 nautical miles), while a detonation height of 50 kilometers would produce an EMP effect out to a radius of about 800 kilometers (432 nautical miles). (Written Statement by Dr. Michael Bernardin, Provost for the Theoretical Institute for Thermonuclear and Nuclear Studies, Applied Theoretical and Computational Physics Division, Los Alamos National Laboratory, before the Military Research and Development Subcommittee of the House Armed Services Committee, October 7, 1999.)
A map presented by another observer shows that a detonation height of 100 kilometers (54 nautical miles) would produce an EMP effect out to a radius of about 1,000 kilometers (540 nautical miles). (Statement of Dr. Gary Smith, Director, The Johns Hopkins University Applied Physics Laboratory, before Military Research and Development Subcommittee of the House Armed Services Committee, July 16, 1996.)
Another published map states that a detonation height of 30 miles would produce an EMP effect out to a radius of 480 miles. A source note attached to the map attributes it to the above-cited July 16, 1997 testimony of Gary Smith. (See page 3 of Jack Spencer, *America's Vulnerability To A Diferent Nuclear Threat: An Electromagnetic Pulse.* Washington, Heritage Foundation, 2000. 7 pp. (Backgrounder No. 1372, May 26, 2000) The document is available on the Internet at [http://www.heritage.org/Research/MissileDefense/ bg1372.cfm]).
Radio-frequency weapons (RFW) could be used against military networks since they transmit high power radio/microwave energy to damage/disrupt electronic components. RFWs fall into two categories, beam and warhead. A beam weapon is a multiple use system that can repeatedly send directional RF energy at different targets. An RF warhead is a single-use explosive device that can be delivered to the target by multiple means, including missiles or artillery shells. RFWs can be assembled with little technical knowledge from commercial off-the-shelf components, such as surplus military radars.[191]

One observer states that, "at least one U.S. source indicates the PLA has developed" non-nuclear radio frequency warheads for ballistic missiles.[192] When asked at a hearing about the

---

[189] CRS Report RL3 2544, op cit, states that "creating a HEMP [high-altitude EMP] effect over an area 250 miles in diameter [i.e., a radius of 125 miles], an example size for a battlefield, might only require a rocket with a modest altitude and payload capability that could loft a relatively small nuclear device."

[190] Even if China does not have the capability to command the early detonation of a warhead on a ballistic missile in flight, it could claim afterward that it did.

[191] *2004 ONI WMC,* p. 39.

[192] *Fisher 7/27/05 testimony,* p. 6. A footnote at this point in Fisher's statement says this information was: "Disclosed to the author by a U.S. source in September 2004." See also page 9.

possibility of China using a nuclear weapon to generate an EMP effect against Taiwan and U.S. naval forces, this observer stated:

> What worries me more, Congressman, is non-nuclear electromagnetic pulse weapons. Non-nuclear explosive propelled radio frequency or EMP-like devices that could be used with far greater frequency and far more effect because they would not run the danger for China of prompting a possible nuclear response. Thereby it would be much more tempting to use and use effectively.
>
> If you could combine a non-nuclear radio frequency weapon with a maneuvering ballistic missile of the type that the Pentagon report describes very briefly this year, that would constitute a real Assassin's Mace weapon. One that, in my opinion, we cannot defend ourselves against and would possibly effectively deny effective military — effective American military intervention in the event of — not just a Taiwan crisis, but other crises as well.[193]

---

[193] Spoken testimony of Richard D. Fisher, Jr., in transcript of *7/27/05 HASC hearing,* in response to a question from Representative Curt Weldon.

In: Economics and Foreign Investment in China
Editor: J.I. Cheng, pp. 67-78

ISBN 1-60021-238-7
© 2007 Nova Science Publishers, Inc.

Chapter 2

JINGWAI JUEZHAN: DISCUSSING YHIS JARGON IN CONJUNCTION WITH ANOTHER CONCEPT, ETC.

Peter Kien-hong Yu[1]

Ming Chuan University in Taipei, Taiwan

PRECIS

1. *Jingwai juezhan*, roughly translated as decisive battle offshore, offshore full-scale engagement, winning of the war off the Taiwanese coast, or outside of Taiwan or offshore engagement with the enemy, is one of the new jargons/slogans put forward by the Chen Shui-bian administration in Taiwan in June 2000.

2. Different interpretations and insights could emerge, if we were to associate this military jargon with another concept, geographic feature, and so on. If we pair it with the political jargon, Republic of China (ROC), we would have noticed that Chen is thinking himself in terms of the president of the ROC on Taiwan, which is at least politically different from national titles like the ROC; the Republic of Taiwan (ROT); Taiwan State (*guo*), the ROC; and so on. This should be a somewhat relief to the Beijing leaders, because the usage *jingwai*, implies that the Chen administration still legally takes the ROC's territory on mainland China into consideration.

3. *Juezhan jingwai* and *jingwai juezhan* are discussed and they are quite different. The former gives one the notion that the Taiwan armed forces may fire the first shot, whereas the latter gives us the impression that the Taiwan armed forces would react to an attack first launched by the Chinese People's Liberation Army (CPLA).

4. The question of where the decisive battle would take place is also related to *jingwai juezhan*. Because the Taiwan armed forces have no intention of initiating an attack after the late 1960s, they have to react to "multiple-wave" and saturation missile attacks from many CPLA's Second Artillery Bases on the mainland as well as from its submarines deployed in waters off eastern Taiwan. When we think in terms of this scenario, the ROC on Taiwan is actually still on the defensive.

---

[1] Pyu8@hotmail.com

5. Cyber warfare is another term that we can associate with *jingwai juezhan*. Armed forces on both sides of the Taiwan Strait plan to paralyze each other's electronic warfare system and facilities with more than 2,000 viruses, so that, for example, missiles cannot be launched. This kind of warfare certainly reaches the mainland. Whether the CPLA will retaliate by other means, such as ordering its naval ships to cross the Taiwan Strait needs to be observed.

In May 2000, Chen Shui-bian officially became the Republic of China (ROC) on Taiwan's new president, who is well known for having advocated "Long Live Taiwan's Independence!" before the March 18, 2000 election.[2] Thereafter, a lot of new jargons/slogans appeared, such as *Zhonghua guo* [(the State of China as opposed to simply *Zhongguo* (China)] as uttered by the then Premier Tang Fei on July 14, 2000, *guojia anquan wang* (national safety net) as coined by the Mainland Affairs Council (MAC),[3] etc. Another jargon deserves our attention, that is, *jingwai juezhan*, which roughly translated, is decisive battle (*juezhan*) offshore or outside of Taiwan (*jingwai*), offshore full-scale engagement, winning the war off the Taiwanese coast, or offshore engagement with the enemy.[4] To be sure, during his presidential campaign and after becoming the President, Chen mentioned this term.[5] But, in the August 2000 version of the National Defense Report, this latest jargon was not mentioned, due to the sensitivity of the matter.[6] In the Hanguang 18 Military Exercise, for example, Taipei for the first time put *jingwai juezhan* into its largest-ever drill into test. It should be noted that Taipei's three-stage strategy used to be the following, which was first put forward by Yu Dawei, the then Minister of National Defense: *zhikong*, *zhihai*, and *fandenglu* (stopping the enemy forces from setting sail toward Taiwan, assaulting them in the ocean, and terminating the rest of them in the beaches.)[7] In this paper, we shall try to discuss this the latest jargon, *jingwai juezhan*, with another concept, etc.

---

[2] In January 2002, Chen made a physical gesture at a function celebrating the 20th anniversary of the founding of a pro-Taiwan's independence organization, Formosan Association for Public Affairs (FAPA).

[3] When the MAC makes a decision related to direct shipping, for example, it has to take the Republic of China (ROC) on Taiwan's security into consideration. See *China Times* (hereinafter CT)(Taipei), August 20, 2000, p.3. The term is also related to developing Taiwan's economy, building Taiwan people's confidence, etc. See *United Daily News* (hereinafter UDN)(Taipei), December 6, 2000, p.3 and *CT*, December 6, 2000, p.2.

[4] Another translation by Damon Bristow is "fighting a decisive battle outside the territory." Applied to the air force, it is called "offshore denial of enemy aircraft," announced on December 26, 2000. In December 2000, the ROC Ministry of National Defense used the term *tanhuanzhan* instead of *xiaohaozhan* in its mid-term plan. See *CT*, December 28, 2000, p.4.

[5] *Straits Times* (hereinafter ST)(Singapore), August 4, 2000, p.54.

[6] *UDN*, September 16, 2000, p.4.

[7] A U.S. Department of Defense's wording is: "maintaining air superiority over the Taiwan Strait and the waters contiguous to Taiwan; conducting effective counter-blockade operations; and, defeating an amphibious and aerial assault on the islands." See chapter 5 of my book, co-authored with Martin L. Lasater, *Taiwan's Security in the Post-Deng Xiaoping Era* (London: Frank Cass Publishers, 2000). In an opinion poll conducted by the then ruling party, Kuomintang (KMT), *jingwai zuezhan* incorporates the *zhikong*, *zhihai*, and *fandenglu*. See *Lianhezaobao* (hereinafter LHZB)(Singapore), November 12, 2000, p.20. In July 2002, the new version of the National Defense Report was publicized, in which *fandenglu* was dropped for the first time.

THE JARGON TOGETHER WITH
ANOTHER CONCEPT AND OTHER THINGS

There are many cross-strait or bicoastal Chinese phenomena that we can relate to *jingwai juezhan*. When we discuss the jargon in conjunction with another concept and other things, different interpretations and insights could emerge. In other words, our understanding of the latest jargon could be deeper. We shall discuss many pairs one by one.

The ROC. The foremost thing in mind is what can be said about *jingwai juezhan* with that of the ROC? Chen said he is the President of the ROC, according to the Constitution.[8] We know that, in May 1991, an amendment was made to the Constitution, that is, the ROC's jurisdiction is limited to the Taiwan area, which includes Jinmen and Mazu, part of the Fujian Province, and Taiping Dao (Itu Aba Island) and Dongsha Dao (Pratas) in the South China Sea, part of the Hainan Province. But, because the National Assembly has not yet relinquished the territory in mainland China including Hongkong and Macao, the ROC's sovereignty is not 100% limited to the Taiwan area. In other words, Taipei has been deliberately playing a political game for many years. Because the President is also the supreme commander of armed forces, Chen was still shouting the following slogans when he was at important military functions: "Long Live Three Principles of the People!" "Long Live the ROC!" and "Achieving the Great Task of Unification!" It is because of the last slogan, the armed forces also chose to use the term *jingwai* before May 20, 2000. That is to say, many armed forces officials at high levels still cling on to a greater China mentality or think about the mainland.[9]

In July 2000, a new book co-authored by Lee argued that, after six rounds of constitutional amendments, the ROC has entered into a new phase, that is, it is no long the ROC *on Taiwan* (as opposed to the ROC) but Taiwan, ROC, which is supposed to be the Second Republic.[10] Although Lee is no longer a President, what he said can still make some impact on some political figures' mind, as the December 2001 elections and the creation of a new political party soon after attest. In March 2003, Lee also said the time to create a new country is 2008. But, the ROC and Taiwan, the ROC are quite different. The ROC can be on mainland China, on Taiwan, or on both the mainland and Taiwan, if not elsewhere such as the Moon and Mars. But, to refer to the ROC as Taiwan, the ROC, it means that there are two states in the political arena at home and abroad. So, Lee said the most accurate way of describing the objective situation is that there is one China but two states.[11] Some opposition parties like the People First Party (PFP) and New Party in Taiwan criticized Lee's latest argument, which is tantamount to two states.[12] But, if Chen were to use the term *jingwai*, he is actually still regarding himself as the President of the ROC *on Taiwan*. To be sure, the ROC was once on the mainland and after the Second World War both mainland China and

---

[8] *CT*, August 1, 2000, p.4.

[9] One ROC naval captain, speaking to June Teufel Dreyer in early 2001, said he will not fight for Chen.

[10] *CT*, July 28, 1999, p.4 and *UDN*, July 22, 2000, p.3. Lee in September 2002 said he was the president of Taiwan, ROC.

[11] *UDN*, July 22, 2000, p.3. He repeated this concept in September 2001.

[12] *Ibid.*

Taiwan.[13] In other words, Chen as opposed to Lee should be better received by the Chinese Communists on the mainland. Of course, Chen mentioned the possibility of another round of constitutional amendment sometime after the December 2001 election. If the Legislative *Yuan* (LY) which took over the job of the National Assembly (NA) in May 2003 indeed constitutionally altered the national territory, Chen's usage of *jingwai juezhan*, to be logical, would have to be changed as well. However, Chen dares not to ask the LY to alter the national territory of the ROC, unless he is re-elected in March 2004, because the mainland leaders regard him as further inching toward Taiwan's independence.[14]

Juezhan Jingwai [15]

The beauty of Chinese characters is that, sometimes, if we invert the phrases, the meaning could be different. A researcher at a Chinese People's Liberation Army (CPLA) Navy institute also noted that, before Chen became the ROC President, the ROC military strategy was changed from *fangwei gushou* (defense and defend) and *youxiao hezu* (effective deterrence). *Juezhan jingwai* is a form of deterrence. Whether it can succeed is another matter. But, the tone is more positive, because it seems that the ROC armed forces are determined to fight the renewed civil war outside of the Taiwan island plus the remote islands such as Penghu Island no matter what. The attack or a saturation of attacks by the CPLA could come from the northeast, the northwest, or elsewhere.

The question of where would the decisive battle take place? This question is an extension of the previous paragraph. According to a National Defense University professor in Beijing, the ROC has three large islands and 58 small geographic features in its possession.[16] Taipei will be increasingly on the defensive militarily. (For example, Taiwan's air force may lose its edge vis-à-vis the mainland air force by 2005.[17]) By June 2002, the ROC has completely installed three Patriot PAC-II batteries, which are basically an anti-aircraft system in the Greater Taipei area, namely, Linkou, Wanli, as well as Nangang and Xindian. It is seeking to install three new PAC-III batteries, which are basically a short-range ballistic missile system[18] in the central and southern part of the island. But, the employment of the term *jingwai juezhan* does not mean that the ROC will deliberately fire the first shot. Of course, we cannot rule out the possibility that a few military officers who, due to one reason or another, turned against the Chen administration, and launched a missile from, for example, Dongyin Dao, which is very close to the mainland and which is under the ROC control.

---

[13] After the December 2001 elections in Taiwan, some people jokingly said the ROC is only on Jinmen because the New Party (NP) only succeeded in getting a legislative seat in the Jinmen district.

[14] In September 2002, PRC officials said they had given up hope on Chen.

[15] In November 1999, the then presidential candidate, Chen Shui-bian, first used the jargon, *juezhan jingwai*. See www.chinatimes.com.tw/news/papers/online/politics/c88b2380.htm, dated November 23, 1999. Taiwan's strategic oil reserve can only last 18 days. See *CT*, September 12, 2000, p.6.

[16] *Zhongguoguofangbao* (note 12), August 2, 2000, p.4.

[17] An expert on air war said it takes only less than 100 hours to see which side can win it. See *UDN*, September 30, 2000, p.2. In May 2002, it was reported that in January 2002 the Pentagon in a report said the CPLA plans to use 48 hours to subjugate Taipei to the negotiations table.

[18] In June 2002, a U.S. Pentagon official at the Heritage Foundation said the PAC-III system has encountered bugs or shortcomings.

In a missile age, the CPLA may well first launch its missiles against Taiwan. In the description of the 2000 National Defense Report published in Taipei in August 2000, a CPLA invasion involves "multiple-wave" and saturation missile attacks. Of course, before missiles hit Taiwan, there is time for Taipei to react. In other words, Taipei, with information gathered from satellite detection, has some 20 to 30 minutes to respond. Before crossing the middle line (as opposed to median line) of the Taiwan Strait, some of the CPLA missiles may well be destroyed by the Patriot missiles of the ROC. It should be added that American researchers revealed in December 2001 that the ROC is conducting research and development of 1,000-kilometer ballistic missiles as well as cruise missiles. To be certain, it is not possible for Taipei to intercept all of the CPLA missiles and, therefore, *jingwai juezhan* could mislead some people into thinking that Taipei could be unharmed or even emerge as a victor after a battle or a war. So, some political figures in Taiwan has mentioned Hongkong and Shanghai, if not other cities as possible targets, hoping officials and residents over there would urge Beijing not to initiate an attack. Thus, the PRC decided to set up an air defense zone or corridor covering Hongkong and its neighboring Shenzhen City in Guangdong Province and armed with guided missiles, etc.[19] Yet, its then Chief of the General Staff, Tang Yao-ming, who was promoted to be the Defense Minister in March 2002, explained that "outside Taiwan" referred to just the area and air space around the Taiwan Strait and it does not include the mainland.[20] In December 2001, the then Defense Minister Wu Shiwen mentioned that the battle should take place in the middle line of the Taiwan Strait, and he ruled out an attack of Hongkong, because the ROC missiles cannot reach that Special Administration Region (SAR).[21] But, we know that the Taiwan Strait is too shallow, lacking depth. So, any military action could quickly involve at least the coastal area of the mainland, especially when we think in the context of Jinmen and Mazu.

On record, the ROC armed forces have deployed missiles on its remote islands, which can hit the coastal area of the mainland. So, strictly speaking, *jingwai* has to include the mainland. As a matter of fact, when Hao Bocun was the Chief of the General Staff, he devised a strategy to bombard the military facilities on the coastal area of mainland China, so as to make, for example, the CPLA air force "deaf and blind."[22]

Objectively speaking, Taipei does not even know where the decisive battle or war would take place. It can be argued that the CPLA's Second Artillery would launch many missiles at the same time from missile bases scattered in mainland China plus from its naval ships off Taiwan's eastern waters. If Taiwan were able to survive after several hundred missiles' attack, the Taiwan Strait may well be the next place. If the CPLA navy successfully crossed the Strait and its marines landed on Penghu Island or Taiwan's beaches, it may well mean the end of the ROC.

In a nutshell, because Taipei knows that it can be exhausted after a period of time, especially its industries will be paralyzed, it does not lose much by putting forward this military term for internal (as opposed to domestic) consumption, so long as its real intention has been relayed to the other side of the Taiwan Strait. As a matter of fact, soon after Lee succeeded Chiang Ching-kuo in January 1988 and beyond the day he stepped down in May

---

[19] *ST*, August 16, 2000, p.21.

[20] *Ibid.*, August 4, 2000, p.54.

[21] www.chineseworld.com/publish/today/11_0900.4w/t/4wtp/(011208)01_tb.htm, dated December 7, 2001.

[22] See chapters 4 and 5 in Lasater and Yu (note 6).

2000, there were still Taiwan messengers or secret envoys working for Lee.[23] It is interesting to know that, according to Hongkong-based *Asiaweek*, Qian Qichen in July 2000 said the PRC does not have a plan to attack Taiwan in five years' time.[24] This ay well be the case, because the CPLA must be able to land on Taiwan in order to defeat the ROC. In July 2001, Beijing succeeded in bidding for the summer 2008 Olympic Games. If the intelligence received by Chen is the same, it only confirms that *jingwai juezhan* is a tactic to rally support of the ROC armed forces behind Chen's back.

Jingwai Juezhan and Non-Jingwai Juezhan

Chinese (Communist) political figures are known for applying dialectics in their word and deed.[25] Chen before the presidential election said he would adopt a new middle road, if elected. In other words, in his mind, there are two new extremes and he is in the "middle." For example, the Republic of Taiwan (ROT) on the left extreme and the ROC (on Taiwan) on the right extreme, which is just the opposite of Lee's framework of thought and action, which is the ROC on the left extreme and the ROT on the right extreme. In other words, Lee was doing something in favor of the ROC on Taiwan, while Chen will seize on opportunities to promote causes in favor of the creation of the ROT, the latest example being the announcement in January 2002 that the phrase issued in Taiwan will be added on the ROC passports in September 2003.[26] So, discussing *jingwai juezhan* and non-*jingwai juezhan* is necessary, with each jargon representing one extreme. Examples of some non-*jingwai juezhan* include battles taking place in Taipei, the air space above the Kaohsiung International Airport in southern Taiwan, and other places. This means that Chen sometimes may stick to *jingwai juezhan* and at other times in the middle (by using another related jargon) or the other extreme, depending on the situation or the time/space sequence. To a non-dialectician, he or she may be confused. But, to a dialectician, he or she knows what is going on at each time/space sequence.

Morale, Equipments, and Training

These three elements determine the war capability of a country's armed forces. Morale is more important than the latter two.[27] In December 1949, the ROC government began its administrative operation in Taiwan. From that time up to the day when Chen Shui-bian became the 10th President, the armed forces in Taiwan were taught about the Three Principles of People (TPP) and other doctrines, because the armed forces were considered part of the

---

[23] *UDN*, July 21, 2000, p.3.

[24] www.mingpaonews.om/20000720/inews/ca41455.htm, dated July 20, 2000.

[25] See my book, *Bicoastal China: A Dialectical, Paradigmatic Analysis* (New York: Nova Science Publishers, 1999) and *The Crab and Frog Motion Paradigm Shift: Decoding and Deciphering Taipei and Beijing's Dialectical Politics* (Lanham, MD.: University Press of America, 2002).

[26] In May 2002, a committee of the Legislative *Yuan* (branch) said it has approved the phrase "Taiwan passport" rather than "issued in Taiwan." In June 2003, it was announced that the proper noun Tiawan would be added on the passport.

[27] Wysiwyg@29/http://www.chienseworld.co...h/today/17_0900.4t/4tt(000901)05_tb.htm, dated August 31, 2000.

ruling party. In other words, they know what to fight for and not to fight for.[28] If Taiwan is for democracy and freedom, the armed forces in Taiwan would fight against the invading CPLA. But, if the armed forces are asked to fight for the creation of the ROT, then it is something else. As of now, most military officers and soldiers arguably are not willing to fight for the ROT. They may collectively retire when the ROT was created. If so, who can fly the jet fighters and man the naval ships? Thus, *jingwai juezhan* does not really help to boost morale.

Cyber Warfare[29]

Computers have been used by most countries' military, including the ROC armed forces[30] and the PLA. The 42nd Group Army of the latter, for example, has recently received advanced electronic equipments to be in charge of harassing Taiwan's southern area, especially Kaohsiung.[31] On January 1, 2001, the former set up a Bureau of Communications, Electronics, and Information, having 5,000 strong information warfare force, so as to counter the mainland's internet force.[32] This is a special war, which does not need to send infiltrators to the enemy's camp. While they are useful, they could also cripple one's capability, such as one's spy satellites, which can counter Theater Missile Defense (TMD)[33] and National Missile Defense (NMD), the latter of which was first put forward in May 1993, that is, after the Persian Gulf War in early 1991. Many internet users including those in Taiwan have this kind of experience.[34] A top Central Intelligence Agency (CIA) official testified in the U.S.

---

[28] On October 10, 2000, Chen, at the ceremony failed to utter the slogan of "Long Live the Three Principles of the People." But, in November 2000, at a graduation ceremony for the armed forces universities and colleges, he uttered the slogan.

[29] This paragraph has been heavily drawn from *ST*, August 8, 2000, p.17 and www.taiwansecurity.org/scmp/scmp-08099.htm, dated August 14, 2000. See also *UDN*, August 23, 2000, p.15, *ZGGFB*, August 23, 2000, p.B2, and James C. Mulvenon and Richard H. Yang, eds., *The People's Liberation Army in the Information Age* (Santa Monica, CA.: Rand, 1999). Russia is well ahead of the West in the development of "radio-frequency weapons" or electro-magnetic device capable of disabling electrical and electronic systems. Referred to as E Bomb, it can be put in a briefcase. See *ST*, December 28, 2000, p.4. According to a report, Cybercrime, Cyberterrorism, Cyberwarfare, released by the Center for Strategic and International Studies, a Washington think tank, it is said that information warfare specialists at the Pentagon estimate that a properly-prepared and well-coordinated attack by fewer than 30 computer virtuoss around the world, with a budget of less than US$10 million could bring the United States to its knees. "Bytes, not bullets, are the real ammo." See *ST*, December 17, 1998, p.6. For an argument that using high technology may not win a war, see *CT*, April 2, 1999, p.15. Deputy Commander of the Second Artillery, Gong Conzhou, wrote a letter to Mao Zedong in June 1975, saying, in the 1970's, the ROC conducts electronic warfare exercises every two months, and Fujian Province's radars were jammed and the troops could not see targets. In December 1975, Ye Jianying reported to Mao on how to counter the enemy's electronic warfare, and Mao liked what Ye said. See *Central Daily News* (hereinafter CDN)(Taipei), April 1, 1997 p.10.

[30] For example, at the 16th Hanguang military exercises in Taiwan, cyber wars was included. See *Taiwan News* (hereinafter TN)(Taipei), August 30, 2000, p.1.

[31] *UDN*, February 3; 2001, p.13. In April 2002, the Central Intelligence Agency (CIA) confirmed that the CPLA is conducting electronic warfare against the United States and the ROC.

[32] *CT*, November 23, 2000, p.4 and http://taiwansecurity.org/TT/TT-112300.htm, dated November 23, 2000 and *Taipei Journal* (hereinafter TJ)(Taipei), November 9, 2001, p.2.

[33] In 2001, the United States dropped the TMD.

[34] More than 10% of computers in Taiwan were hacked by the mainland, according to a secret investigation by the Taiwan authorities. See www.mingpaonews.com/20001026/inews/ca41445c.htm, dated October 26, 2000.

Congress, saying even his agency cannot predict computer attacks.[35] This is because many hackers try to infiltrate and sabotage computers with viruses (or electromagnetic pulses), like the "I Love You" virus and its derivatives. As of July 2002, there are more than 61,300 viruses. Computer experts in the military also take cyber drills or try to launch an information war to paralyze the enemy's military command, energy, transportation and banking systems. Sometimes, they lure hackers to fall into their virus traps. The ROC armed forces for the first time in August 2000 at the Hanguang 16 Military Exercise[36] and their counterpart on the mainland had simulated computer virus offensives in exercises. It is claimed that none of the viruses had paralyzed the Taiwan military's computer systems.[37] The Taiwan military authorities have worked out about 2,000 types of computer viruses, just like their counterpart on the mainland. The former may also seek help from the United States. When time becomes opportune, the ROC armed forces' electronic warfare system and facilities, which are located on the east side (as opposed to the west side) of Taiwan will be tapped on. If so, this is a form of *jingwai juezhan*. If successful, the CPLA Second Artillery with their cripples computers may not be able to launch its missiles.

Taiwan's *Xinfang* (The Ability to Cope with Pressure, so as to Avoid Being Caved in)

Mentally, Taipei thinks that it has been pushed to a corner by Beijing. Time is not on its side. Its territory under its control is much smaller than Beijing's and it may also become an outcast in the international community, if it does not provide more foreign aid to other countries in exchange for having diplomatic ties. Besides, one of its core negotiators from the Lee days, Shi Hwei-yow, admitted that the ROC is gradually losing its bargaining chips.[38] To avoid cave in, *jingwai juezhan* can be used for domestic consumption, so as to make political figures psychologically feel more secure and confident about their future. From January 1, 2002, the first ROC modern psychological warfare unit based in Taoyuan County's Army General Headquarters would be in operation so as to counter the PRC's military build-up. It is modelled on the 4th Psychological Operations Group of the U.S. Army.

Jinmem and Mazu

Those are two remote islands under the jurisdiction of the ROC. For many decades, residents on those islands were sandwiched between the ROC and the PRC. By uttering the slogan *jingwai juezhan*, most Jinmen and Mazu residents should again feel uncomfortable. If Chen only wants to save the lives and properties of the Taiwan residents, he should not have used the word *jingwai*, because those islands are too close to mainland China and too far

---

[35] *ST*, June 23, 2001, p.8.
[36] *Guangjiaojing* (hereinafter GJJ)(Hongkong), September 2000, p.59.
[37] *Chengming* (Hongkong), No.275 (September 2000), p.68.
[38] *CT*, August 3, 2000, p.2.

away from the Taiwan island. An attack of the mainland coast may also affect the interests of those remote islands under Taipei's jurisdiction.[39]

Arms sales. Taiwan's defense is dependent upon the United States and, to a lesser extent, other countries like Israel, Holland, and France. If the PRC succeeded in stopping U.S. arms sales of advanced weapons to the ROC, then *jingwai juezhan* is a hollow or empty jargon, because credibility in conducting a counter-attack is called into question. Of course, Beijing has had a hard time in doing that, because, even though the August 17, 1982 communique between the United States and the PRC still exists, the U.S. Congress has approved sales of weapons to the ROC. In addition, the American Congress is contemplating enhancements to Taiwan's security.

Deterrence. Jingwai Juezhan is certainly related to deterrence.[40] Deterrence is a form of psychological warfare, combined with threats and promises. The main purpose is to avoid war. But, the Chinese version and the foreign version are different. To the latter, you have to show what you have, hoping that your enemy would not attack you for fear of losing the battle or war, because your (potential) enemy can see that your weapons are superior, numerous, etc. To the Chinese, one has to hide what they have. In so doing, the enemy dares not to launch an attack, because he or she does not know what you have.[41] However, there is change. In January 2002, a Taiwan academic trusted by Chen said the ROC President wants to develop surface-to-surface missiles capable of reaching the mainland. Chen is thinking of having cruise missiles and surface-to-surface missiles with a range of 1,000-kilomters but such weapons would not be used for a pre-emptive attack.[42] If the ROC on Taiwan cannot beef up its defense by upgrading its naval ships, air fighters, and other weaponry systems etc., it cannot defend itself and survive for a longer period of time. If it cannot defend itself, its enemy may take military actions first. So, *jingwai juezhan* does not really help to deter Taipei's (potential) enemy. As a matter of fact, a pro-Beijing monthly in Hongkong said *jingwai juezhan* is Taipei's scheme to embroil foreign armed forces in a renewed Chinese civil war.[43]

On purpose, some Taiwan political figures have identified Hongkong and Shanghai as possible targets of attack, if Taiwan were to be first attacked by the PLA. (In passing, it may well be noted that, in August 1958, Washington planned to attack Shanghai, Hangzhou, Nanjing, and Guangzhou with nuclear weapons.)[44] In April 1961, the ROC Chief of General Staffs, Peng Mengqi, was checking whether there are canons which can fire nuclear weapons in remote islands.[45] In April 1963, the U.S. planned to bombard the mainland's nuclear facilities.[46]) By doing so, most Hongkong and Shanghai residents' feeling toward Taiwan would be negative. But, if they treasure what they have got especially after Deng Xiaoping's southern inspection tour in early 1992, they may turn to their leaders for help, asking the latter not to help the CPLA in its attack against Taiwan. If that were to turn out to be the case,

---

[39] Taiwan plans to buy water from Fujian Province. See *UDN*, August 13, 2000, p.2. In May 2002, Fujian Province delivered water to Jinmen and Mazu free of charge due to draught in the area.

[40] *CT*, November 1, 2000, p.13.

[41] *Yazhou Zoukan* (hereinafter YZZK)(Hongkong), July 24-30, 2000, pp.28-29.

[42] See the January 14, 2002 issue of *Taipei Times* (hereinafter TT)(Taipei).

[43] *GJJ*, September 2000, p.58.

[44] www.chineseworld.com/publish/to.../4ha(000721)07_tb.ht, dated July 20, 2000.

[45] *World Journal* (hereinafter WJ)(New York), September 3, 2001, p.A2.

[46] *LHZB*, January 14, 2001, p.30.

Taiwan becomes safer and its *jingwai juezhan* strategy would have to be regarded as least as being partially successful.

The United States. Washington has been actively involved in Chinese (Communist) politics since the early 20th century. It is fair for Beijing to say that Taipei could not have changed its military posture without Washington's (and even Tokyo's) tacit agreement or endorsement, because most of the ROC's military hardwares come from the United States.[47] That is to say, some of the weapons must be offensive, such as the submarines. Thus, Taipei has approved a seven billion New Taiwan dollars program to upgrade its Indigenous Defense Fighter (IDF) to a joint counter-offensive platform (JCP), which would be capable of carrying offensive weapons.[48] Besides, for sometime already, the United States wants to directly or indirectly bring Taiwan into its TMD program or a similar version of it.[49] Taipei wants to purchase the Aegis radar and battle management systems, which is part of the TMD. Washington certainly understands Chen's usage of the jargon, *jingwai juezhan*.[50] It was for the first time involved in the planning, organization, and implementation of the Hanguang 18 Military Exercise. By uttering the slogan, Taipei is trying to be part of the TMD.[51] In this connection, according to the latest Guidelines for U.S.-Japan Defense Cooperation, Japan could also play a bigger role after and even before an incident in the Taiwan Strait, as the then American President William J. Clinton promised in July 2000 to reduce the number of troops in Okinawa. Of course, it is not that easy for the United States to succeed in directly bringing in the ROC, because, if Taiwan can be part of the U.S. strategy, it would constitute a violation of the PRC's sovereign claim. Beijing would certainly react to the American move. So, by associating *jingwai juezhan* with the United States, it seems that Chen's *jingwai juezhan* is just on the paper, an empty shell. But, we cannot rule out the possibility that Taiwan may well become a U.S. chip or proxy in fighting for the United States at the frontline.

Japan. We cannot rule out the possibility of the Japan Maritime and Air Self-defense Force's involvement at the time of an armed conflict between both sides of the Taiwan Strait. The Japanese Maritime Safety Agency (JMSA) which was created in May 1948 and which is under the Ministry of Transport with its coast guard ships may also be involved. After defeating Iraq for its invasion of Kuwait in early 1990s, Japan's Maritime Self-defense Force swept mines in Persian Gulf. The Taiwan Strait is much closer to Japan than to the Middle East. So, *jingwai juezhan* could be applied to situations close to the Japanese waters and air space. So, to only think about the Taiwan Strait and the mainland is not enough. Because the United States can, at most,only provide the ROC with intelligence and logistical support. So, other countries could be involved. Australia could be called upon by the United States in July 2000 to play a role, and it seems that it will. Decades ago, Canberra also contemplated an aerial bombardment of Kunming, provincial capital of Yunnan.[52] But, Washington has made it clear that it would not come to the Taiwan side, unless the PRC fired the first shot. In other words, if Taipei first declared *de jure* independence, then Washington cannot help it. So, it is not possible for Chen to execute this latest *jingwai juezhan* strategy, even if Taipei acquired

---

[47] *ST*, August 4, 2000, p.54.

[48] *Ibid.*

[49] After the Persian Gulf War in January 1991, the Pentagon set up an office in June 1994 to work on the idea of National Missile Defense (NMD) for the United States and TMD.

[50] *Chengming*, No.274 (August 2000), p.73.

[51] *GJJ*, October 2000, p.24. The concept outer-space missiles has been mentioned on page 22.

[52] See Lasater and Yu (note 6).

the C^{4}ISR (command, control, communication, computerization, intelligence, surveillance and reconnaissance) capability.

Looking from the CPLA perspective, it must quickly bring about a rapid capitulation once a war breaks out, hence the term *shouzhan ji juezhan*. A CPLA spokesman in August 2000 said maritime, amphibious and land drills involving submarines, frogmen, gunboats, paratroopers, and attack helicopters are necessary to prevail in future local wars under high-technology conditions.[53] It has been estimated that by 2010, the CPLA will be able to target more than 1,000 missiles, including cruise missiles, against Taiwan.[54] If the CPLA, indeed, wants to initiate an attack of Taiwan, then Chen's strategy is necessary. Yet, we also see that the CPLA does not even have a lot of marines, which can land on Taiwan shores or even Penghu Island. It is said a ratio of 5:1 or at least 3:1 is needed for the CPLA to succeed. According to the August 2000 National Defense Report, published in Taipei, the CPLA currently has 70,000 troops deployed in Fujian Province, and it can rapidly move 250,000 more to that Province from other military regions, such as Jinan. In this connection, mainland China can mobilize up to 400,000 troops for a land battle with Taiwan and its air force can transport two parachute regiments to Taiwan.[55] So, it is quite not possible for the CPLA to launch a successful landing attack against Taiwan in the next few decades.

World Trade Organization (WTO). According to the WTO agreement, each member can decide whether or not to have tariff with another member. Thus, it took the PRC from July 1986 to November 1999 to sign documents with the United States on how to deal with each other. So far, Taipei can choose to delay direct trade and commerce with Beijing. But, without trade and commerce with the mainland, Taiwan may not be able to earn more "foreign exchange reserve" as it could. In any case, after the PRC became a full member of the WTO in December 2001, its will to attack Taiwan decreases, because it has to take the benefit and cost into serious consideration. If the CPLA does not have a solid attack plan, there will be no renewed civil war. As a result, *jingwai juezhan* is just a way for Chen to divert some people's attention.

CONCLUDING REMARKS

On the whole, the jargon *jingwai juezhan* is barely acceptable, because it can be applied to cyber war, which has to involve computers on the mainland. It is a form of deterrence, however controversial. The main reason for controversy is because tension flared up between both sides of the Taiwan Strait since July 1995, especially Lee's pronouncement of the "special state to state relationship" policy in July 1999. But, Taipei's (potential) enemy should fully understand this newest jargon, *jingwai juezhan*. As mentioned earlier, the purpose of deterrence is to avoid war. If a war broke out between both sides of the Taiwan Strait, it simply means that the jargon has failed to do its intended job. The ROC's survival cannot be based on this jargon alone. In other words, there should be other concepts and so on at work, which may strengthen, complement, detract, etc. *jingwai juezhan*. For this reason, we should not be too alarmist when we see *jignwai juezhan*. Besides, it is a working concept,

---

[53] *Ibid.*, August 4, 2000, p.19.

[54] *CT*, July 21, 2000, p.13.

[55] *TJ*, August 25, 2000, p.2.

subject to modification, refinement, and so on as time goes by. In other words, if we were to think about the WTO first, then everything else discussed before that part seems to become secondary. If so, Chen is not serious about *jingwai juezhan*, because the WTO could also benefit Taiwan, which became an official member economy in January 2002.

In any case, because the ROC cannot possibly win a protracted war vis-à-vis the PRC, *jingwai juezhan* is for Chen to figure out who can go to his side in the remaining presidential term.[56] According to a pro-Beijing magazine in Hongkong, there are currently about 30% of native Taiwanese generals in the ROC's armed forces.[57] Some of them eager for promotions may want to move closer to him. If Chen can succeed in controlling the armed forces or win their trust, he can further consolidate his power in the second presidential term.[58]

ABOUT THE AUTHOR

Peter Kien-hong YU received his Ph.D. in Politics from New York University in October 1983. He became a full professor at the National Sun Yat-sen University (Taiwan, R.O.C.) in September 1992. In August 2002, he became Dean of Research and Development at the Wenzao College, Kaohsiung City, Taiwan, Republic of China. Starting August 2003, he is a professor of international affairs at Ming Chuan University in Taipei. He had authored and edited more than ten books, the most recent ones in English are *Bicoastal China: A Dialectical, Paradigmatic Analysis* (1999) and *Taiwan's Security in the Post-Deng Xiaoping Era* (2000) and *The Crab and Frog Motion Paradigm Shift: Decoding and Deciphering Taipei and Beijing's Dialectical Politics* (2002). He has about 80 academic journal papers and book chapters published in the West.

---

[56] *Jingwai juezhan* is related to Taiwan, as a piece of land in which its inhabitants should cherish. See *Liberty Times* (hereinafter LT)(Taipei), November 18, 2000, p.2. The first draft of this paper was completed in summer 2000. In December 2000, it was reported that the Chief of the General Staff, Tang Yaoming, is a supporter of *Jingwai juezhan*. Tang met Chen after the presidential election in March 2000. See *CT*, December 10, 2000, p.2.

[57] *GJJ*, September 2000, p.60.

[58] According to one of his confidants, if Chen were able to beat James C. Soong again in March 2004, the DPP would be able to rule Taiwan for the next 20 years.

In: Economics and Foreign Investment in China
Editor: J.I. Cheng, pp. 79-91

ISBN 1-60021-238-7
© 2007 Nova Science Publishers, Inc.

Chapter 3

HOW DOES FDI AFFECT ECONOMIC GROWTH IN A TRANSITIONAL COUNTRY? THE CASE OF CHINA[*]

Kevin Honglin Zhang[1]

Department of Economics, Illinois State University
Normal, IL 61790-4200 USA

ABSTRACT

How does inward foreign direct investment (FDI) affect a transitional economy? This study attempts to analyze the role of FDI in China's income growth and market-oriented transition. We first identify possible channels through which FDI may have positive or negative effects on the Chinese economy. Using a reasonable growth model and cross-section and panel data in the period of 1984-98, we provide an empirical assessment, which suggests that FDI seems to help China's transition and promote income growth, and that this positive growth-effect seems to rise over time and to be stronger in the coastal than the inland regions.

Keywords: *Foreign direct investment; economic growth; and transition.*

1. INTRODUCTION

Since market reforms began in 1978, China has achieved an impressive success in economic growth with an average rate at 9.5% in 1978-99, the highest in the world in that period. China's economic achievement seems to owe much to the adoption of radical initiatives encouraging inward foreign direct investment (FDI). From an almost isolated economy, China has become the second largest recipient of FDI in the world (next only to the

[*] A different version of the paper was presented at the conference of Developing through Globalization at Shanghai, China in July of 2000. I am grateful of comments from the participants and of Yu Chen's research assistant work. Comments from Yingyi Qian, Shang-Jin Wei, and two referees are helpful in revising the paper. The usual disclaim applies.

U.S.) since 1993, with cumulative FDI inflows as much as $305 billion by the end of 1999 (UNCTAD, 2000). The following indicators may suggest the significance and contributions of FDI to the Chinese economy in 1998: FDI flows constituted 15% of gross fixed capital formation, foreign-invested enterprises produced 15% of total industrial output, and created 44% of China's entire exports (SSB, 1999; UNCTAD, 1999).

While there has been an increasing body of the literature on FDI in China (e.g., Lardy 1995; and Pomfred, 1997), systematic treatments of the role of FDI in Chinese economy seem to have been limited. Especially few studies have been devoted to empirically analyzing the impact of FDI on China's income growth and market-oriented transition.[2] This study attempts to close the gap by providing a quantitatively assessment of effects of FDI on the Chinese economy. We first identify possible channels through which FDI may affect Chinese economy and transition. Then using cross-section and panel data in 1984-98, we estimate a reasonable growth model in which the direct effects (e.g., raising productivity and promoting export) and externality effects (e.g., facilitating transition and diffusing technology) of FDI on the Chinese economy are emphasized.

Two features characterize this study. First, empirical specifications used in this study not only indicate usual effects of FDI on China's economic growth, but also enable one to analyze externality effects of FDI on the Chinese economic reforms. The importance of FDI in the Chinese economy, combined with China's smooth transition and rapid income growth in the last two decades, seems to suggest that in no other transitional economy has FDI played such a dynamic and significant role (Lardy, 1995; Promfred, 1997).

Second, estimations are conducted with both cross-section and panel data at the provincial level for more informative and reliable results. Breaking down the entire period (1984-98) into three sub-periods allows us to investigate structural changes over time in the impact of FDI and other growth factors on the Chinese economy. The panel approach allows one to capture province-specific differences that are not reflected in cross-section estimates.

The main results may be summarized as follows. The overall impact of FDI on income growth and the externality effect on the transition are significantly positive, and they seem to increase over time. Regional differences, specially due to biased FDI policies, favor the coastal region. The marginal product of foreign capital seems to be significantly larger than that of domestic capital.

2. THE ROLE OF FDI IN CHINA'S ECONOMIC GROWTH AND TRANSITION

The impact of FDI on the Chinese economy may be analyzed in the framework of both neoclassic theories and dependency theories. We first look at contributions of FDI to Chinese economy in two aspects: the usual effects on income growth and a special role in the market-

---

[1] Phone: (309) 438-8928,Fax: (309) 438-5228,Email: khzhang@ilstu.edu.

[2] There are a few exceptions. Using city-level data in 1980-90, Wei (1995) finds positive effects of FDI on the Chinese economy through technology spillovers. A recent study by Zhang (1999) tests the long-run link and short-run dynamics between FDI and Chinese economic growth. Branstetter and Feenstra (1999) provide an empirical analysis with political economy approach toward effects of FDI and trade on the Chinese economy.

oriented transition. Then we discuss potential negative effects of FDI from perspectives of the dependency theories.

2.1. The Impact on Economic Growth

Standard propositions of the neoclassical theories suggest that FDI is likely to be an engine of host economic growth, because (a) inward FDI may enhance capital formation and employment augmentation; (b) FDI may promote manufacturing exports; (c) By its very nature, FDI may bring into host economies special resources such as management know-how, skilled labor access to international production networks, and established brand names; and (d) FDI may result in technology transfers and spillover effects (Markusen and Venables, 1999; UNCTAD, 1992).

In the case of China, the most prominent contribution of FDI has been expanding China's manufacturing exports.[3] Increases in foreign-invested enterprises (FIEs) not only augment China's export volumes, but also upgrade its export structure.[4] While China's exports were ranked as the 26th in the world in 1980, with the volume of $18 billion and 47% of the exports as manufactured goods, the corresponding numbers in 1998 were the 9th in ranking, $184 billion, and 89%. As indicated in Table 1, exports by FIEs in China rose 66.7% annually in 1980-98, and the value of their exports in 1998 (almost all of them as manufacturing goods) were $88.6 billion, comprising 44% of China's total exports in that year (SSB, 1999).

Table 1. Importance of FDI and Foreign-Invested Enterprises (FIEs) in China

	1991	1995	1998
FDI flows as a ratio of gross domestic investment (%)	3.9	15.1	15.2
Exports by FIEs (billions of US dollars)	12.1	46.9	88.6
Share of exports by foreign-invested enterprises in total exports (%)	17.0	31.3	44.1
Share of industrial output by FIEs in total industrial output (%)	5.0	11.7	14.9
Number of employees in FIEs (million persons)	4.8	16.0	18.0
Tax contributions from FIEs as share of total tax revenue (%)	4.1	10.0	13.2

Notes: The numbers of the tax contributions by FIEs in 1991 and 1998 are actually for 1992 and 1997, respectively, due to unavailable data for the two years.

Sources: Computed from *China Statistics Yearbook* by SSB (1997, 1998, and 1999), and *World Investment Report* (1998 and 1999) by UNCTAD.

---

[3] The view of exports as an engine of growth has been recognized for long time in both academic and policy circles (for example, Feder, 1982).

[4] Naughton (1996) argued that China's dualistic trading regime has led to a "crowding out" of domestic firms exports by FIEs due to more favorable policies for the latter. This may be true in some particular industries to a certain extent, but overall effects of FDI on exports seem to have been positive because of China's export-oriented FDI strategy and the relocation of labor-intensive production from Taiwan and Hong Kong to China. In 1999, exports by FIEs (most of them are joint ventures) were US$88.6 billion, comprising 45.5% of China's total exports (Zhang and Song, 2000; Lardy 1995).

FDI seems also to have enhanced China's economic growth through raising capital formation, increasing industrial output, generating employment, and adding tax revenue. The ratio of FDI flows to gross domestic investment increased from a negligible level in the 1980s to 4% in 1991, and then to 15% in 1998 (SSB, 1999). Table 1 shows that the share of industrial output by FIEs in total industrial output grew from 5% in 1991 to 18.6% in 1997. FDI also has reduced China's unemployment pressure and contributed to government tax revenues. By the end of 1998, FIEs employed 18 million Chinese, comprising 11% of total manufactured employment. Tax contributions from FIEs rose with FDI flows, and its share in China's total tax revenues increased from 4% in 1992 to 13% in 1997 (SSB, 1998).

2.2. The Impact on Transition

The neoclassical theories argue that markets are usually a better way to organize economic activities than centrally planned economies (Mankiw, 2001). FDI seems to have spillover effects on China's economic transition toward market-oriented systems in the following aspects (Zhang, 1993).

a) *Diversifying the Ownership Structure*. China's reforms in the ownership structure involved changes from one with predominantly state ownership towards a more desirable mix of state-owned, collective and private ownership. As indicated in Table 2, increasing FIEs have played a significant role in transiting of China's ownership structure. In 1992 state-owned enterprises (SOEs) accounted for 48% of the total domestic output, collective enterprises for 38%, and private enterprises (including foreign-invested enterprises), rising from negligible shares in earlier years, for 13%. The proportion of gross industrial output produced by SOEs declined from 78% in 1978 to 34% in 1994 and to 28% in 1998 (SSB, 1999).[5]

b) *Establishing Market-Oriented Institutions*. FDI in China seems to have stimulated the transition through introducing a market-oriented institutional framework. To effectively attract and utilize foreign capital, China liberalized its FDI regime in the 1980s by establishing special economic zones and coastal open cities. This liberalization exerted constant pressure in the direction of introducing market mechanisms in other sectors. For example, the legal framework specifically pertaining to FDI has prompted numerous laws and regulations governing domestic economic activities as well. This is especially true in relaxing foreign exchange restrictions, establishing a regulatory framework for the protection of intellectual property rights, and reforming accounting systems (Pomfret, 1997).

c) *Facilitating Reforms of State-Owned Enterprises (SOEs)*. FDI in China might have played a unique role in rejuvenating and reforming SOEs either directly through joint ventures with SOEs or indirectly through demonstration effects from the operations of FIEs. Foreign investors are expected to introduce market-oriented management systems, such as incentive schemes, production organization systems, accounting methods and risk

---

[5] Among China's top 500 manufacturers of China in 1993, near 14% of them (69) were foreign-invested enterprises. Although the number for 1998 is not available, it is likely to be larger than that in 1993 because FIEs' share in gross industrial output rose from 8% in 1993 to 15% (SSB, 1999).

management, which are in line with those practiced in market-based economies. Since many of FIEs in China are joint ventures with SOEs, their potential impact on SOE reforms should be considerable.

Table 2. Importance of Foreign-Invested Enterprises (FIEs) in China's Ownership Structure, 1998

	SOEs	Collective	Private	FIEs	Others
Total Investment in Fixed Assets (%)	54.1	14.8	13.2	10.5	7.4
Gross Industrial Output Value (%)*	28.2	38.4	17.1	14.9	0.8
Gross Output Value of Construction (%)*	36.3	58.3	0.4	1.1	4.9
Urban Employment (%)	43.8	9.5	15.6	2.8	28.3
Average Annual Money Wage (Yuan of RMB)	7668	5331	8972	10897	6133
Domestic Trade (%)*	48.5	21.0	23.0	0.9	6.6

Notes: * the numbers are for 1997.
Sources: *China Statistical Yearbook* (1997, 1998, and 1999) by SSB.

In addition, FDI seems to be conducive to the transition by stimulating competition and fostering China's integration into the world economy. The entry and rise of foreign-invested enterprises are expected to break China's state monopolies and oligopolistic structure. With forward and backward linkages between domestic firms and foreign-invested enterprises, China's integration with the world economy has been deepened. Foreign-invested enterprises also helped promote exports through their established world marketing networks (Zhang and Song, 2000).

2.3. Negative Effects of FDI

The Marxist and dependency stances may treat FDI made by multinational corporations (MNCs) as one mechanism for exploitation of and gaining controls over developing countries by western industrialized countries.[6] Economic arguments of this view suggest that FDI may be detrimental to Chinese economy, because (a) rather than closing the gap between domestic savings and investment, FDI might actually lower domestic savings and investment; (b) in the long run FDI may be to reduce China's foreign-exchange earnings on both current and capital accounts; (c) contributions of foreign-invested enterprises' public revenue may be considerately less than it should be as a result of transfer pricing and variety of investment allowance provided by the Chinese government; (d) the management know-how and technology provided by MNCs may in fact inhibit developing local sources of these scarce skills and resources due to the foreign dominance in Chinese markets.

The true significant criticism of FDI may be conducted on more fundamental levels of the long-term national welfare. This includes, for example, (a) MNCs may suppress domestic firms and use their advantages in technology to drive out local competitors; (b) MNC activities may reinforce China's dualistic economic structure and exacerbate income

---

[6] For more discussions, see Biersteker (1978) and surveys by Helleiner (1989) and Caves (1996).

inequalities due to their uneven impact on development (Zhang and Zhang, 2000); (c) MNCs may influence government policies in directions unfavorable to China's development by gaining excessive protection, tax rebates, investment allowances, and the cheap factory sites and social services; and (d) powerful MNCs may gain controls over Chinese assets and jobs such that they could exert considerable influences on political as well as economic decisions at all levels in China.

3. MODEL SPECIFICATIONS

Although further theoretical and qualitative insights about the impact of FDI on the Chinese economy would be valuable, empirical analyses are needed as well for a better understanding of the relationship between FDI and the Chinese economic growth. Adapting the methodology used in Feder (1982) and Levin and Raut (1997), we may estimate the impact of FDI by specifying an aggregate production function as follows:

$$(1) \qquad Y = AL^{\beta_1}K^{\beta_2}, \qquad A = B\left[1 + \theta\left(\frac{F}{Y}\right)\right]F^{\alpha}$$

where Y = GDP, L = labor input, K = stock of domestic capital, F = stock of FDI, and A = total factor productivity level. This specification permits total factor productivity (A) to be endogenously determined by the stock of FDI and the share of FDI stock in GDP, as well as exogenous influences represented by the residual productivity factor (β). Following the standard procedure in the literature, we take the natural logarithm, then the first difference of this production function, and finally slightly manipulating items in the right-hand side. With the addition of a constant term (β_0) and an error term (ε), we obtain the following expression describing the determinants of the growth rate of GDP:

$$(2) \qquad \dot{Y} = \beta_0 + \beta_1\dot{L} + \beta_2\left(\frac{I}{Y}\right) + \beta_3\left(\frac{I_F}{Y}\right) + \beta_4\Delta\left(\frac{F}{Y}\right) + \varepsilon$$

where a dot over a variable indicates its rate of growth, and I and I_F are domestic investment and FDI flows, respectively. β_1 represents output elasticity of labor, β_2 and β_3 are marginal products of domestic capital and FDI, respectively. Thus influences of externalities of FDI on the transition and technology diffusions are captured by the coefficient of I_F/Y (β_0). The coefficient (β_4) of changes in the ratio of FDI stock to GDP ($\Delta F/Y$) reflects the superior productivity of foreign-invested enterprises.[7]

Two more variables have been suggested in recent growth models as determinants of growth: initial development levels (y_0 as per capita GDP) and human capital (H) (Barro and Sala-i-Martin, 1995). In particular, the models predict a negative link between initial per

---

[7] The major postulates of Feder (1982) are made: (a) the economy consists of two sectors, FDI sector and the rest of the domestic economy; (b) the output of the FDI sector generates an externality effects; (c) labor and capital serve as the conventional inputs in both sectors; and (d) production functions and relative marginal products of the inputs differ across the two sectors.

capita GDP and long-run growth rate of GDP, and the positive impact of human capital on income growth. Then the regression model is expanded as follows.

$$(3) \qquad \dot{Y} = \beta_0 + \beta_1 \dot{L} + \beta_2 \left(\frac{I}{Y} \right) + \beta_3 \left(\frac{I_F}{Y} \right) + \beta_4 \Delta \left(\frac{F}{Y} \right) + \beta_5 y_0 + \beta_6 H + \varepsilon$$

Studies of FDI and growth also postulate a positive link between FDI and human capital, since the application of the advanced technology embodied in FDI requires a sufficient level of human capital in host economies (e.g., Borensztein, et al., 1998). We incorporate such complementarities between FDI and human capital by assuming A in the aggregate production function (1) is of the following form:

$$A = B \left[1 + \theta_0 \left(\frac{F}{Y} \right) + \theta_1 H \left(\frac{F}{Y} \right) \right] F^{\alpha}$$

By applying the same procedure in equation (1) to this function, we have equation (3) to be

$$(4) \qquad \dot{Y} = \beta_0 + \beta_1 \dot{L} + \beta_2 \left(\frac{I}{Y} \right) + \beta_3 \left(\frac{I_F}{Y} \right) + \beta_4 \Delta \left(\frac{F}{Y} \right) + \beta_5 y_0 + \beta_6 H + \beta_7 H \Delta \left(\frac{F}{Y} \right) + \varepsilon$$

4. THE DATA AND THE MAIN RESULTS

Equation (4) constitutes the basis for our cross-section and panel analyses of growth effects of FDI at provincial levels in 1984-98. The empirical specifications may be modified slightly based on patterns of FDI and economic growth in China. First, there are significant regional variations in economic performance and distribution of FDI within China, as indicated in Table 3. The coastal region enjoys higher growth rate than the inland region by 1.4-3.9% during 1984-98. At the same time, most of FDI (87-89% of total) went to the coastal region.[8] To capture the regional differences in the economic performance and the FDI distribution, we include a regional dummy (D) in estimates to control policy-induced biases of economic growth.

Second, as shown also in Table 3, growth rates of GDP and FDI flows changed substantially over the fifteen years (1984-98). National GDP grew at the rate of near 12% in the first five years, then slowed down at 8%, and went up again at 9.5% in the last five years. FDI flows are characterized as a boom in the 1990s in contrast with relative small amount in the 1980s.[9] To bring out any possible structural variations over time, separate cross-section estimations are to be conducted for three sub-periods: 1984-88, 89-93, and 92-97.

---

[8] Researchers have identified various factors to explain the skewed geographic pattern of FDI within China. Among them are government's biased open-door policy toward the coastal region, higher development levels in the coastal region, and historical and cultural links between provinces and FDI sources (e.g., Guangdong-Hong Kong and Fujian-Taiwan). See Zhang (2001).

[9] The factors that caused the FDI boom in the 1990s included further liberalization of China's FDI regime and the explosive growth of domestic economy, along with the worldwide rise in FDI outflows in the first half of the

Table 3. FDI Flows and GDP Growth Rates in China by Provinces, 1984-98

Provinces	Growth Rates of GDP (%)			Shares of FDI in Total (%)		
	1984-88	1989-93	1994-98	1984-88	1989-93	1994-98
Coastal Areas	*12.28*	*11.90*	*12.23*	*90.17*	*89.32*	*87.28*
Beijing	11.5	8.6	10.9	8.86	3.77	3.97
Tianjin	9.8	7.4	13.0	2.63	2.09	4.53
Shanghai	9.4	8.7	12.8	11.32	8.83	8.88
Hebei	11.4	11.2	13.1	0.54	1.38	2.27
Liaoning	12.8	7.5	8.8	3.07	4.74	4.43
Shandong	12.3	12.5	12.9	1.31	6.65	6.20
Jiangsu	15.3	12.3	13.4	2.71	9.89	12.75
Zhejiang	15.7	12.4	14.1	1.34	3.08	3.28
Fujian	13.8	15.1	15.6	6.06	11.26	9.84
Guangdong	15.9	16.0	13.1	47.59	31.44	27.21
Hainan	11.8	18.5	7.2	2.76	3.82	2.01
Guangxi	7.6	12.6	11.9	1.98	2.37	1.91
Inland Areas	*10.67*	*7.99*	*10.78*	*9.83*	*10.68*	*12.72*
Jinlin	12.3	6.4	11.2	0.10	0.69	0.96
Heilongjiang	7.6	6.7	9.4	1.05	0.80	1.27
Inner Mongolia	11.6	7.9	10.2	0.16	0.07	0.16
Shanxi	9.6	8.1	10.2	0.11	0.29	0.36
Anhui	11.4	9.0	14.1	0.27	0.67	1.01
Jianxi	11.3	9.6	12.9	0.30	0.68	0.87
Henan	10.6	9.1	12.3	1.20	1.10	1.33
Hubei	11.8	8.9	13.3	0.52	1.70	1.81
Hunan	9.4	8.2	10.8	0.60	1.22	1.60
Sichuan	11.2	8.5	10.0	1.01	1.65	1.64
Guizhou	10.5	7.2	8.5	0.11	0.17	0.12
Yunnan	12.0	8.5	10.1	0.19	0.27	0.39
Tibet	6.4	6.6	13.7	0.00	0.00	0.00
Shaanxi	10.8	7.3	9.4	3.49	0.92	0.88
Gansu	12.1	8.5	9.9	0.20	0.22	0.13
Qinghai	9.2	5.3	8.6	0.00	0.01	0.01
Ningxia	11.9	7.0	10.3	0.00	0.04	0.05
Xinjiang	12.3	11.1	9.2	0.54	0.15	0.11
Nation	*11.96*	*8.10*	*9.54*	*100.00*	*100.00*	*100.00*
Total FDI Flows (billions of US$)				*6.76*	*49.26*	*205.73*

Notes: According to Chinese government, the coastal region includes 3 municipalities (Beijing, Tianjin, and Shanghai) and 9 provinces as in the table. The rest is the inland region (SSB, 1998).

Sources: Data for 1984-1995 are taken from *China Regional Economy* (1996) by SSB and data for 1996 through 1998 are from *China Statistical Yearbook* (1997, 1998, and 1999) by SSB.

Third, panel analyses are to be employed to control for province-specific effects, since the fixed-effects estimation enables us to focus on relationships within provinces over time. To avoid potential problems of time-series data with non-stationarity, cointegration, and

---

1990s and China's political stability (Lardy, 1995). Another relevant factor is so-called "round-trip FDI" between Hong Kong and China. While Hong Kong was returned to China as a special administration area from Britain in 1997, its direct investment in China has been still treated as FDI. It was observed that part of Hong Kong's FDI turned out to be the investment carried by subsidiaries based in Hong Kong but owned by Chinese central or local governments to take advantage of preferential treatment under the name of FDI. While no accurate figures for this type of FDI are available, they were estimated to be not large relative to total HKDI (UNCTAD, 1996).

autocorrelation, we use average values of all variables for three sub-periods, rather than 15 years of time series (Macnair, et al., 1995).

The data were collected for 28 regional units for the period 1984-98, since the information on FDI is not available for many provinces for years before 1984. In addition to 21 provinces, the sample includes three municipalities (Beijing, Tianjin, and Shanghai) and four autonomous regions (Inner Mongolia, Guangxi, Ningxi, and Xinjiang) that have provincial status. The province of Qinghai, the autonomous region of Tibet, and the newly established municipal city of Chongqing are dropped from the sample due to unavailability of the data.

All data on variables used in the estimations are taken from or calculated based on *China Statistical Yearbook* (1997, 1998, and 1999) and *China Regional Economy* (1996) by State Statistical Bureau (SSB) of China. The growth rate of real GDP for each province is taken as a proxy for $\dot{Y}$. The growth rate of population is used in place of $\dot{L}$, and human capital (H) is measured by shares of secondary school enrollments in total population.[10] The domestic investment-output ratio (I/Y) is computed as nominal gross fixed capital formation divided by the nominal GDP. The FDI-output ratio (I_F/Y) is computed as the ratio of nominal realized FDI flows (in U.S. dollars) to nominal GDP that is converted into U.S. dollars. Data on changes in the ratio of FDI stock to GDP ($\Delta(F/Y)$) are calculated in a two-step procedure. First, data on nominal realized FDI stock in each province are obtained by accumulating over years, with adjustments based on data on nominal national FDI stock, which are from *World Investment Report* (UNCTAD, various years from 1992 through 1999). Second, we compute the ratio of nominal FDI stock to nominal GDP and then take differences of the ratio. Per capita real GDP levels in 1984, 1989, and 1994 are used as the initial levels of economic development (y_0) for the three sub-periods. The regional dummy (D) takes value of one if the province is located in the coastal region and zero for others. For cross-section estimations, growth rates over the relevant periods are obtained by fitting exponential trend equations, and the ratios are computed by taking mean values of the basic variables over the relevant periods.

We estimate two variants of equation (4) for the purpose of comparisons: one without FDI variables and the other with FDI variables. The main regression results of the two specifications with the cross-section and panel data are presented in Table 4 and Table 5,[11] from which the following points are easily discerned. First, in all relevant cases, the comparison of results from the two models highlights the superior explanatory power of the model with FDI variables over the model without FDI variables. In particular, the adjusted R^2 increases by 23-25% (from 0.58-0.61 to 0.73-0.78) in the cross-section and panel estimations when the specifications including FDI as independent variables are used. The finding suggest that FDI seems to be one of factors that affected the Chinese economy

---

[10] There is a concern about growth rate of population as measurement of $\dot{L}$ due to inter-province floating population. Unfortunately, no accurate figures on such persons are available. Similarly, data on schooling years of labor forces at provincial levels are incomplete, although they are better proxy of human capital (H) than student enrolment shares in population.

[11] The estimates reported here might be troublesome due to the feedback from the dependent variable. A full-scale treatment of the issue requires causality tests with reasonable long time-series data, which is impossible for the present work due to limited years covered. Instead, we can test, based on the approach suggested by White (1980), at a simple level whether there are specification errors of the kinds mentioned. The result of White test indicates that the values of the test statistic are too small to justify non-acceptance of the null hypothesis of correct model specifications, suggesting absence of the feedback.

Second, the variable of $\Delta(F/Y)$, which indicates the superior productivity of foreign-invested enterprises, has significantly positive coefficients in all relevant estimates. The overall picture of cross-section estimates in Table 4 is similar to that of panel estimates in Table 5. The results are consistent with the widespread belief that more productive foreign capital seems to enhance China's economic growth (Lardy, 1995; and Pomfret, 1997).

Table 4. Results of Cross-Section Estimations: 1984-88, 1989-93, and 1994-98

Independent Variables	1984-88		1989-93			1994-1998
	Without FDI	With FDI	Without FDI	With FDI	Without FDI	With FDI
$\dot{L}$	0.73*	0.77**	0.71**	0.69*	0.68	0.63
	(1.88)	(2.33)	(2.26)	(1.84)	(1.49)	(1.67)
I/Y	0.12**	0.13**	0.14*	0.12*	0.12*	0.13*
	(2.87)	(2.28)	(1.77)	(1.88)	(1.72)	(1.91)
y_0	-0.16*	-0.14*	-0.12	-0.11	-0.09	-0.08
	(-1.79)	(-1.85)	(-1.50)	(-1.58)	(-1.25)	(-1.47)
H	0.01	0.008	0.009	0.01	0.01	0.01*
	(1.20)	(1.17)	(1.35)	(1.35)	(1.60)	(1.79)
D	0.16*	0.18**	0.17**	0.21***	0.20**	0.27***
	(1.80)	(2.22)	(2.34)	(3.35)	(2.51)	(3.97)
I_F/Y		0.21		0.25**		0.28**
		(1.63)		(2.66)		(2.46)
$\Delta(F/Y)$		0.16**		0.20***		0.23***
		(2.24)		(4.25)		(4.05)
$H \cdot \Delta(F/Y)$		0.06		0.07*		0.08**
		(1.14)		(1.87)		(2.48)
Adjusted R^2	0.59	0.73	0.60	0.74	0.58	0.73
F-Statistic	12.89	9.46	11.56	16.13	12.45	15.78

Notes: The number of observation is 28 for all estimations. The coefficient estimates of constant terms are omitted to save the space. The dependent variable is average rate of growth of real GDP (%). The asterisks ***, **, and * indicate levels of significance at 1%, 5%, and 10%, respectively.

Third, externality effects of FDI (measured by coefficients of (I_F/Y)) are significantly positive in all relevant cases except the sub-period of 1984-88. This findings thus lend a support to the observation that the presence of multinational corporations themselves may not only result in technological diffusion and transfers, but also facilitate China's transition toward a market economy. Moreover, significantly positive coefficients of the interaction variable ($H\Delta(F/Y)$) in most relevant cases suggest that there might exist complementary effects between FDI and human capital.

Fourth, effects of three FDI variables on the Chinese economy are clearly larger in the 1990s than in the 1980s, as suggested in Table 4. The coefficient of $\Delta(F/Y)$ rises from 0.16 to 0.23 in the three sub-periods, representing an increase of 44%. The coefficient of I_F/Y goes up as well over time from 0.21 to 0.28 (rising by 33%). The same story may be found for the interaction variable ($H\Delta(F/Y)$). The result is anticipated from the consideration that the substantially greater amount of FDI flows during the 1990s than in the 1980s might have led to a growing role of FDI in the Chinese economy.

Table 5. Results of Panel Estimations: 1984-98

Independent Variables	Model without FDI		Model with FDI	
	Coefficients	t-Statistics	Coefficients	t-Statistics
L	1.06*	1.95	0.98	1.57
I/Y	0.13**	2.30	0.12**	2.89
y_0	-0.14*	-1.93	-0.12*	-1.81
H	0.004	0.74	0.005	0.97
D	0.24**	2.66	0.26***	5.07
I_F/Y			0.31**	2.90
$\Delta(F/Y)$			0.22**	2.53
$H \cdot \Delta(F/Y)$			0.07*	2.07
Adjusted R^2	0.61		0.78	
F-Statistic	31.38		35.60	

Notes: The number of observation is 84 (28 provinces and 3 periods). The coefficient estimates of constant terms are omitted to save the space. The dependent variable is average rate of growth of real GDP (%). The asterisks ***, **, and * indicate levels of significance at 1%, 5%, and 10%, respectively.

Fifth, the result of the regional dummy (D) in both the cross-section and panel estimations shows that favorable FDI policies and natural resource conditions are beneficial to economic growth in the coastal region. Rising values of the coefficient of D and its significance over time suggest that growth effects of FDI induced by policies and regional differences seem to be larger in the coastal region in the 1990s. This point is consistent with findings of recent studies that FDI contributed China's widening regional income-gap (Zhang and Zhang, 2000).

Finally, the coefficients of Δ (F/Y) are numerically larger than those of domestic investment (I/Y) in the panel estimates as well as the cross-section estimates, with a greater differential in 1994-98. This result thus supports predictions of FDI theories that marginal product of FDI should be greater than that of domestic capital, because a multinational firm must possess some special advantages such as superior technology to overcome inherent disadvantages and high costs of foreign production (Caves, 1996; Zhang and Markusen, 1999).

In summary, overall effects of FDI on the Chinese economy seem to be positive and not negligible. This finding confirms the Chinese government's perception about the role of FDI in the Chinese economy. According to the Chinese official estimations (SCI, July 31, 2001), out of 9.7% of the average growth rate of real GDP in 1980-99, 2.7% came from direct and indirect contributions of foreign-invested enterprises, which constitutes more than a quarter (27.84%) of total growth rate in that period.

Tow points are worth notice. First, other factors that affect China's economic growth may exist but were excluded from this investigation. This work, therefore, should not be treated as an exhaustive study of economic growth in China but, rather, as a narrowly focused investigation of the merits of FDI. Second, perhaps the case of China is somewhat unique in the sense of its advantages in large country-size, strong government, massive FDI from overseas Chinese, and effective FDI strategy, all of which seems to be lacking in many other developing countries and transitional economies. These advantages provided China with a great bargaining power over multinational corporations such that China could be able to maximize gains from FDI and to minimize negative effects of foreign-invested enterprises (Zhang, 2000).

5. CONCLUDING REMARKS

The main purpose of this study is to test empirically the widespread belief about the beneficial growth-effects of increased foreign direct investment in China. An effort has been made to base the present work on reasonable empirical and theoretical foundations. Besides the discussions of potential positive and negative effects of FDI on the Chinese economy, a reasonable growth model is specified, and cross-section and panel data for a recent period have been used. Subject to the caveats that are appropriate for studies with aggregate data, the most notable aspect of the regression estimates is a favorable effect of FDI on growth rate of real Chinese GDP. FDI seems to contribute to China's economic growth through direct effects (such as raising productivity and promoting export) and positive externality effects (such as facilitating transition and diffusing technology). The effects of foreign-invested enterprises in the Chinese economy seem to increase with FDI inflows from the 1980s to the 1990s, and to be larger in the coastal region than that in the inland region. Finally, the marginal product of foreign capital seems to be larger than that of domestic capital.

REFERENCES

Barro, Robert and Xavier Sala-i-Martin (1995), *Economic Growth*, Cambridge, MA: MIT Press.

Biersteker, Thomas (1978), *Distortion or Development: Contending Perspectives on the Multinational Corporation*, Cambridge, MA: MIT Press.

Borenszten, E., J. De Gregorio, and J-W. Lee (1998), How Does Foreign Investment Affect Economic Growth?" *Journal of International Economics*, 45: 115-135.

Branstetter, Lee, G. and Robert Feenstra (1999), "Trade and foreign direct investment in China: A political economy approach," NBER Working Paper # 7100.

Caves, Richard (1996), *Multinational Enterprises and Economic Analysis*, the 2nd edition,

Cambridge, MA: Cambridge University Press.

Feder, Gershon (1982), "On Exports and Economic Growth," *Journal of Development Economics*, 12: 59-73.

Helleiner, G. (1989), "Transnational corporations and direct foreign investment," in H. Chenery and T. N. Srinivasan, ed, *Handbook of Development Economics*, Elsevier Science Publishers B.V., 1441-1480.

Lardy, Nicholas R. (1995) "The role of foreign trade and investment in China's economic transformation," *The China Quarterly*, 144: 1065-1082.

Levin, Andrew, and Lakshmi Raul (1997), "Complementarities between exports and human capital in economic growth: evidence from the semi-industrialized countries," *Economic Development and Cultural Changes*, 46 (1): 155-174.

Macnair, E, J. Murdoch, C. Pi, and T. Sandler (1995), "Growth and defense: pooled estimates for the NATO alliance, 1951-1988," Southern Economic Journal, 61 (3):846-860.

Mankiw, N. Gregory (2001), Principles of Economics, Fort Worth, TX: Dryden Press

Markusen, James and Anthony Venables (1999), "Foreign direct investment as a catalyst for industrial development", European Economic Review, 43 (2): 335-356.

Naughton, Barry (1996), "China's emergence and prospects as a trading nation," Brookings Papers on Economic Activity, 2: 273-343.

Pomfret, Richard (1997), "Growth and transition: Why has China's performance been so different?" Journal of Comparative Economics, 25: 422-440.

State Center for Information (SCI) (2001), Economic Reports, The World Journal, July 31, 2001.

State Statistical Bureau (SSB) (1996), China Regional Economy: A Profile of 17 Years of Reform and Opening-Up, China Statistics Press, Beijing, China.

State Statistical Bureau (SSB) (1997, 1998, and 1999), China Statistical Yearbook 1997, 1998, and 1999, China Statistics Press, Beijing, China.

United Nations Conference on Trade and Development (UNCTAD) (1992 through 1999), World Investment Report (various years, 1992 through 1999), New York: United Nations.

Wei, Shang-Jin (1995), "The open door policy and China's rapid growth: Evidence from city level data," in T. Ito and A. O. Krueger eds. Growth Theories in Light of the East Asian Experience, The University of Chicago Press.

White, Halbert (1980), "A heteroscedasticity-consistent covariance matrix estimator and a direct test for heteroscedasticity," Econometrica, 48: 817-838.

Zhang, Kevin H. (1999), "How does FDI interact with economic growth in a large developing country? The case of China," Economic Systems, 23 (4): 291-303.

Zhang, Kevin H. (2000), "Why does China succeed in attracting and utilizing FDI?" mimeo.

Zhang, Kevin H. (2001), "What attracts foreign multinational corporations to China?" Contemporary Economic Policy, 19 (3): 336-346.

Zhang, Kevin H. and James Markusen (1999), "Vertical multinationals and host-country characteristics", Journal of Development Economics, 59: 233-252.

Zhang, Kevin H. and Shunfeng Song (2000), "Promoting exports: The role of inward FDI in China," China Economic Review, 11 (4): 385-496.

Zhang, Xiaobo and Kevin H. Zhang (2000), "How does globalization affect regional inequality within a developing country? Evidence from China," a paper presented at International conference of Developing through Globalization in 2000.

Zhang, X. James (1993), "The role of foreign direct investment in market-oriented reforms and economic development: the case of China," Transnational Corporations, 2 (3): 121-148.

In: Economics and Foreign Investment in China
Editor: J.I. Cheng, pp. 93-108

ISBN 1-60021-238-7
© 2007 Nova Science Publishers, Inc.

Chapter 4

OVERVIEW OF THE CHINESE ECONOMY*

Jim Saxton

ABSTRACT

Since economic reform began in 1978, the People's Republic of China (PRC) has sought the benefits of capitalism without surrendering government control of the commanding heights of the PRC's economy. The PRC has largely adhered to openness to international trade and investment, one of the characteristics of successful market economies. Not surprisingly, the PRC's greatest strength is its integration with the global economy.

Although the PRC has made some progress toward achieving other characteristics of successful market economies, the PRC retains many of the detrimental characteristics of command economies. In particular, the PRC's four major state-owned banks and other depository institutions have extended too many questionable loans to the state-owned enterprises and the state-influenced enterprises based on industrial policy, *guanxi* (i.e., connections) with government officials, or outright corruption. Along with below-market interest rates and distorted prices, non-market lending has sustained the PRC's unusually high rate of investment in capital assets (i.e., equipment, software, and structures) of 43.6 percent of GDP in 2004. In turn, this high investment rate has boosted the PRC's real GDP growth rate to 9.5 percent in 2004.

However, many state-owned enterprises and state-influenced enterprises are unprofitable. Protected through *guanxi* from bankruptcy and foreclosure, many state-owned enterprises and state-influenced enterprises are either unable or unwilling to service their debts. Consequently, non-market lending has saddled the PRC's four major state-owned banks and other depository institutions with enormous portfoliosof non-performing loans. Private economists estimate that the cost of resolving the PRC's bad loan problem would be about 40 percent of the PRC's GDP.

Non-market lending encouraged the state-owned enterprises and the state-influenced enterprises to invest in too many capital assets and the wrong types of capital assets to produce goods and services to satisfy market demand. The eventual liquidation of the resulting overinvestment or malinvestment poses a significant long-term risk to the continuation of the PRC's economic growth. Given the PRC's integration with the global

---

* Excerpted from A Joint Economic Committee Report dated July 2005.

economy, a significant slowdown or recession in the PRC could diminish the prospects for economic growth in the United States and other countries around the world.

I. INTRODUCTION

In 1978, the People's Republic of China (PRC) embarked upon incremental reforms that transformed its command economy into a mixed economy.[1] Essentially, Chinese leaders have sought the benefits of capitalism without relinquishing government control of what Soviet leader Vladimir Illyich Lenin, British Prime Minister Clement Attlee, and Indian Prime Minister Jawaharlal Nehru separately described as the "commanding heights" of the economy.[2] However, this strategy embraces contradictions that pose considerable risks not only for the Chinese economy, but also for the global economy. This study analyzes both the strengths and the weaknesses of the PRC's economy in light of the following characteristics exhibited by successful market economies:

- Freedom of individuals to seek employment with firms or to establish firms;
- Private ownership and control of resources;
- Freedom of firms to compete with other firms and enter new geographic or product markets;
- Resource allocation and product distribution through market-determined prices;
- Secure property rights, uncorrupt formulation and administration of laws, and impartial courts to adjudicate disputes;
- Efficient bankruptcy system to redeploy underemployed individuals and misallocated resources to more valuable uses; and
- Openness to international trade and investment.

The PRC has largely adhered to openness to international trade and investment, one of the characteristics of successful market economies. Not surprisingly, the PRC's greatest strength is its integration with the global economy. Although the PRC has made some progress toward achieving each of the other characteristics of successful market economies, the PRC retains many of the detrimental characteristics of command economies. In particular, the four major state-owned commercial banks (SOCBs) and other depository institutions have made too many questionable loans to the state-owned enterprises (SOEs) and the state-influenced enterprises (SIEs)[3] based on central government industrial policy, *guanxi* (i.e., connections) with central, provincial, and local government officials, or outright corruption by bank executives and managers. Along with below-market interest rates and distorted prices, non-market lending has sustained the PRC's unusually high rate of investment in capital assets (i.e., equipment, software, and structures) of 43.6 percent of GDP in 2004.[4] In turn, this high investment rate has boosted the PRC's real GDP growth rate to 9.5 percent in 2004.[5] However, many SOEs and SIEs are unprofitable. Protected through their *guanxi* from bankruptcy or foreclosure, many SOEs and SIEs cannot or will not service their debts to the four major SOCBs and other depository institutions. Consequently, non-market lending has saddled the four major SOCBs and other depository institutions with enormous portfolios of non-performing loans (NPLs). Private economists estimate that the cost of resolving the PRC's bad loan problem would be about 40 percent of the PRC's GDP.[6] Moreover, non-market lending has encouraged the SOEs and the SIEs to invest in too many capital assets and the wrong types of capital assets to produce goods and services to satisfy market demand. The eventual liquidation of the resulting overinvestment or malinvestment poses a significant long-term risk to the continuation of the PRC's economic growth. Given the PRC's integration with the global economy, a significant slowdown or recession in the PRC could diminish the prospects for economic growth in the United States and other countries around the world.

II. STRENGTHS

Since economic reform began in 1978, the PRC has largely integrated into the global economy. From 1979[7] to 2004, the value of PRC's goods exports grew by an average of 17.9 percent a year.[8] Consequently, the PRC's share of world goods exports (excluding intra-European Union exports) increased from 1.2 percent in 1979 to 9.3 percent in 2004.[9] While the growth in the PRC's goods exports may seem impressive, it is actually quite typical for Asian economies during early stages of their development. Graph 1 compares the PRC's export performance after its take-off in 1979 to the export performances of Japan, South Korea, and Singapore after their take-offs in 1955, 1968, and 1970, respectively.[10] The PRC's two-way trade in goods and services expanded from 15.2 percent of GDP in 1982[11] to 74.2 percent of GDP in 2004.[12] Table 1 demonstrates that the PRC is far more dependent on international trade than the United States or other major economies with large populations.

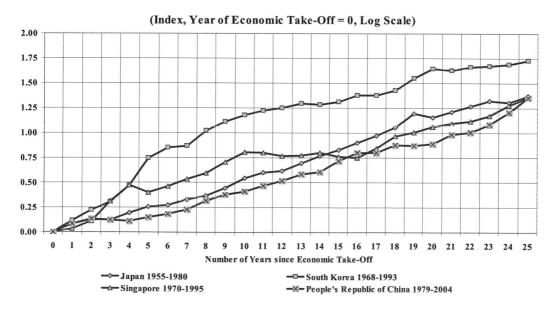

Graph 1. Growth of Real Exports of Goods from Japan, South Korea Singapore, and the People's Republic of China during Similar Periods of Economic Development.

Table 1. PRC's Dependency on International Trade[13]

Major Economy with Large Population	Two-Way Goods and Services Trade as a Percent of GDP in 2004
Brazil	31.2%
European Union (25)	25.6%
India	33.7%
Japan	22.8%
PRC	74.2%
Russia	57.0%
United States	24.8%

Likewise, the PRC relies heavily on inward foreign direct investment for economic growth. From 1982[14] through 2004, the PRC received $531.8 billion in inward foreign direct investment.[15] Chinese affiliates of foreign multinational firms:

-   Employed 10 million urban workers in 2004;[16]
-   Accounted for 8.8 percent of the PRC's gross investment in capital assets in 2003;[17]
-   Produced 31.2 percent of the PRC's gross industrial output[18] in 2003;[19] and
-   Accounted for 57 percent of the PRC's goods exports and 58 percent of its goods imports in 2004.[20]

Because of the PRC's success in expanding exports and attracting inward foreign direct investment, real GDP grew by an average of 9.4 percent a year from 1979 to 2003, by 9.5 percent in 2004, and at an annualized rate of 9.5 percent in first quarter of 2005.[21] According to the World Bank, the PRC's economic reforms have lifted about 400 million Chinese individuals out of poverty from 1981 to 2002.[22]

III. WEAKNESSES

A. Price Distortions

The PRC's government significantly distorts prices in three factor markets. These policies contribute to a significant misallocation of resources in the PRC.

1. Interest Rates

Although some liberalization has recently occurred, the PRC still regulates interest rates at the four major SOCBs and other depository institutions, keeping both nominal and real interest rates low for both depositors and borrowers when compared with interest rates in other developing countries. Because of the scarcity of alternative investments, low interest rates do not prevent the four major SOCBs or other depository institutions from gathering deposits. However, low interest rates do encourage Chinese firms to borrow heavily from the four major SOCBs or other depository institutions and invest in capital assets. Thus, interest rate controls have helped to boost the PRC's investment rate in capital assets from 25.8 percent of GDP in 1990 to an incredible 43.6 percent of GDP in 2004.[23]

2. Energy

The PRC keeps energy prices below market-determined levels. The PRC requires state-owned oil companies to use some of their profits from domestic oil production to subsidize oil imports. Consequently, state-owned oil companies have not increased domestic prices for gasoline and other refined petroleum products in line with recent increase in world prices.[24]

3. Land

In the PRC, the government effectively controls all land. In rural areas, peasants may lease land, but not formally own it. Because peasants lack legal title to the land that they farm, they cannot use it as collateral to finance agricultural equipment or other improvements that might increase farm productivity and output. In urban areas, real estate developers frequently conspire with provincial or local government officials to seize nearby agricultural lands or raze existing urban neighborhoods as sites for new projects. In exchange for various payoffs, provincial or local government officials force peasants off their leased farmland or urban dwellers out their apartments with little compensation. Consequently, real estate developers may gain control over project sites for a fraction of their market value.[25] These below-market land prices along with interest rate controls have stimulated a boom in new construction. From 2000 to 2004, the amount of new floor space under construction increased by 14.7 percent a year.[26] In many Chinese cities, this stimulus has caused real estate developers to build new projects far in excess of the actual demand for new office, industrial, residential, or retail space. For all types of new construction, 28.3 percent of floor space completed in 2004 stood vacant.[27]

B. State-Owned and State-Influenced Enterprises

Early economic reforms that introduced the price system and profit incentives to the SOEs did not significantly improve their performance. Consequently, President Jiang Zemin announced the *zhuada fangxiao* policy (i.e., grab the big, dump the small) at the Fifteenth Party Congress in 1997. Under this policy, the PRC retained three types of large SOEs under central government ownership:

- SOEs that produce armaments or other goods and services directly related to national security;
- SOEs in industrial sectors that the central government has targeted for economic development; and
- Inefficient and unprofitable SOEs that employ large numbers of Chinese workers.
- The remaining SOEs, especially small and medium-sized SOEs, were converted into:
- Township and village enterprises owned by local governments;
- Cooperatives owned by their employees;

-     Private domestic enterprises often sold to provincial or local government officials or their families; and
-     Joint enterprises owned by a state-owned enterprise or a collectively owned enterprise in conjunction with other types of enterprises.

Because of the *zhuada fangxiao* policy, the number of SOEs fell by 44.6 percent over six years to 31,750 in December 2004.[28] However, this policy did not significantly improve SOE performance. Thirty-five percent of the remaining SOEs were unprofitable in 2004.[29] The PRC incorporated many large SOEs in industrial sectors that the central government has targeted for economic development. These firms, which the PRC describes as shareholding enterprises, have issued a minority of their shares to domestic and foreign investors through initial public offerings (IPOs). While these shareholding enterprises have some of the characteristics of private corporations (e.g., shareholders, boards of directors, annual reports), the central government still controls a majority of their shares, elects a majority of their directors, and exercises effective control over their operations. On December 31, 2004, the PRC controlled 69.0 percent of the market value of all shareholding enterprises through non-marketable shares.[30] In the *Australian Financial Review*, Stephen Wyatt (2005) concluded:

> In fact, the entire privatization of China's state-owned enterprises is still more hype than reality. So far, only minority stakes of state-owned groups have been listed, leaving the government with primary control. … The government's strategy is still to list minority shares in state-owned groups in order to raise capital and import better governance while ultimately retaining control … [31]

The PRC allows individuals to establish sole proprietorships, partnerships, or corporations. The PRC now has more than 3.3 million private domestic firms.[32] However, privately owned firms are generally small, employing an average of 14 employees.[33] Private domestic firms are concentrated in service industries, oriented to local markets, and are not generally engaged in international trade or investment.[34] Although some privately owned domestic firms are manufacturers, they shun direct competition with the SOEs or the SIEs in industrial sectors that the central government has targeted for economic development.[35] The SOEs and the SIEs still control a large part of the PRC's economy. The SOEs and the SIEs:

-     Employed 99 million urban workers in 2004;[36]
-     Accounted for 76.7 percent of the PRC's gross investment in capital assets in 2003;[37] and
-     Produced 53.9 percent of the PRC's gross industrial output in 2003.[38]

Chinese laws and regulations often lack clarity. Their enforcement may be arbitrary and sporadic. Government policy influences court decisions. In this legal environment, property rights are insecure. Individuals and private firms must depend on their *guanxi* with central, provincial, or local government officials to protect themselves and their property. From 1949 to 1976, Chinese leader Mao Zedong exercised strict control over all central, provincial, and local government officials in the PRC. However, economic reforms since 1978 have given provinces and localities a significant degree of economic independence, reducing central government control over provincial and local government officials. Given the PRC's weak rule of law and the lack of democratic accountability, provincial and local government officials can exploit their *guanxi* to enrich themselves and their families through widespread corruption. In the words of a Chinese proverb, "the mountain is high, and the emperor is far away." Among other things, provincial and local government officials have:

- Bought the privatized assets of SOEs through rigged sales at a fraction of their market value;
- Demanded bribes from individuals and private firms to enforce or refrain from enforcing certain laws and regulations;
- Pressed branch managers of the four major SOCBs and other depository institutions to make loans to the business interests of provincial or local government officials or their families on favorable, non-market terms; and
- Suppressed the distribution of products competing against the products of firms controlled by provincial or local government officials or their families.

Transparency International reported that the PRC scored 3.4 out of 10 on its *Corruption Index 2004*, 71st of the 146 countries rated.[39] The burden of official corruption is very high. Chinese economist Angang Hu[40] estimated that corruption costs the PRC about 15 percent of its GDP a year in lost tariff and tax revenues and skimmed government funds.[41] The *China Economic Quarterly* (2005) reported that provincial and local government officials extracted from private firms the equivalent of 91 percent of their profits in 2003 through non-tax costs, including fees, *tanpai* (i.e., forced expenditures on unwanted provincial or local goods or services), or *zhaodai* (i.e., entertainment of provincial or local government officials).[42] A weak rule of law, the lack of democratic accountability, and the disintegration of comprehensive central government planning give the SOEs and the SIEs significant competitive advantages over private domestic firms. Generally, large SOEs and SIEs have *guanxi* with Chinese leaders, central government ministries, or prominent provincial or local government officials. These patrons use their influence to secure favorable laws, better regulatory treatment, and preferential access to loans from the four major SOCBs and other depository institutions for the SOEs and the SIEs.

Many SOEs and SIEs face a "soft budget constraint" (i.e., the four major SOCBs and other depository institutions lend to the SOEs and the SIEs without regard to their ability to repay their loans). Some SOEs and SIEs receive policy loans,[43] while other SOEs and SIEs benefit from their *guanxi* with central, provincial or local government officials. Frequently, local government officials have more sway over the lending decisions of local branch managers of the four major SOCBs and other depository institutions than do either senior bank executives in Beijing or Shanghai or central government officials from the People's Bank of China (PBC) or the China Banking Regulatory Commission (CBRC). Despite some recent efforts of the central government officials to curb such non-market loans, the flow of non-market loans from the four major SOCBs and other depository institutions to the SOEs and the SIEs largely continues. These non-market loans allow many unprofitable SOEs and SIEs to continue operations or to invest in new capital assets when market discipline would force these SOEs and SIEs to shutter operations or to forgo the acquisition of capital assets. Although, bankruptcy is a necessary part of the process of creative destruction described by economist Joseph Schumpeter in *Capitalism, Socialism, and Democracy* (1975, orig. pub.

1942)[44] that promotes economic growth in market economies, bankruptcy is relatively rare in the PRC. The PRC's bankruptcy process strongly favors debtors over creditors, making any significant recovery of debts from bankrupt firms extremely difficult. Despite their weak financial conditions, most SOEs and SIEs can avoid bankruptcy or foreclosure. In practice, only the SOEs or the SIEs whose patrons have lost favor with Chinese leaders (e.g., Guangdong International Trust and Investment Corporation (GITIC) in 1999) ever declare bankruptcy.[45]

C. Bad Loan Problem and Dysfunctional Banking System

1. Scope of the Bad Loan Problem

Before 1979, the PRC had one bank, the People's Bank of China, which accepted deposits and lent funds to SOEs under central government direction. During the next decade, the PRC divided the PBC into a central bank with responsibility of formulating and implementing monetary policy and four major SOCBs:

- Agricultural Bank of China (ABC)
- Bank of China (BOC)
- People's Construction Bank of China (PCBC)
- Industrial and Commercial Bank of China (ICBC)

In 1994, the PRC transferred "official" policy lending from these four major SOCBs to three specialized state-owned policy banks:

- Agricultural Development Bank of China (ADBOC)
- China Development Bank (CDB)
- Export-Import Bank of China (EIOC)

Thereafter, the four major SOCBs were to suppose to operate on a market basis. Since then, approximately one hundred-twenty other commercial banks, owned by a mixture of provincial governments, local governments, and other shareholders, have opened. In addition, the PRC has about 75 thousand credit unions.

The PRC relies heavily on banks and other depository institutions to allocate its national savings:

- Deposits are the dominant form of savings. On December 31, 2004, deposits in all banks and other depository institutions were $2.906 trillion or 170.9 percent of GDP.[46]

. Loans are the primary source of funds for business investment. On December 31, 2004, loans from all banks and other depository institutions were $2.143 trillion or 126.0 percent of GDP.[47] In contrast, the market value of all marketable shares listed on the PRC's stock exchanges on December 31, 2004, was $141 billion or 8.3 percent of GDP.[48] The four major SOCBs dominate the PRC's banking market. Table 2 shows that the combined assets of the four major SOCBs were 53.7 percent of the assets of all banks and other depository institutions on December 31, 2004.[49]

Table 2. Assets of the PRC's Banks and Other Depository Institutions on December 31, 2004[50]

Type	Total Assets (in billions of U.S. Dollars)	Market Share
State-Owned Banks	$2,044	53.7%
Joint Shareholding Banks	$568	14.9%
Other Urban Commercial Banks	$206	5.4%
Other Depository Institutions[51]	$987	25.9%
All Banks and Other Depository Institutions	$3,805	100.0%

Banks and other depository institutions accumulated an extraordinarily large "legacy" of non-performing loans (NPLs) from past non-market lending, whether through policy loans, *guanxi* loans, or outright corruption. The China Banking Regulatory Commission reported that NPLs at the four major SOCBs and other commercial banks were $221 billion or 12.3 percent of GDP on March 31, 2005.[52] However, the CBRC estimate excludes:

- $87 billion of NPLs which remain from $169 billion of "legacy" NPLs that the four state-owned asset management companies (AMCs) bought at face value from the four major SOCBs in 2001;[53]
- Non-market loans to the SOEs and the SIEs made by the four major SOCBs and other commercial banks in recent years that are likely to become NPLs; and
- NPLs at policy banks, finance companies, and credit unions

Private estimates of the size of the PRC's bad loan problem are staggering. Standard and Poor's (2004) estimated that the PRC's NPLs comprise 40 percent of all loans.[54] In other words, the PRC's NPLs are equal to 55 percent of GDP.[55] Alternatively, Roubini and Sester (2005) estimated that the PRC's NPLs range between 46 percent of GDP and 56 percent of GDP.[56] Chinese leaders are aware of the enormous challenges confronting their banking system. Since 1998, the PRC has injected $277 billion of government funds into its four major SOCBs:

- $33 billion through swap arrangements in August 1998; $169 billion through the AMCs in 2001;
- $45 billion through swap arrangements in December 2003; and
- $30 billion equity injection into the ICBC in April 2005.[57]

Moreover, the PRC is currently seeking private capital from both domestic and foreign investors to recapitalize its banks. In 2004, HSBC bought a 19.9 percent stake in the Bank of Communications for $1.7 billion. On June 17, 2005, Bank of America announced its intention to buy up to a 9 percent stake in the PCBC for $3 billion. The PRC is planning an IPO to sell additional shares in the PCBC later this year. IPOs for the ABC, the BOC, and the ICBC are likely to follow. Nevertheless, the ultimate cost of resolving the PRC's bad loan problem is huge. Standard and Poor's (2004) estimated that the total cost of resolution would be $650 billion or about 40 percent of GDP.[58] Moreover, Standard and Poor's (2005) estimated that the cost of recapitalizing of two of the four major SOCBs, the ABC and the ICBC, would be between $110 billion and $190 billion.[59] Other private sector estimates for resolving the PRC's bad loan problem are similar to Standard and Poor's. Even assuming a generous recovery rate of 20 percent, Roubini and Sester (2005) estimated the central government would need to issue additional debt ranging between 35 percent of GDP and 45 percent of GDP to resolve its bad loan problem.[60] At the end of 2004, central government debt was about 30 percent of GDP.[61] Under this favorable recovery assumption, resolution would more than double central government debt to between 65 percent of GDP and 75 percent of GDP.[62] Moreover, the interest expense for this additional debt would add approximately 2 percent of GDP a year to the central government's annual budget deficit, increasing it from 1.4 percent of GDP in 2004 to approximately 3.5 percent of GDP a year.[63]

Furthermore, the PRC lacks a credit culture that will prevent a reoccurrence of these bad loan problems. Realizing that the continued patronage of central, provincial, or local government officials virtually ensures a flow of new loans from the four major SOCBs and other depository institutions to maintain operations regardless of financial performance or invest in new capital assets regardless of expected returns, many SOE and SIE executives have developed a cavalier attitude toward servicing their debts. Indeed, domestic firms that pay interest and principal punctually are at a disadvantage with their competitors that ignore their debt obligations. Because many SOE and SIE executives regard loans as "free money," SOE and SIE investment decisions reflect less concern about future profitability than would be the case in a market economy.

2. Macroeconomic Consequences of the PRC's Dysfunctional Banking System

Large-scale non-market lending by the four major SOCBs and other depository institutions to the SOEs and the SIEs limits the availability of credit cards, installment loans, and mortgage loans to Chinese consumers. Individuals must save to buy a car or a home. Moreover, many insurance and annuity products are not yet widely available. Individuals must save still more to self-insure against life's risks. Thus, Chinese individuals save a very high percentage of their income. Consequently, the PRC has a very high national saving rate. It has increased steadily from 34.0 percent of GDP in 1985 to 48.0 percent of GDP in 2004.[64] The unnecessarily high national savings rate contributes to what Chairman of the Council of Economic Advisers Ben S. Bernanke describes as a "savings glut" in Asia.[65] Large-scale non-market lending by the four major SOCBs and other depository institutions to the SOEs and the SIEs restricts the availability of loans to private domestic firms. This limits the ability of Chinese entrepreneurs to invest in new capital assets, expand their businesses, and hire additional workers. Instead of lending to Chinese individuals and private domestic firms, the four major SOCBs and other depository institutions essentially channel the bulk of Chinese savings to support unprofitable SOEs and SIEs and to fund uneconomic SOE and SIE investments in new capital assets. In the short term, such non-market lending to the SOEs and the SIEs maintains production and creates investment that increases the PRC's gross domestic product (GDP) in the short term. However, economic growth is sustainable over the long term if and only if firms:

- Produce goods and services that the market demands; and
- Invest in capital assets that have a positive net present value (i.e., the expected future revenues generated by a capital asset exceeds its current and expected future costs discounted by a rate that reflects the real interest rate, expected future inflation, and the risk associated with such investment).

The rapid accumulation of capital assets among the SOEs and the SIEs suggests that widespread overinvestment (i.e., the acquisition of too many capital assets for producing goods and services given expected future demand) and malinvestment (i.e., acquisition of the wrong types of capital assets for producing goods and services to meet expected future demand) may be occurring in the PRC.

Table 3. PRC's Extraordinarily High Investment Rate[66]

Economy	Gross Investment in Capital Assets as Percent of GDP in 2004 (2003 for India)
Australia	24.5%
Brazil	19.6%
Canada	20.1%
Chile	20.6%
European Union (25)	19.5%
Hong Kong	22.0%
India	22.7%
Indonesia	21.0%
Japan	23.8%
Korea (South)	29.4%
Malaysia	20.4%
Mexico	20.2%
New Zealand	22.7%
PRC	43.6%
Philippines	16.6%
Russia	17.9%
Singapore	25.8%
Taiwan	20.1%
Thailand	25.8%
United States	19.3%

Table 3. demonstrates that the PRC's investment rate (i.e. gross investment in capital assets as a percent of GDP) is way out of line with investment rates in Brazil, the European Union, the United States, and other Asia-Pacific economies. Non-market factors, including central government industrial policy, below-market interest rates, distorted prices, *guanxi* lending, and outright corruption, have driven the PRC's investment surge. Recent economic data, including the high vacancy rate for new construction, suggest that a significant portion of these newly acquired capital assets may be overinvestment or malinvestment.

An economic boom caused by overinvestment and malinvestment cannot sustain itself indefinitely. The inevitable liquidation of overinvestment and malinvestment will impose significant costs on the PRC in terms of lost output, employment, and income and could slow economic growth in the United States and other countries around the world.

D. Sources for Gdp Growth

Economic growth in the PRC is mainly attributable to increases in the quantities of factor inputs rather than efficiency gains or innovation. Since 1978, the migration of unemployed or underemployed peasants from rural communities to cities increased the supply of labor available for industrial jobs. Meanwhile, low interest rates, non-market lending by the four major SOCBs and other depository institutions to the SOEs and SIEs, and inward foreign direct investment have caused a rapid accumulation of capital assets. As the quantity of capital assets increased for each hour worked, the PRC's labor productivity grew by an average of 6.9 percent a year from 1979 to 2004.[67] However, Jinghai Zheng and Anagang Hu (2004) found that the growth in PRC's total factor productivity[68] decelerated dramatically from 3.2 percent a year for 1978-1995 to 0.6 percent a year for 1995-2001.[69] Total factor productivity measures the growth in output that is not attributable to increases in factor inputs such as labor and capital assets. Thus, total factor productivity represents the gains from efficiency improvements and technological innovation. The combination of a high rate of labor productivity and a dropping rate of total factor productivity means that the marginal productivity of new capital assets is falling. This is further evidence that domestic firms are investing in too many capital assets or the wrong types of capital assets given the PRC's comparative advantage in plentiful, low-cost labor.

IV. CONCLUSION

Since economic reform began in 1978, Chinese leaders have sought the benefits of capitalism without relinquishing government control of the commanding heights of the PRC's economy. The resulting mixed economy has both strengths and weaknesses. Because Chinese leaders have largely adhered to openness to international trade and investment, the PRC's main economic strength is its integration into the global economy.

The PRC's numerous deviations from the characteristics of successful market economies have generated all of the PRC's economic weaknesses. The PRC's four major SOCBs and other depository institutions have extended far too many questionable loans based on non-market criteria to the SOEs and the SIEs. Along with below-market interest rates and distorted prices, non-market lending has sustained the PRC's unusually high rate of investment in capital assets of 43.6 percent of GDP in 2004. In turn, the PRC's high investment rate has boosted the real GDP growth rate to 9.5 percent in 2004. However, many SOEs and SIEs are unprofitable. Protected through their *guanxi* with central, provincial, or local government officials, many SOEs and SIEs cannot or will not service their debts to the four major SOCBs and other depository institutions. Consequently, non-market lending has saddled the four major SOCBs and other depository institutions with enormous portfolios of NPLs. Private economists estimate that the cost of resolving the PRC's bad loan problem would be about 40 percent of the PRC's GDP. The SOEs and the SIEs are apparently investing in too many capital assets or the wrong types of capital assets to produce goods and services to satisfy market demand. The high vacancy rate in new construction and slumping total factor productivity suggest widespread overinvestment and malinvestment in the PRC. The eventual liquidation of this overinvestment and malinvestment poses a significant long-term risk to the continuation of the PRC's economic growth. Given the PRC's integration with the global economy, a significant slowdown or recession in the PRC could diminish the prospects for economic growth in the United States and other countries around the world.

ENDNOTES

1   While Hong Kong and Macau are special administrative regions of the People's Republic of China, the economies of Hong Kong and Macau are not considered part of the economy of the People's Republic of China. Therefore, economic statistics about the People's Republic of China do not include data from Hong Kong or Macau.

2   In November 1922, Soviet leader Vladimir Illyich Lenin coined "commanding heights" during his speech to the Fourth Congress of the Communist International in St. Petersburg (then known as Petrograd). In this speech, Lenin defended his New Economic Policy that permitted the resumption of small-scale trade and private agriculture in the Soviet Union against militant communists who attacked Lenin for compromising with capitalism. Although the New Economic Policy allowed some elements of a market economy to function, Lenin declared that the state would control the "commanding heights," the most important elements of the Soviet economy. The British Labour Party adopted "control of the commanding heights of the economy" to describe its policy of nationalizing many British industries after World War II. Then, Prime Minister Jawaharlal Nehru used this expression to describe the similar policies of the Congress Party in India. Daniel Yergin and Joseph Stanislaw, *The Commanding Heights: The Battle Between Government and the Marketplace That is Remaking the Modern World* (New York, NY : Simon and Schuster, 1998): 12.

3   State-owned enterprises are firms owned by the central government. State-influenced enterprises (SIEs) include collectively owned enterprises, township and village enterprises, cooperative enterprises, shareholding enterprises, and joint enterprises. Collectively owned enterprises are firms owned by provincial or local governments. Township and village enterprises are small firms owned by local government in rural areas. Cooperative enterprises are firms owned by their managers and employees. Shareholding enterprises are former state-owned enterprises that have incorporated and issued a minority of their shares to investors. Joint enterprises are firms owned by at least one state-owned enterprise or collectively owned enterprise and at least one other state-owned enterprise, collectively owned enterprise, shareholding enterprise, cooperative enterprise, private domestic enterprise, or individual.

4   Author's calculation based on data from China National Bureau of Statistics/Haver Analytics. This study uses economic data collected and disseminated by the various statistical agencies of the central government of the People's Republic of China. Despite recent quality improvements, Chinese economic data remains less accurate and reliable than comparable U.S. data.

5   Ibid.
6   Scott Bugie, John Chambers, Ryan Tsang, Daria Alexeeva, and Aurélie Thiellet, *Global Financial System Stress: Likelihood of Future Bank Crises Recedes, but Vulnerabilities Remain* (New York: Standard and Poor's, July 8, 2004): 15, found at http://ratingsdirect.com/Apps/RD/controller/Article?id=385155andtype=andoutputType=print.
7   The year 1979 is the first year in which data for the PRC is available.
8   Author's calculation based on International Monetary Fund/Haver Analytics data.
9   Ibid.
10   Ibid.
11   The year 1982 is the first year in which data for the PRC is available.
12   Author's calculation based on International Monetary Fund/Haver Analytics data.
13   Author's calculations based on data from U.S. Bureau of the Census, U.S. Bureau of Economic Analysis, Banco Central do Brasil, European Central Bank, Eurostat, Bank of Japan, and Japanese Ministry of Finance, and the Central Bank of the Russian Federation/Haver Analytics and Economist Intelligence Unit.
14   The year 1982 is the first year in which data for the PRC is available.
15   Author's calculation based on State Administration of Foreign Exchange and China National Bureau of Statistics/Haver Analytics data.
16   China National Bureau of Statistics/Haver Analytics.
17   Author's calculation based on China National Bureau of Statistics/Haver Analytics. The year 2003 is the last year in which complete data is available.
18   Gross industrial output measures the value of industrial goods and services produced during a period. Gross industrial value-added subtracts the value of intermediate inputs and the value-added tax from gross industrial output.
19   Ibid.
20   Congressional Research Service.
21   Author's calculation based on China National Bureau of Statistics/Haver Analytics data.
22   [U]sing the World Bank's $1/day income measure, the number of poor is estimated to have dropped from about 490 million to 88 million over the same period, a decline in poverty incidence from 49 percent in 1981 to 6.9 percent in 2002. World Bank, Shanghai Poverty Conference: Case Study Summary (2004), found at http://www.worldbank.org/wbi/reducingpoverty/docs/newpdfs/case-summ-China-8-7PovertyReduction.pdf.
23   Author's calculations based on China National Bureau of Statistics/Haver Analytics.
24   Nouriel Roubini and Brad Sester, *China Trip Report* (April 2005): 17, found at www.regmonitor.com.
25   Ibid.
26   Author's calculations based on China National Bureau of Statistics/Haver Analytics.
27   Ibid.
28   Ibid.
29   Ibid.
30   Author's calculation based on data from China Securities Regulatory Commission, Shanghai Stock Exchange, and Shenzhen Stock Exchange/Haver Analytics.
31   Stephen Wyatt, "Privatization More Hype than Reality," *Australian Financial Review* (June 7, 2005).

32 "Private Enterprise: Faster, Higher, Stronger," *China Economic Quarterly* (First Quarter 2005): 46.

33 Ibid: 47.

34 Ibid.

35 Gordon G. Chang, *The Coming Collapse of China* (New York: Random House, 2001): 144-165.

36 China National Bureau of Statistics/Haver Analytics.

37 Author's calculation based data from China National Bureau of Statistics/Haver Analytics. The year 2003 is the last year in which investment data by enterprise type is available.

38 Ibid.

39 *Transparency International Corruptions Practices Index 2004*, found at http://transparency.org.

40 The name of this Chinese economist is in western fashion with the family name last.

41 Julie Chao, "China is Losing Battle with Corruption," *Milwaukee Journal Sentinel* (December 8, 2002).

42 *China Economic Quarterly* (First Quarter 2005): 48.

43 Policy lending occurs when banks make loans to individuals, firms, organizations, or governments based on government regulations or suasion rather than market criteria. Under policy lending, banks grant borrowers larger loans, lower interest rates, or more favorable terms than banks would willingly grant in the absence of government regulation or suasion.

44 Joseph A. Schumpeter, *Capitalism, Socialism, and Democracy* (New York: Harper, 1975, org. pub. 1942): 82-85.

45 Chang (2001): 98-102.

46 Author's calculation based on data from China National Bureau of Statistics and Money and Banking Statistics, People's Bank of China/Haver Analytics.

47 Ibid.

48 Author's calculation based on data from China National Bureau of Statistics, China Securities Regulatory Commission, Shanghai Stock Exchange, and Shenzhen Stock Exchange/Haver Analytics.

49 Author's calculation based on data from China Banking Regulatory Commission, found at http://www.cbrc.gov.cn/english/module/viewinfo.jsp?infoID=966.

50 Ibid.

51 Other depository institutions include credit unions, rural commercial banks, foreign banks, finance companies, trust companies, and policy banks.

52 Author's calculation based on data from China National Bureau of Statistics and Money and Banking Statistics, People's Bank of China/Haver Analytics.

53 Author's calculation based on China Banking Regulatory Commission data, found at http://www.cbrc.gov.en/english/viewinfo.jsp?infoID=968.

54 Bugie, Chambers, Tsang, Alexeeva, and Thiellet (2004): 15.

55 Author's calculation.

56 Roubini and Sester (April 2005): 10-14.

57 "Beijing Tops Up Bad-Loan Banks Again," Reprinted in the Sydney Morning Herald from the New York Times (January 8, 2004), found at http://ww.smh.com.au/articles/2004/01/07/1073437347723.html; Ryan Tsang and Paul

Coughlin, *Recapitalization of China's ICBC and ABC Could Cost US$100 Bil. and up to US$190 Bil.* (New York: Standard and Poor's, April 25, 2005): 1, found at http://www2:standardandpoors.com; and Brian Bremner with Dexter Roberts, "Wanted: A Big Broom for China's Banks," *Business Week* (May 9, 2005).

58 Bugie, Chambers, Tsang, Alexeeva, and Thiellet (2004): 16.

59 Tsang and Coughlin (April 25, 2005): 1.

60 Roubini and Sester (April 2005): 15.

61 Derived from IMF, International Financial Statistics and State Statistical Yearbook.

62 Author's calculations.

63 Author's calculations.

64 International Monetary Fund.

65 Ben S. Bernanke, "Remarks at Homer Jones Lecture," (April 14, 2005), found at http://www.federalreserve.gov/boarddocs/speeches/2005/20050414/default.htm.

66 Author's calculations based on data from national statistical agencies/Haver Analytics.

67 Author's calculations based on data from China National Bureau of Statistics/Haver Analytics.

68 This assumes a weight for capital of 0.6 and labor of 04 for growth accounting.

69 Jinghai Zheng and Angang Hu, "An Empirical Analysis of Provincial Productivity in China (1979-2001)," Working Paper in Economics (SwoPEc), no. 127, ISSN 1403-2465 (March 2004).

In: Economics and Foreign Investment in China
Editor: J.I. Cheng, pp. 109-150

ISBN 1-60021-238-7
© 2007 Nova Science Publishers, Inc.

Chapter 5

CHINA, THE UNITED STATES AND THE IMF: NEGOTIATING EXCHANGE RATE ADJUSTMENT[*]

Jonathan E. Sanford

ABSTRACT

In recent years, the United States and other countries have expressed considerable concern that China's national currency (the yuan or renminbi) is seriously undervalued. Some analysts say the yuan needs to rise by as much as 40% in order to reflect its equilibrium value. Critics say that China's undervalued currency provides it with an unfair trade advantage that has seriously injured the manufacturing sector in the United States. Chinese officials counter that they have not pegged the yuan to the dollar in order to gain trade advantages. Rather, they say the fixed rate promotes economic stability that is vital for the functioning of its domestic economy.

On July 21, 2005, China announced a new foreign exchange system which is intended to allow more flexibility and to permit the international value of the yuan to be established by market forces. The yuan was increased in value by 2% and a "managed float" was introduced. However, the value of the yuan has changed little since then. Despite the publication of many studies, scholars do not agree whether or by what percent the yuan is undervalued. The wide range of estimates suggests that there is no reason to believe that any particular figure is correct. It is not clear that the U.S. trade deficit would be lower or U.S. manufacturers would benefit if China raised the value of the yuan. In the short run, U.S. producers might be able to sell higher-priced products to U.S. consumers if the inflow of Chinese goods were reduced. In the long run, though, as long as the United States is a net importer of capital, it will have a trade deficit and other countries will ultimately replace China as suppliers of low-cost goods to the U.S. market.

The Treasury Department has strongly urged China in recent years to adopt procedures that would allow the yuan to rise in value. Congress is considering legislation that would penalize China if its currency is not revalued. The United States has pursued the yuan-dollar exchange rate issue as a bilateral U.S.-China issue. Other countries are also affected by the presumably undervalued yuan — some more than the U.S. — but they have allowed the United States to take the lead.

---

[*] Excerpted from CRS Report RL33322 dated March 13, 2006.

There are at least five ways the United States could deal with the yuan exchange rate issue. Some of these would involve other countries more explicitly in the process. First, the United States could continue pressing China publicly to raise the value of the yuan on the assumption that change will not occur without foreign pressure. Second, it could stop pressing China publicly, on the expectation that China might move more rapidly towards reform if it is not pressured. Third, the United States could restrict imports from China pending action to revalue the yuan. Fourth, the U.S. could ask the IMF to declare that China is manipulating its currency in violation of IMF rules. Fifth, the United States could refer the issue to the World Trade Organization (WTO), asserting that the United States has been injured by unfair trade practices linked to the undervaluation of China's currency. The WTO, in turn, could authorize trade remedies (tariffs on Chinese goods, for example) aimed at correcting this abuse. This report will be updated as new developments arise.

SCOPE AND CONTENT

Overview

In recent years, there has been growing concern in the United States and elsewhere that China may be manipulating the value of its currency to gain unfair trade advantages. Many believe that China's national currency, the yuan or renminbi (RMB), may be seriously undervalued compared to the dollar and other major currencies.[1] The United States and other countries have urged China to raise the value of its currency. Chinese officials say they want to make their exchange rate system more flexible, but they say China also needs long-term stability in its currency value in order to avoid internal dislocations. Discussion of this question has taken place at the International Monetary Fund (IMF) and at other multilateral fora such as the periodic meetings of the G-8 (the seven largest industrial countries plus Russia.) The United States and other countries have also spoken directly to China on a bilateral basis about this issue.

The key issue is what — if the yuan is undervalued — China and the world should do about it. China is currently undergoing a major shift from a state-dominated to a market-based economy. It has pursued a policy of export-led growth in order to generate the employment and income necessary to facilitate change in the overall structure of its economy. It has priced its currency in order to facilitate that policy. In July 2005, China adopted reforms aimed at giving market forces a possible role in the valuation of the yuan. Most observers say the initial changes (a 2% rise in value) were too small and they note that little change has occurred since. Chinese officials retain firm control over the mechanisms which produce the yuan-dollar exchange rate and the criteria they use in this process remain opaque. International discussions have sought to persuade China to accelerate the process but — while the concerns of other countries may bear weight in the thinking of Chinese officials —there are no effective "teeth" in the International Monetary Fund that could compel China to change its policies and procedures more rapidly than it wishes to do so.

Many in the United States believe that the large volume of Chinese exports to the United States is damaging the U.S. manufacturing sector and feeding the U.S. trade deficit. They believe that the undervalued yuan is an important reason why China is able to price its goods so competitively and why production in many areas is shifting to China. Other analysts believe that — by virtue of its undervalued currency — China is damaging the world trading system and denying export opportunities to other countries whose currencies are more fairly priced. Congress is considering legislation which would place countervailing duties or special tariffs on Chinese goods entering the U.S. in order to offset the trade benefits China presumably gains from its present exchange rate policies.

THIS REPORT IN FOUR PARTS

Events and Issues

This report has four parts. The first part discusses the issues and events surrounding the yuan-dollar controversy. It describes the actions which Chinese authorities have taken to revalue the yuan and, arguably, to lay the groundwork for a larger future role for market forces in its valuation. It also describes the methods the Chinese authorities have used and still use to hold the value of the yuan at the level they prefer. This section discusses the efforts the International Monetary Fund, the U.S. Government and other governments have made to encourage or press China to revalue its currency. It also reviews the U.S. Treasury Department's discussion of China in its semi-annual report on currency manipulation and legislation currently pending in Congress which would levy special duties on Chinese goods if the yuan is not increased considerably in value.

Five Questions which Frame the Controversy

The second part of this report looks at five central questions. First, is the yuan undervalued and, if so, by how much? This question may be harder to answer than many people assume. Most economists agree the yuan is undervalued, but the 17 studies reviewed in this report show widely different conclusions. Some say the yuan is slightly *overvalued*, others say it is 15% or 25% or perhaps 49% *undervalued*, while several say it is impossible to make an accurate computation. The data are poor, China is changing rapidly, and scholars use different assumptions in their studies. Moreover, new economic data published in December 2005 seem to render all previous studies obsolete, as they give a very different picture of the Chinese economy than was available before. In recent studies, IMF experts say the yuan is undervalued but they also say it is impossible to know how large the distortion might be. The IMF also says that it is impossible to separate the trade effects of that distortion from the other factors (labor costs, productivity, etc.) which also affect the price of Chinese goods.

Without some objective way of determining what the "real" value of the yuan might be, it may be difficult for China and other countries to agree what size increase is "enough." Likewise, without knowing the proper rate, it might be difficult to design special U.S. tariffs which the world would consider fair and compensatory rather than arbitrary or punitive. It might be helpful if China, the United States and other countries could agree on criteria by which to decide how an appropriate exchange rate for the dollar and yuan might be determined.

Second, does China manipulate the value of the yuan? The IMF rules state that countries may not manipulate the value of their currency in order to gain unfair trade advantage. The second section of this report examines China's behavior in light of the five standards the IMF uses to judge whether manipulation is taking place. For whatever reason, the IMF has not publicly declared that China is manipulating its currency. However, China's actions seem to meet three of the IMF's criteria in this regard. The IMF has no "teeth," however, nor any means other than persuasion to make countries comply with its rules. In this context, it is not clear that an IMF announcement that China was violating its rules would help or hinder the current discussions aimed at persuading China to raise the value of the yuan.

Third, how fast could China revalue the yuan if it wanted to? Theoretically, the People's Bank of China could raise the exchange value of the yuan to any specified level overnight. However, Chinese officials are concerned about the growth and employment effects any change in the value of the yuan may have on their economy. A too-rapid increase might have serious negative effects on employment, output and growth. Some also worry that "hot money" could complicate the process of revaluation and may require China to delay any changes until the perceived speculative pressure abates. Many experts believe that a gradual and measured approach to currency revaluation is appropriate for China. The IMF says, for example, that emerging market countries generally do not handle rapid and large exchange rate movements well and that serious dislocations can occur. Others believe, however, that basic fairness to other countries requires China to raise the value of its currency. Some analysts believe China could suffer serious damage to its economy if it does not change is economic strategy. Its heavy reliance on export-led growth makes it vulnerable, for example, to a slowdown in world demand. Higher currency values would stimulate growth of its domestic economy.

Fourth, has China "cooked the books" in terms of its trade surplus? Some analysts believe that China's actual net income from trade is many times larger than that which China's publishes in its official trade statistics. Indeed, data published by the IMF show that, while China reports that it had a net trade surplus of $41 billion in 2004, its trading partners report that they had a combined trade deficit of $267 billion with China. Some people say that a trade surplus this large is proof that China's currency is substantially undervalued.

Others would ask, however, where — if China is accruing an extra $200 billion annually in trade income beyond the amounts accounted for in its balance of payments figures — that money might be. It might be hard, for example, for China to hide all this additional income year after year in secret undeclared foreign exchange reserves without somebody discovering that it exists.

Trade date for other countries also show (though on a smaller scale) this same mismatch between the amount reported by exporter countries and the amounts reported by those who import their products. Bad data collection by individual countries and methodological problems in the reporting system seem to be better explanations for these discrepancies than is the uniform prospect that exporters fudge their data while importers report their incoming trade data correctly.

Fifth, would the U.S. economy benefit if China revalued the yuan? Correcting the international value of the yuan may improve the efficiency of international trade. But will it reduce the U.S. trade deficit and strengthen the U.S. manufacturing sector? Most economists believe not. The U.S. and Chinese economies have become increasingly interdependent in recent years. China is pursuing a policy of export-led growth and the United States provides a ready market for its goods. Meanwhile, the United States imports large quantities of capital from abroad (by borrowing or by opening its economy to foreign investment) and — in order (more money chasing the same quantity of goods) to avoid turning that imported money into inflation — it must also import goods and services for the imported money to buy. If China raised the value of the yuan, its exports to the United States will likely shrink and the amount of money it could place in the U.S. economy would decline.

Temporarily, the decline in these imports might allow U.S. producers to take some of the market (albeit at higher prices) previously supplied by China. From a longer perspective, though, it is likely that production will shift to other low-cost countries and these will ramp up their exports in order to supply the U.S. market previously supplied by Chinese goods. On the other hand, the inflow of foreign goods will decline and U.S. manufactured goods might be more competitive in U.S. and foreign markets if the U.S. savings rate increased, the United States borrowed less and received fewer investments from abroad, and the international value of the dollar declined.[2]

Three Dilemmas for China

The third section of this report looks at some of the monetary and financial dilemmas which affect China's views about exchange rate policy.

First, what should China do about its foreign exchange (forex) reserves? China has $819 billion in foreign exchange reserves (rough 70% in dollars). These are an important source of income, influence, and future spending power. However, they are also a problem. For one thing, the growth in China's forex reserves fuels domestic inflation. For every dollar the People's Bank of China buys (to hold down the value of the yuan and to increase its reserves), it injects 8 yuan into China's economy. China's reserves grew by $100 billion in 2005, so this is a lot of new "printing press" money. The central bank has tried with limited success to bottle up the inflationary effect of this money with public debt transactions and tight monetary policy. If China raised the value of the yuan, the growth in its foreign exchange reserves would slow or stop and — if it relaxed its monetary policy — the growth and reform prospects of its internal economy might be enhanced.

On the other hand, revaluation would cost China a great deal of money. If the yuan increased in value by 20%, the purchasing power of China's foreign reserves would go down corresponding. It would lose, from China's perspective, about 1.3 trillion yuan (about $200 billion) in purchasing power. If China began withdrawing assets from the U.S. market and converting them to other currencies, in order to reduce its exposure, it would lose money because its actions would push down the value of the securities and the dollars it sold. When it purchased other currencies and foreign assets to replace its former U.S. holdings, it would lose money again because its actions would also push up their prices. Chinese officials may want to reduce the inflationary pressure which comes from growth in their foreign exchange reserves but they may not be happy about the prospect of major financial losses if they revalue or if they move their current assets elsewhere.

Second, where is the money coming from that fuels those growing reserves?

Many people believe that exports and incoming foreign investment account for most of the increase in China's foreign exchange reserves. Some suggest, however, that "hot money"

— speculative inflows of foreign funds seeking to profit from revaluation of the yuan — may account for most of the growth in China's reserves.

Depending on the source of the money, the policy implications for China are very different. If trade and investment are the main source of the funds, then — if Chinese officials want to slow the growth in reserves — they should raise the value of the yuan. However, if speculative inflows are the primary source, then China's policy choices are more difficult. A large quick revaluation would stop the speculative pressure but it might also damage China's economy. Gradual increases would allow the Chinese economy to adjust but it might also encourage speculators to bring more money into China in hopes of profiting as the currency goes up in value. A refusal to consider any change in the value might discourage the speculators over a long period of time But if the status quo prevailed during that period, this would also make China's trading partners angry and give them reasons to doubt whether Chinese officials are sincere when they say they want to revalue the yuan.

Third, would revaluation strengthen or weaken China's banking system?

China's banks are riddled with bad debt and their competitiveness weakened by years of state control. If the yuan were increased in value, would the shock cause Chinese banks to strengthen their procedures or would it put the system at risk? A change in exchange rates which weakened the export sector without simultaneously stimulating domestic commerce could hold bad news for China's banks.

Some experts point out that Chinese banks hold only a small portion of their assets in foreign currencies and the government has recently established asset management companies (similar to the mechanisms the U.S. Government used in the 1980s to resolve the U.S. savings and loan crisis) to take bad debt off the books of the banks. However, export-related activities account for a major share of the customers in China's banking system. Nevertheless, most experts agree that bad debts (non-performing assets) account for perhaps 30% of the assets of Chinese banks and they say the government will need to spend hundreds of billions of dollars in yuan to recapitalize and restructure the major banks. The IMF says that the strength of China's banking system should not be an impediment to a gradual increase in the value of the yuan. However, Chinese officials have expressed reservations and may not be willing to revalue the yuan very quickly until their concerns about the impact on their national banking system have been alleviated. External pressure to revalue rapidly might be seen as an effort by foreigners to create more opportunities for their firms to buy ailing Chinese banks.

Policy Options for the United States

The fourth part of this report identifies five major options which U.S. policy-makers might consider if they want to encourage China to revalue the yuan. They are not mutually exclusive, though it might be difficult for some of them to be pursued simultaneously.

First, the United States could continue pressing China publicly for further changes in its foreign exchange system, in order that the yuan's value would better reflect market conditions and economic realities. If Chinese reformers need outside pressure to help them persuade other officials to consider reform, this strategy might help. Second, as a reciprocal of the first option, U.S. policy-makers might refrain from pressing China to move more quickly with its reforms. This might be an effective strategy if the Chinese proponents of change find that outside pressure strengthens the hand of those resisting reform.

Third, the United States could levy special tariffs on Chinese imports in an effort to encourage China to be more accommodating in their discussions with the United States about the yuan. However, such duties may violate WTO rules. Also, Chinese exporters may be able to absorb some of the cost of the new duties. Further, if the yuan were revalued, the price of Chinese exports would need not increase by the same rate as did the yuan. Chinese exports include a high proportion of inputs imported from other countries. The price of those inputs would not change if the yuan went up in value. To break even, producers in China would only need to increase the price of their exports by an amount which reflects the higher dollar-equivalent cost of Chinese-produced inputs and labor paid in yuan.

Fourth and fifth, the United States might refer the dollar-yuan controversy to the IMF or the World Trade Organization. As noted above, this issue has been discussed at the IMF for some time. Proposed changes in the power of the IMF might give it more authority over country exchange rate policies, including authority to address problems of manipulation. Whether China would be the main country affected, whether the United States and other countries would allow the IMF to determine their exchange rates, and what impact these rule changes might have on the policies of the countries with the world's largest economies are matters for speculation.

An appeal to the WTO might be based on the grounds that China's undervalued currency allegedly constitutes a subsidy to its export sector. The WTO can evaluate trade disputes and it can authorize countries to levy trade penalties in order to enforce its decisions. However, it has no authority to judge exchange rate issues. The WTO and IMF have an agreement, though, specifying that any exchange rate issues which arise in WTO deliberations shall be referred to the IMF and the IMF's decision shall be final. In effect, the WTO would be the enforcer if the IMF decided that a country was manipulating its currency to gain unfair trade advantage.

ISSUES AND EVENTS

Yuan-Dollar Exchange Rate Issue

The Controversy. In 1994, the People's Bank of China (PBC) lowered the value of its currency from 5.8 to about 8.3 yuan to the dollar. During the next decade, despite the rapid growth and modernization of the Chinese economy and the enormous expansion of its exports, the pegged value of the yuan remained essentially unchanged. The PBC bought dollars in the market in order to keep the value of the yuan virtually unchanged. Many argue that this constitutes manipulation.

Arguments Pro and Con. Many argue that China is manipulating the value of its currency in order to gain unfair trade advantage.[3] They believe this has seriously injured the manufacturing sector in the United States and contributed significantly to the U.S. trade deficit.

The act of currency manipulation is often hard to see. However, the effects of manipulation on currency prices is more apparent. Critics of China's exchange rate policies argue that China's currency is perhaps 25% to 50% undervalued compared to the U.S. dollar. They cite various studies which support their view. They say the undervalued yuan adds to the U.S. trade deficit and hurts U.S. output and employment. Many have urged the Administration to put pressure on China in order to make it stop manipulating the yuan. They say China should either raise the value of the yuan by official action ("revalue") or let it trade freely in foreign exchange markets ("float") so that the free market can determine its real international value.

The issue of manipulation is controversial. The IMF says, in its Articles of Agreement (Article IV), that countries shall "Avoid manipulating exchange rates or the international monetary system in order to prevent effective balance of payments adjustment or to gain an unfair competitive advantage over other members."[4] Member countries are supposed to comply with this requirement. In addition, the U.S. Omnibus Trade and Competitiveness of 1988 requires that the Secretary of the Treasury determine whether other countries "manipulate the rate of exchange between their currency and the United States dollar for the purpose of preventing effective balance of payments adjustments or gaining unfair competitive advantage in international trade."[5]

Chinese officials argue that the fixed exchange rate between the yuan and the U.S. dollar is not intended to promote exports but rather to promote economic stability. They worry that, if the value of the yuan increased sharply against the dollar or if its value fluctuated widely in world currency markets, China could suffer a major economic crisis that would seriously injure its prospects for growth, employment, and economic reform. Chinese officials have not entered into the debate concerning the "real" value of China's currency, though some say there is no convincing evidence that the yuan is undervalued. They could cite econometric studies (see below) which support the view that China's currency is slightly overvalued or perhaps only a little undervalued compared to the dollar.

Many economists doubt that China's actions have had any appreciable impact on the long-term value of the dollar. The dollar plays a broad role in international finance and the amount of dollars in circulation globally is very large. A recent survey by the world's leading central banks indicated that the daily trading of foreign currencies totals more than $1.9 trillion, 90% of which is in dollars.[6]

China Announces a Change. On July 21, 2005, China's central bank announced a new exchange rate system for China's currency. First, it increased the value of the yuan, which rose from 8.28 to 8.11 to the dollar.[7] Second, the yuan would be referenced, not just to the dollar but to a basket of currencies, and it would be allowed to vary by 0.3% each day above or below a central parity. Third, the central bank said that "the closing price of...the US dollar traded against the RMB [yuan]...after the closing...of the market each working day" would become "the central parity for the...following working day."[8] This seemed to be an exchange system which economists call a "crawling peg."

If the new procedure had been allowed to function as announced, the yuan could have increased in value by 30% in five months. On July 27, 2005, however, the central bank announced that no further changes in the value of the yuan should be expected. Rather, it said, China's new system would be a "managed float." The central bank would compare the value of the yuan to a "basket" of currencies issued by its major trading partners. However, the Chinese authorities made it clear that they would decide what the value of the yuan would be and they would determine when and how liberalization might occur. The yuan might fluctuate compared to other currencies, but they said its dollar value would be fixed.

Too Small? To many observers, the 2% increase in the value of the yuan announced in July 2005 was too small and the process for possible future increases was too obscure and uncertain. Some might argue that the changes in the new system reflect the current debate about economic policy within the Chinese leadership. Some Chinese officials may believe that reform, including liberalization of the yuan, is in China's best interest. Others may believe that China must continue the policy of export-led growth and the advantages of the old system should not be disposed of lightly.

From this perspective, some might say the new system was adopted in order to buy time, to delay reform, and to forestall outside pressure. China was scheduled to discuss its exchange rate policies with the IMF executive board in August 2005 and the advent of a new system gave the Chinese something new to present. The IMF board was critical of China's exchange rate policies in 2004 and IMF staff had strongly urged China in mid-2005 to introduce market forces into China's exchange rate regime. The change was also announced just before Congress was scheduled to consider several bills which sought to put pressure on China if it did not revalue its currency. Arguably, a series of ambiguous steps which seemed to herald change might buy China time to consider its options and lay its plans. It might give the IMF board a reason not to press for faster action and it might persuade Congress to postpone action on the pending bills.[9]

Alternatively, instead of seeing the new system as the product of internal debate, one might say that it is obscure because it seeks to confuse and frustrate speculators. The inflow of "hot money," is serious. An official with China's State Administration of Foreign Exchange reportedly observed that "Whether we [can] effectively refrain speculation on yuan is the key to the success or failure of the reform."[10] If China wants to avoid instability and sharp changes in currency prices, its actions must not invite speculators to bring in more foreign currency and buy more yuan. In effect, China must do what the speculators expect — increase the value of the yuan —without encouraging them to capitalize on their expectations.

The old system offered speculators a one-way no-risk bet, since there was little chance the yuan would fall in value whereas there seemed a real possibility that the value would eventually rise, perhaps substantially. This offered potentially large rewards to those who owned yuan or yuan-denominated assets.[11] The inflow of speculative money puts pressure on China to revalue the yuan to reduce the flow.[12]

However, if the increase were not sudden and massive, speculators might be encouraged to buy more yuan in hopes of profiting as it goes up in value. As long as there is a general expectation that the yuan is underpriced and as long as these speculative flows continue, Chinese officials are reluctant to allow the market to determine the yuan's value. They worry that it might increase too much in value ("overshoot") if it were opened suddenly to market forces and this could also have negative consequences for the Chinese and world economies.

New Initiatives since July 2005

More recently, the Chinese authorities have taken other steps that could allow market forces to eventually play a role in the valuation of the yuan. In mid- 2005, they created a system of non-deliverable forward contracts which let individuals take positions and make predictions as to the future value of the yuan.[13].

In January 2006, China's State Administration of Foreign Exchange (SAFE) authorized 13 local and foreign banks[14] to buy and sell yuan for dollars in the yuan spot market. An experiment allowing some banks to trade yuan for euros and Hong Kong dollars had begun in

2005. The new arrangement is supposed to improve liquidity and allow market forces a role in the valuation of the yuan. Under the new rule, the opening price for the yuan would be determined by the average closing price of the 13 banks (with the two most extreme eliminated.) In principle, this would allow yuan to move up or down in value in response to market forces. However, observers note that the central bank remains the biggest trader in the yuan-dollar market and any bank which quotes too high a rate will be vulnerable if it floods the market with yuan in order to keep the rate at its preferred price.

In December 2005, the Chinese authorities took two additional steps that would either reduce the demand for yuan or increase the demand in China for dollars. The central bank announced that it was raising the interest rate for deposits held in U.S. or Hong Kong dollars, widening the gap between those rates and those paid for accounts denominated in yuan.[15] This was aimed at discouraging speculators from buying yuan in hopes they can turn a profit by converting them back into dollars if, in the near future, the yuan should increase substantially in value.

The central bank also announced that it would soon scrap the existing limits on the amounts that Chinese firms could take out of the country.[16] This could marginally push down the value of the yuan when Chinese firms sold their national currency in order to purchase the dollars needed to expand their overseas operations.

Market Expectations

The dollar exchange rate for the yuan has changed by only a little more than one-half of 1% since the new system was introduced, going from Rmb 8.11 to the dollar on July 21, 2005 to Rmb 8.0424 to the dollar on February 26, 2006. The People's Bank of China retains firm control of the exchange rate through its transactions in foreign exchange markets. In January 2006, futures contracts suggested that traders believed the value of the yuan would rise 2.1% (to Rmb 7.86 to the dollar) in six months and 4.3% by the end of 2006. A global markets analyst for Goldman Sachs predicted, by contrast, that the value of the yuan would increase by 9% (to Rmb 7.34) by the end of the year.[17] The Economist Intelligence Unit said the yuan would rise 4.4% in 2006 (to Rmb 7.9) and 3.7% in 2006 (to Rmb 7.6.)[18]

These predictions assume that the People's Bank of China will bring these results about through its exchange market transactions or (to say the same thing) that it will not act to prevent market forces from generating these rates of exchange.

INTERNATIONAL VIEWS

Efforts by the IMF

The IMF staff proposed, in its June 2005 report on its recent Article IV consultations, that China should revise its foreign exchange policies and allow the market to play a larger role in the valuation of the yuan.[19]. The IMF executive board had the report prior to its formal review of China's policies, though the actual document was not published until September.

The IMF executive board discussed China's new exchange rate policies during its August 2005 annual Article IV consultation review. Many people believe that China announced its new policies two weeks before that meeting in order to show they were addressing the issue. The previous year, during its August 2004 review of China's policies, the board had said that greater exchange rate flexibility was in China's best interests.[20] It also welcomed China's statement that it would "introduce, in a phased manner, greater exchange rate flexibility." Some observers suggest that it might have been awkward for China to go to the 2005 meeting and report that it had done nothing.

In its August 2005 review, the IMF executive board "welcomed the change in the exchange rate regime — an important move toward greater exchange rate flexibility — and encouraged the authorities to utilize the flexibility afforded by the new arrangement." It reiterated its earlier point that greater exchange rate flexibility was both necessary and in China's best interests.[21] It also said that "a more flexible exchange rate, not simply a revaluation, is the key to providing scope for monetary policy independence and enhancing the economy's resilience to external shocks." According to the summary of the board discussion, most directors supported a gradual and cautious approach but many others recommended that China move quickly to a foreign exchange level which reflects underlying market forces.

Other Countries' Views

No other country has taken as strong a public position on the Chinese exchange rate issue as has the United States, even though the low cost of Chinese exports has been a source of concern to interests in their countries as well. Nevertheless, some other countries reportedly have been vigorous in their private discussions with Chinese officials, urging them to give market forces a larger role in determining the value of the yuan. Their public statements have tended to show patience with China's concerns. Some observers suggested that they preferred to let the United States do the "heavy lifting."

Some countries have spoken out. In early June 2005, for example, David Dodge, Governor of the Bank of Canada, called on China to free its currency from the fixed rate against the U.S. dollar or to risk sparking U.S. and European trade protectionism.[22] At the same time, Japan's finance minister urged China to reform its tight currency peg on grounds that the current yuan-dollar exchange rate was hurting the Chinese economy and causing it to overheat.[23].

European ministers reportedly have been more accommodating in their remarks. For example, Chinese Premier Wen Jiabao told an Asia-Europe ministerial meeting in June 2005 that China would adopt a more flexible currency policy only when it believed itself ready. European ministers replied, in their public statements, that they hoped it would not take too long[24] but they agreed that China should not be pressured and it had the right to determine when and how it would reform its currency.[25].

Since July 2005, observers have been waiting for an announcement by China that it would further liberalize its exchange rate policy. The IMF executive board urged this at its discussion of China's policies in August 2005. The governing boards of the IMF and World Bank urged it at their joint annual meetings in late September 2005. Treasury Secretary Snow urged it during his October 2005 trip to China. President Bush reiterated the point during a state visit to China in November 2005.

In September 2005, the finance ministers of the G-7 countries said, in the communique following a meeting in Washington, D.C., that "we welcome the recent decision by the Chinese authorities to pursue greater flexibility in their exchange rate regime."[26]. This was the first time a G-7 communique had called on China by name to take action. "We expect the development of this more market-oriented system to improve the functioning and stability of the global economy and the international monetary system," they added. China's President told the G-8 leaders that China wanted to base the yuan's value on market forces but it would do this on its own time and not as a result of foreign pressure.[27]

The G-7 finance ministers were even more specific in their communique following their meeting in London on December 3, 2005. They said that "further implementation of China's currency system would improve the functioning and stability of the global economy and the international monetary system." They said, in language not directly mentioning China, that such disparities, along with high oil prices, were a threat to a "solid" world economy.[28] They also said that "exchange rates should reflect economic fundamentals" and that they would monitor exchange markets closely. This was much stronger language than the "welcome" the ministers had expressed three months earlier.

Individual leaders were even more specific in their remarks. European Central Bank president Jean-Claude Trichet said at the time that the G-7's public comments were "in continuity with the message that we have been giving." He also said, referring to Asia, that "this part of the world has to contribute to the solution of global imbalances."[29] Japan's finance minister, Sadakazu Tanigaki, said, at the same time, that "we believe China needs some time to get accustomed to their new currency regime, but a considerable time has already passed. I expect China to make its currency a bit more flexible."[30] Treasury Secretary Snow said, on this occasion, that "this rigidity constrains exchange rate flexibility in the region and thus poses risks to China's economy and the global economy." Jin Renqing, China's finance minister, did not comment directly but did say that China would over time allow market forces to play a greater role in determining the value of the renminbi.

U.S. Views. In the United States, both the Administration and Congress have spoken to the issue of China's currency.

Action by the Executive Branch. In January 2004, President George W. Bush told a crowd in Toledo, Ohio that "we expect countries like China to understand that trade imbalances mean that trade is not balanced and fair. They have got to deal with their currency."[31] On July 21, 2005, responding to China's announcement that it was adopting a new exchange rate system, Treasury Secretary John Snow said that he welcomed the announcement but "we will monitor China's managed float as their exchange rate moves to alignment with underlying market conditions."[32] He agreed that the initial 2% change was small, but he said the important thing was China's willingness to change. "This is the start of a process," he said, "and the Chinese have indicated they want to get their currency based on markets rather than a peg."[33]

The United States has urged the IMF to press China to introduce market forces in its foreign exchange process more quickly. (This is discussed further in Part IV below.) In January 2006, at the World Economic Forum in Davos, Switzerland, Under Secretary Tim Adams told Bloomberg Television that China was not doing enough. "China needs to undertake serious reforms. They're on the road to reform but they need to move faster."[34]

He also told a panel at the Forum that the United States had never asked China to float its currency as it does not think the Chinese financial system could withstand it. Rather, he said, the United States had urged China to allow more flexibility in their exchange rate. "All we've asked them to do is what they've agreed to do and what they know is in their best interest to do," he said.[35]

The Omnibus Trade and Competitiveness Act of 1988 (sec. 3004) requires the Secretary of the Treasury to determine, in consultation with the International Monetary Fund, whether countries are manipulating their currency in order to gain unfair trade advantage. In May 2005, Treasury reported that China was not manipulating its currency.[36] Some observers said the Treasury Department was more critical of China in this report than earlier in part due to congressional pressure. "If current trends continue without substantial alteration [i.e., revaluation]," the report said, "China's policies will likely meet the statute's technical requirements" for designating China as a country which unfairly manipulates its currency value. Nevertheless, the report said that Chinese authorities had assured Treasury Secretary Snow that they were laying the groundwork for a future revaluation of the yuan. It was on this basis that the Department found that China was not manipulating its currency. Snow reportedly gave China six months to rectify the situation and he called for an immediate 10% revaluation.[37] No such change occurred.

In November 2005, Treasury reported that China's actions "are not sufficient and do not represent fulfillment of the Chinese authorities' [earlier] commitment."[38] It said, though, that Chinese authorities had pledged in October 2005 "that they would enhance the flexibility and strengthen the role of market forces in their managed floating exchange rate regime." It also said that "President Hu told President Bush that China would unswervingly press ahead with reform in its exchange rate mechanism." Therefore, by implication, they were not manipulating the yuan. The Chinese authorities should act, the report concluded, "by the time this report is next issued" (i.e., in six months.)

The Treasury Department's report did not discuss what impact China's new multi-currency exchange rate system might have on U.S. credit markets. Under the new system, China will not need to hold or acquire as many dollars as before in order to stabilize the price of its currency. To stabilize the value of the yuan compared to the currency basket, it may need to buy euros or yen or some other currency instead. If China is accumulating fewer dollars than before, it will have less need to purchase dollar-denominated assets. Many analysts believe that if China's future purchases of U.S. securities go down, the sellers of dollar-denominated notes and bonds may find that they need to offer higher interest rates than before in order to attract new buyers for the securities previously bought by China. This might lead to an increase in market interest rates in the United States.

Action by Congress

In late 2005, Congress passed legislation which urged the President to create a comprehensive plan to address diplomatic, military and economic issues relating to China.[39] In particular, it said the Administration should encourage China to revalue its currency further against the U.S. dollar by allowing the yuan to float against a trade-weighted basket of currencies. Congress is currently considering several bills which would require the

United States to limit trade with China if it does not revalue the yuan or direct the President to take the yuan-dollar exchange rate issue to the IMF or WTO for action.

Three bills are prominent among this legislation. In July 2005, the House of Representatives passed legislation (H.R. 3283) introduced by Representative Phil English which would make imports from non-market economies (such as China) subject to U.S. countervailing duty.[40] Exports from China which were found to be subsidized on account of exchange rate manipulation might be subject to these trade rules and monetary penalties could be assessed which would raise the price of those goods in U.S. markets. The bill also required the Treasury Department to define the term "currency manipulation" for the purpose of U.S. law and to report periodically on China's implementation of its new exchange rate regime.[41]

The House is also considering another bill (H.R. 1498), introduced by Representatives Tim Ryan and Duncan Hunter, that would make it clear under U.S. law that exchange rate manipulation by China would make goods imported from that country actionable to U.S. countervailing duties.[42] No action has been taken on the bill, though it currently has 158 co-sponsors.

The Senate is also considering legislation that would limit China's access to the U.S. market if it does not stop manipulating the value of its currency. Senators Charles Schumer and Lindsey Graham proposed on April 6, 2005, for example, that Congress enact a 27.5% tariff on all Chinese products entering the United States if China does not raise the value of its currency.[43] This is deemed to be the average degree of undervaluation identified by several studies. The Senate voted 67-33 for this proposal, as a rider on another bill, but it was later introduced as a separate bill (S. 295). Originally scheduled for consideration in mid-2005, action was postponed. The bill is expected to come up again for consideration by the Senate in sometime in 2006.

FIVE KEY QUESTIONS

Is the Yuan Undervalued? by How Much?

The IMF said in its 2004 evaluation of the Chinese economy that it was "difficult to find persuasive evidence that the renminbi [yuan] is substantially undervalued."[44] Since then, many economic studies have been published seeking to determine the yuan's "equilibrium" exchange rate. (This is the exchange rate that would prevail if the value of the yuan was not controlled and if the U.S. and Chinese economies were both at macroeconomic equilibrium.) The results of these studies differ widely. Consequently, there is sufficient research available to support any position about the value of the yuan that one might wish to take.

The IMF's China experts found in their 2005 evaluation that the yuan is undervalued and the rate of undervaluation is increasing. More flexibility is needed, they said, to avoid disruption of the domestic economy.[45] The difficulty, however, one expert told the author, is the lack of any reliable way of knowing how large the distortion may be or how its effects can be separated from the other factors (such as labor costs and productivity) which affect the international price of Chinese goods.

In a market economy, the exchange rate of a currency (vis-a-vis another currency) can be affected by many things. These including interest rates, trade relationships, institutional arrangements the international flow of money between currency markets, and interventions (purchases or sales of currency) by the central bank. Market forces will balance these factors and establish an exchange rate which is supposed to reflect the actual value of goods and services in one country compared to those in another country but sometimes — depending on other considerations affecting the economy of either country — it does not.

The task of assessing exchange rates is more difficult when market forces are constrained and currency values are set by official action. A simple method would have one look at the price of a single product in world markets, on the theory that properly functioning currency markets should adjust to equalize product costs. One example is the *Economist*'s well known "Big Mac Index," a light-hearted procedure which compares the cost of McDonald's hamburgers around the world.[46] By its calculation, based on the price of hamburgers sold in both markets, the yuan is 59% undervalued compared to the U.S. dollar. Most economists agree that this index provides only a general suggestion of the relative valuation of currencies.[47] The disparity in hamburger prices around the world can also be read as a comment on the valuation of the U.S. dollar. The *Economist* says that the index shows that the U.S. dollar is more overvalued now, compared to most other currencies, than at any time since measure was introduced 16 years ago.

A more substantive effort to calculate the equilibrium value requires construction of an econometric model for the countries whose currencies are being compared. Much statistical information is required as well as a clear concept of the way the institutions and sectors relate to each other. Often, information is not available and analysts have to substitute data based on their understanding as to how each economy works and what the correct number would be if it were available. [48]

In 2005, the Chinese Currency Coalition published a report citing eight reports or statements (in addition to the Big Mac Index) which said that, to varying degrees, the yuan was substantially undervalued.[49] Two of the sources dated from 1998 or 2000. The others dated from 2002 or 2003. These included (in addition to the hamburger index) a reference saying that the World Bank thought the yuan was 75% undervalued and other studies, statements or testimony to Congress saying the yuan was priced 10% to 40% below its "real" value.[50]

The IMF published a paper in late 2005 which compared eight major studies released in 2004 and 2005 that sought to calculate China's "real" exchange rate on the basis of macroeconomic and econometric analysis.[51] One scholar found, in two studies using 2003 data, that the yuan was either slightly undervalued or slightly overvalued that year. He found in a later study (using the next year's data) that the yuan was 5% overvalued in 2004. Another analyst found, using the same data, that the yuan was only slightly undervalued in 2004. By contrast, others scholars have found, using essentially the same statistics, that the yuan has been substantially undervalued in recent years. One team concluded, for example, that the yuan was pegged (in a study using 2002 data) at a rate that 18-to-49% and (in another study using 2003 data) 23% below its "real" value. Another researcher found, in a study using 2000 data, that the yuan was undervalued by 35% that year. Yet another scholar concluded, on the basis of 2004 data, that the official rate that year was 15-to-30% below its "real" market equilibrium value.

Meanwhile, Funke and Rahn, two scholars from Hamburg University in Germany, found "compelling evidence that the renminbi is not substantially undervalued."[52] They seem to have employed the same econometric equilibrium modeling techniques used by scholars cited in the recent IMF paper. The claims by some that China's currency is grossly undervalued are incorrect, they argue. Rather, they say, it seems in some circles to be "politically expedient to scapegoat the Chinese currency for economic difficulties elsewhere." Higgins and Humpage, two economists with the Federal Reserve Bank of Cleveland, report that it "is next to impossible"to determine the equilibrium exchange rate for developing countries through econometric modeling. [53] China is particularly difficult, they say, because institutions and patterns of economic activity are changing very rapidly.

Data on the Chinese economy are incomplete, uncertain or unreliable. In late December 2005, China announced that — when services previously omitted from official statistics were taken into account — its gross domestic product (GDP) was 17% larger than expected. This was like discovering a province the size of Turkey or Indonesia that was previously not counted in national statistics. The new data make the Chinese economy the sixth largest in the world in dollar terms. If it grows by 10% in 2006 and its currency appreciates by a like amount, China could surpass Germany, Britain and France to become the world's third largest economy.[54] All the previous macroeconomic ratios — investment to GDP, exports as a share of GDP, rate of growth, etc. — changed with the advent of the new data. None of the studies cited above used the new data. Thus, even if they are correct in their use of the old data, their calculations do not reflect this more recent data on the Chinese economy.

The variations in the conclusions of the 17 studies mentioned above may be due in large part to the way scholars define the relationships among the different segments of the Chinese economy and the different assumptions they use to fill in gaps when they lack adequate information. Without careful analysis of the methodology and assumptions used in each study, there is no way of knowing whether the results of any of these studies are more accurate than others.[55]

It appears that few of the participants in the debate about the value of China's currency have studied the methodologies or the assumptions of the various studies. Rather, it seems that advocates select the studies they quote more because they like their conclusions than because they believe they are the best research available. Few of the participants in the debate cite findings which support conclusions other than those they support or provide reasons why their preferred studies are superior on substantive grounds to others which disagree.

Is China Manipulating its Currency?

The IMF and Exchange Rate Policy. In the past thirty years, the role of the IMF in the international financial system has changed. Until the early 1970s, the IMF had a central role in determining world exchange rates. All currencies had a fixed value ("par value") compared to the U.S. dollar and the U.S. dollar was worth a specified amount of gold. If countries wanted to change their par value compared to the U.S. dollar, the IMF had to first approve. Since 1976, however, with passage of the Second Amendment to the IMF Articles of Agreement, each country is free to determine the exchange rate system it will use. Some countries have floated the value of their currency in world money markets, others have fixed the value of their currency to that of another major country, and others have pursued a mixed strategy.

IMF Surveillance. The IMF is no longer the arbiter of world exchange rates. Rather, in the modern world, it exercises surveillance over exchange rates in order to encourage and to help countries comply with the basic rules. Article IV of the IMF charter prohibits countries from manipulating their exchange rates in order to gain unfair trade advantage. It also says that "the Fund shall exercise firm surveillance over the exchange rate policies of members, and shall adopt specific principles for the guidance of all members with respect to those policies." Its current principles for surveillance were adopted by the IMF executive board in 1979 and have been revised periodically since.[56] The principles say that countries may peg the value of their currency to another currency but they cannot do this in ways which violate the requirements of Article IV. Basically, the pegged rate needs to reflect a country's underlying economic realities. These include, for example, changes in the volume and composition of its domestic output, in the size, composition and direction of its foreign trade, in its domestic rates of growth and national income, in the size of its reserves and in shifts in its domestic fiscal and monetary policies, relative rates of productivity and of change and technological advance.

Countries are allowed, under the guidelines, to use their exchange rates to promote growth and development. The IMF rules for surveillance say the Fund's appraisal of country policies "shall take into account the extent to which the policies of a member, including its exchange rate policies, serve the objectives of the continuing development of orderly underlying conditions that are necessary for financial stability, the promotion of sustainable economic growth, and reasonable levels of employment." However, countries are also required to "take into account in their intervention policies the interests of other members, including those of the countries in whose currencies they intervene." In other words, countries can use exchange rate policy to help sustain growth and employment in their domestic economy but they cannot use an unrealistic exchange rate to prevent balance of payments (BOP) adjustment or to gain unfair trade advantages. Adjustment includes such things as increased imports, capital inflows to fund BOP deficits or outflows to offset BOP surpluses, increased domestic interest rates or price levels, and the accumulation of excess reserves. If one country does not adjust its BOP imbalance, the burden of adjustment will be thrown upon its trading partners through monetary contraction, unemployment and the like.

China and Manipulation. The IMF has six criteria which might be used to identify situations where countries are manipulating their currencies in order to gain unfair trade advantage. Any one of the criteria would be sufficient to note the likely presence of manipulation. It appears that China's foreign exchange practices are congruent with at least four of the IMF criteria.[57]

Persistent Intervention. The IMF says (its criterion number 1) that "protracted large-scale intervention in one direction in the exchange market" is one indication that a country may be manipulating the value of its currency. Countries may intervene in foreign exchange markets to counter short-term disorderly conditions that cause disruptive short-term movements in the exchange value of their currencies. However, the IMF guidelines say that persistent one-way intervention"might indicate the need for discussion with a member."[58]

If China's currency were properly priced and the goal were exchange rate stability, the central bank would intervene in the market in both directions, buying and selling yuan in order to dampen the effect of temporary shocks and to spread the effects of change over a longer period of time. Instead, China routinely sells yuan in order to keep the market price from rising. It rarely buys yuan to keep the market price from sinking too low. This would seem to be the kind of "protracted large-scale intervention in one direction" which the IMF specified in its first operational definition of manipulation.

An Unchanging Peg. The IMF's second criterion which indicates that a country might be manipulating its currency is "behavior of the exchange rate that appears to be unrelated to underlying economic and financial conditions including factors affecting competitiveness and long-term capital movements." Countries may peg the value of their currency to another currency but the pegged rate needs to reflect the country's economic realities. These include, for example, changes in the volume and composition of its domestic output, in the size, composition and direction of its foreign trade, in its domestic rates of growth and national income, in the size of its reserves and in shifts in its domestic fiscal and monetary policies, relative rates of productivity and of change and technological advance.

The yuan-dollar exchange rate was largely unchanged from1994 to 2005. Since reforms were announced in mid-2005 it has changed very little. Some might argue that the fact that China held its exchange rate constant during this period is evidence that China was not manipulating the yuan through fine-tuning of its valuation. However, manipulation can be as much a *lack* of change as an *act* of change.[59]

Whether an unchanging exchange rated is a violation of Article IV depends on the way the country holds the rate constant. China did not have to micro-manage the daily rate for its currency in order to maximize its export opportunities. They merely sold yuan whenever the yuan-dollar exchange rate increased beyond the level the central bank desired. Chinese authorities used domestic monetary policy and other domestic economic practices to offset the effects of the fixed yuan-dollar rate.

Economic conditions have changed markedly in China since 1994. Production and consumption patterns changed. Import and export patterns changed. The relative value of goods and services and the relative value of labor, capital and other factors of production changed. The international value of China's currency should have changed as well to reflect these changes. Among other things, this would have produced price signals that could have changed consumption and production patterns, promoted efficient and effective utilization of resources, and improved the Chinese people's standard of living and level of real income. The behavior of the yuan-dollar exchange rate after 1994 "appears to be unrelated to underlying economic and financial conditions" and is therefore consistent with the IMF's second criterion for identifying currency manipulation.

Prolonged Foreign Lending. The IMF's fourth criterion says that "excessive and prolonged short-term official or quasi-official lending for balance of payments purposes" can be evidence that currency manipulation is taking place. Prolonged borrowing for the same purpose is also evidence of manipulation.

Since 1994, China's foreign exchange reserves have grown sixteen-fold, from $53 billion to $819 billion. Some of the funds in China's foreign exchange reserves are equity investments. Most, however, are loans to foreign governments or private borrowers. For example, China's investment in U.S. Government debt has more than tripled in the past five years, from $71 billion in 2000 to $242 billion in 2005. By definition, these are loans to the U.S. Government and they are short-term, in the sense that they can be liquidated at any time through sales in security markets. They help the United States cover its balance of payments (current account) deficit and they help China adjust its balance of payments in a way which does not require it to spend its international income on purchases of goods and services from abroad. At least on the part of China, this appears to be the kind of behavior "to prevent effective balance of payments adjustment" (in the words of Article IV) that meets the IMF's fourth test for currency manipulation.

Influence on Capital Movements. The IMF's fifth criterion says that a conversation with a country might be in order if it evidences "the pursuit, for balance of payments purposes, of monetary and other domestic policies that provide abnormal encouragement or discouragement to capital flows." Many observers say that the growing size of China's reserves shows that its government is promoting an abnormal outflow of capital for BOP purposes.

The Chinese government purchases large amounts of foreign exchange in order to maintain the price of its currency. Thus, foreign money is less available to Chinese citizens and firms than it might be otherwise. Consequently, instead of being cleared on the current account through imports and other current activity, China's balance of payments is cleared through the capital account by large additions to China's foreign exchange reserves.

Many analysts agree that China's reserves are larger than its normal trade or financial needs would require. They are larger, for example, than any need China is likely to face if its international income suddenly declined — as a result, for instance, of an economic shock originating elsewhere in the world economy — and it needed money for a while to pay for imports or to service debt. In this light, many would argue with reference to the IMF criterion noted above, that continued expansion of China's foreign exchange reserves is not just an encouragement for the outward flow of capital but an encouragement for "abnormal" flows as well.

Some would argue in addition that the continued growth of China's reserves is inconsistent with provisions of the IMF charter. Article IV also stipulates that all members shall seek to promote stability by fostering orderly underlying economic and financial conditions and a monetary system that does not tend to produce erratic disruptions." Every dollar that China adds to its reserves is a dollar that some other country adds to its foreign debt. Arguably, the accumulation of large reserves and large debts does not enhance the stability of the world financial and trading system. Countries with large foreign exchange reserves do not import as much as they could and debtor countries have difficulty retiring their foreign obligations by trade. In that sense, high reserves are not a formal trade barrier but they have the same effect. They hamper "the expansion and balanced growth of international trade" (one of the purposes, stated in its Articles of Agreement, for which the IMF was created.) China is not the only country accumulating large reserves but many would argue that its practices are a source of concern.

China's View. Chinese officials say they are not seeking unfair trade advantage. They only want exchange rate stability to protect their economy from destabilizing change. The result, however, is the same. Chinese officials say that, whatever the technicalities might be, the economic benefits of stability are important and are shared by many countries. Moreover, they could argue, their efforts to influence exchange rates through intervention in currency markets differ little in their effect from similar action which countries with floating exchange rates take to influence their currencies' exchange rates — changes in interest rates and other policies, for example. Furthermore, they might say, Japan and other Asian countries also buy dollars in order to keep down the value of their currencies and to stimulate their exports.

Arguably, they would argue, it is unfair to single out China in this regard when others do the same thing and their trade impact on the U.S. economy is at least as great as that of China.[60]

HOW FAST SHOULD CHINA REVALUE?

If China can continue to contain the inflationary pressures caused by rapid growth in its economy and its foreign exchange reserves, it can probably delay for some time any need for a major change in the dollar value of its currency. Unlike countries with overvalued currencies, it will not run out of foreign exchange if it postpones the decision. Rather, its foreign exchange reserves will grow.

China could increase the value of the yuan overnight to a much higher level if it wished to do so. However, Chinese officials are concerned that too-fast and too-steep an increase could hurt the growth rate, employment rate, and reform prospects of the Chinese economy. Chinese officials say they want to shift away from export led growth towards an economic program focused more on growth in the internal economy. However, they do not want to slow down the export sector until their internal economy is able to provide the growth they need to continue the transformation process now underway. These considerations seem to suggest that revaluation should take place gradually. However, if speculative capital flows are a problem, as discussed below, they may want to delay the process considerably.

Most experts agree that China's current situation is not sustainable and they cannot postpone revaluation of the yuan indefinitely. If nothing is done to slow the growth of China's foreign exchange reserves, for instance, inflation may eventually push up domestic prices in China and raise its export prices. Experts differ, though, as to how quickly China should move towards a market-based exchange system. The IMF says a gradual approach is needed. In July 2005, the IMF staff proposed that China adopt a phased approach in moving towards full exchange rate flexibility.[61] More recently, the director of the IMF's research department urged a deliberate pace.[62] Experience has shown, he said, that emerging markets do not handle large, rapid exchange rate movements well. In China, he suggested, rapid change might disrupt or bankrupt major segments of the economy — particularly the banking system — and make reform a long, drawn-out and painful process.

Other experts believe that policy reform must occur more quickly. Some say that China's undervalued currency is hurting other countries and fairness requires rapid action to remedy the situation. Some suggest that China risks a financial crisis if it does not revalue soon.[63] One says that rapid revaluation is needed because China's emphasis on export-led growth makes it vulnerable to any slowdown in global demand.[64] Otherwise, they say, China risks being another "Asian miracle" country, like those that went bust during the Asian financial crisis in the 1990s.

Many also believe quick action is needed because the current economic relationship between the United States and China is unstable and harbors serious risk. Roubini and Setser argue, for instance, that change is inevitable and the only question is how it will take place.[65] A smooth landing is possible, they say, if Chinese officials lessen China's emphasis on exports and the accumulation of reserves and U.S. policy makers reduce their country's dependence on foreign loans and capital. Otherwise, they believe, some unforseen event may trigger a crisis which could have serious negative consequences for both countries.

IS CHINA HIDING ITS REAL TRADE SURPLUS?

Some people argue that China's trade surplus is many times larger than the amount which China publishes in its official statistics. The China Currency Coalition says, for instance, that China's trade balance was nearly six times larger in 2003 than its official statistics suggest.[66] IMF data show that in 2004 the 156 countries it categorized as "world" had a combined trade deficit with China of $267 billion, roughly six and one-half times more than trade surplus of $41 billion that China reported that year.[67] If China's trade income were the larger of these figures, this would be strong evidence the yuan is undervalued.

In theory, the net trade figures reported by exporter and importer countries should match. In practice, the data are often inconsistent. There is strong reason to believe that methodological reasons account for much of the discrepancy in data. Perhaps countries keep better count of their imports than their exports. Perhaps the figures are confused and intermingled when products are imported and re-exported or when inputs from several sources are channeled through a final exporter countries.

The IMF's *Direction of Trade Statistics* (DOTS) shows, in any case, that —when the exports of all countries to every country are subtracted from the imports every country receives from all countries, the world had a $269 billion trade deficit with itself in 2004.[68] Other countries show similar disparities between the trade balances they report and those reported by their trade partners.[69] In 2005, the IMF executive board noted weaknesses in China's BOP statistics in its annual Article IV review in 2005 and it urged the Chinese authorities to take advantage of Fund's technical assistance to help improve them.[70]

The China Currency Coalition says, however, that China is "hiding the ball" by deliberately reporting incorrect trade statistics. It believes the figure reported by importer countries more accurately reflects China's net income from trade. This is further evidence, the Coalition says, that the yuan is seriously overvalued.

If this is correct, China must be receiving over $200 billion more each year from trade income than it reports. In that case, the money must be somewhere. China could not have spent this money on imports, as it would have then shown up in the trade statistics of the exporter countries. It seems unlikely that Chinese exporters would have brought this additional foreign currency back into China. If they had, the People's Bank of China would have had to spend three times more yuan than the amount officially announced to keep the yuan at the pegged rate. The inflationary impact of these additional yuan would be substantial and would have manifested itself through rapidly increasing domestic price levels.

Alternatively, the presumed $200 billion in extra annual revenue might have been held abroad. This would require the cooperation of Chinese officials, since it would mean that roughly 80% of China's trade income each year does not come back to China. It seems unlikely that China has been giving the money away, since this would make it the world's largest foreign aid donor (ten times the size of the United States) and international effects of its generosity would be evident. Possibly, if the money exists and is not the product of a methodological flaw, the government of China might have accumulated it annually into secret foreign exchange reserves. This would mean, again if the money exists, that China has perhaps $1 trillion in clandestine funds invested in other countries (over and above its announced official reserves.) Even if China were only using this money to acquire revenue, not influence, it would be difficult to hide. If the assets were registered as Chinese at the time of purchase, for instance, they would likely show up in host country statistics.

As another possibility, if the government of China does not control the money, then it might be held by Chinese citizens and companies. In any other country, the fact that people prefer to hold foreign currencies rather than their own currency might be taken as evidence of capital flight. It might suggest that people "in the know" believe the yuan is overpriced and likely to crash. Keeping their assets in foreign currencies would be a way of protecting themselves against that eventuality. For China, however, the general view is one suggesting that the yuan will be going *up* in value and foreign currencies will go *down* in value compared to it. It seems unlikely that Chinese insiders would see the situation so differently from the common view or that they would have been able to hold a secret this big for so long.

The above scenarios are not be impossible, but they seem unlikely. It seems more likely that the $200 billion difference in the trade data reported by China and its trade partners is not real money. Rather, it is probably the result of methodological and procedural error. China's real export figures may be higher or its trading partners' import figures may be lower than the reported amounts. We do not know. Caution in the use of published data would seem appropriate. It is probably not a good idea, though, to ignore or discard the existing body of world trade and finance statistics just because some of the data do not match. The IMF and its member countries might scrutinize their procedures to see whether errors and inaccuracies of this sort can be reduced or eliminated over time.

WOULD REVALUATION HELP THE U.S. ECONOMY?

A Symbiotic Relationship

The dollar-yuan exchange rate is not determined in a vacuum. Rather, the relationship between the two currencies reflects the broader relationship between the countries which issue them. Even if they are chosen by official action, exchange rates are the consequence of each country's economic priorities and the way those priorities interact. The United States needs to import capital from abroad to finance its present level of economic activity without incurring higher interest rates. Consequently, the international value of the dollar must be relatively high in order to encourage the inflow of capital. China needs to encourage exports in order to stimulate economic growth and facilitate economic reform. Therefore, the value of the yuan must be low enough to encourage export growth. So long as these are the main issues on each country's economic agenda, major changes in yuan-dollar exchange rate or the U.S. trade deficit are unlikely.

The U.S. Imports Capital

The United States does not save enough domestically to finance simultaneously its preferred levels of consumption and investment and to cover the Federal budget deficit. By contrast, other countries (including several in Asia) save more than their economies can effectively absorb. The United States needs more capital than it can generate on its own to sustain the U.S. economy and foreigners need safe and profitable ways to invest their surplus funds. This generates a continual inflow of foreign funds into the United States. The inflow of funds, in turn, helps generate more demand for imported goods. The U.S. current account deficit equals about 6% of GDP and requires the United States to import more than $2 billion daily from abroad.[71]

This capital inflow pushes up the exchange value of the dollar, which lowers the relative price of imports and generates a corresponding inflow of foreign goods. It is a basic principle of economics that countries which are net borrowers of money from the world must be net importers of goods and services as well.[72] If the value of the yuan increased, the volume of Chinese exports and Chinese capital flows to the United States would likely decrease.[73] In the short run, U.S. producers would probably take over a share of the market previously supplied by Chinese goods, though consumers would likely have to pay more for those goods than they did for Chinese imports. Profits and employments in those firms would likely increase. If China's trade balance declined, under this scenario, its rate of investment in the United States would also likely decline. In that case, many economists believe, U.S. interest rates would probably increase. This would likely have a negative impact, they expect, on the housing market and (with interest taking a larger share of household income) on consumer purchases.

Over the longer run, foreign production is likely to shift from China to other low-cost countries. As their exports to the United States increase, producers in these other countries would likely recover much of the market previously supplied by the Chinese. On the other hand, higher interest rates in the United States might stimulate an inflow of capital from other foreign sources. One can only speculate whether interest rates would eventually decline to their former level and what the impact these changes would have on the U.S. economy.

China Wants Growth

China, for its part, also has priorities other than an accurate valuation of the yuan. Chinese officials believe they need to pursue a policy of export-led growth. They believe their domestic economy is otherwise too inefficient to generate the levels of employment and resources needed for economic reform and conversion of the economy to a market-based system rather than one based on state-ownership and control. They worry that the domestic economy cannot otherwise absorb the unemployment being generated by reform in the rural sector and state-owned enterprises. They also worry that their banking system would be unable to allocate capital effectively or to cope with the speculative pressure that might follow the introduction of a more flexible exchange rate system and more open capital markets.

China's economy has been growing at a rate of about 9% annually for the past decade. Most experts believe this rate cannot be sustained indefinitely, given both the present levels of productivity and the strain and inflationary pressure such growth places on the economy. China needs to slow down its growth rate in order to consolidate recent gains and to correct imbalances. They say that raising the value of the yuan would help. It would slow the growth in reserves, lower inflationary pressures, reduce the cost of imports, raise per capita income, reduce distortions and encourage the flow of resources from the export sectors to the domestic economy. However, Chinese officials are reluctant to shift from a policy of export-led growth to one based more on internal growth until they believe their domestic economy is more efficient and productive and economic reform has further progressed.

According to the IMF, most Chinese officials believe they eventually need to liberalize the yuan and shift more to a policy of domestic led growth.[74] Senior Chinese officials told the press in December 2005 that the value of the yuan would be increasingly influenced by the market and the trend is for China's currency to appreciate over time.[75] Yu Yongding, a member of the central bank's policy committee, said at the time that there is a risk that inflation could be ignited if the exchange rate is not allowed to appreciate. He also said that China's foreign exchange reserves had been growing too fast.

Many in the Chinese leadership believe their country is not yet ready for substantial changes in the value of the yuan. In any case, they say, efforts to resolve the imbalances in the world economy will require concerted action by many nations and China should not be expected to solve them alone.[76]

THREE DILEMMAS FOR CHINA

Intervention and Reserves

The People's Bank of China intervenes in the market to buy foreign exchange and sell yuan in order to hold the value of its currency at a relatively constant level. As a result, China has accumulated foreign exchange reserves which now total more than $819 billion. At the present rate of growth, its reserves will surpass those of Japan and total $1 trillion by the end of 2006.[77] If the bank did not sell yuan, the value of China's currency would rise and its volume of exports would fall. Many of China's export industries reportedly operate on very slim profit margins and many might go bankrupt if the yuan rose substantially in price.[78]

Much attention has been paid to the size of China foreign exchange reserves. Many see them as a potential financial threat to other countries. Many believe the growth in China's reserves proves that its currency is undervalued and manipulated.

However, the growth in China's reserves causes problems as well. For one thing, it puts great pressure on China's monetary system. China cannot have an independent monetary policy, since its domestic money supply grows at the size of its foreign reserves expands. For every dollar bought by the central bank to maintain the peg, the People's Bank of China creates new 8 yuan which it gives to the seller. The PBC has reportedly intervened in the currency market at a rate equal to about 12% of China's GDP.[79] The IMF says that only about half the liquidity caused by the increase in reserves has been sterilized (that is, removed from circulation through sales of government bonds.)[80] Thus, the central bank has had to hold down the growth of credit and lending by state banks in order to keep this excess liquidity from causing inflation. The June 2005 IMF Article IV staff report urged China to wring more excess liquidity from the system and to tighten monetary policy still further.

The growth in China's reserves also creates another problem. Roughly 70% of its reserves are held in dollars or dollar-denominated securities. If the yuan should go up in value compared to the dollar, the value of China's reserves will go down and China would lose a great deal of money.[81] The State Agency for Foreign Exchange announced in mid-January 2006 that it would be "actively exploring more efficient use of our FX [foreign exchange] reserve assets" and "widening the foreign exchange reserves scope." It said it wanted to "optimize the currency and asset structure" of China's reserves and to "actively boost investment returns."[82] Some market analysts thought this meant that China intended to sell some of its dollar-denominated assets.[83] Their alarm abated, however, when it became clear that China simply planned to invest a smaller portion of its new reserves in dollars and more in the currencies of other trading partners.

WHERE'S THE MONEY COMING FROM?

Hot Money or Trade?

China's foreign exchange reserves are growing because the country's central bank is buying dollars and other foreign currencies in order to stabilize the market price of the yuan. The question is where the foreign currency is coming from. Many argue that the growth in China's reserves is the result of its trade policies as well as the inflow of foreign investment. Recent research suggests, however, that speculative inflows ("hot money") may be responsible for over three-quarters of the net increase in China's foreign exchange reserves since 1998.

Table 1. Composition of China's Buildup in Foreign Exchange Reserves (billions of U.S. dollars)

	(1) Average 1998-2000	(2) Average 2001-2004	(3) Amount of Change
Foreign reserve increase [a]	8.5	122.8	114.3
Current Account balance	23.7	42.2	18.5
Capital Account Balance	0.3	69.3	69.0
Of which FDI [b] net	*38.5*	*46.6*	*8.1*
Of which other	*-38.2*	*22.7*	*60.9*
Errors and Omissions	-15.4	11.4	26.8
Non-FDI* capital account balance [c]	*-53.6*	*34.1*	*87.7*

Source: Prasad and Wei.

a. Foreign reserve increase is the sum of the current account and capital account balances plus errors and omissions.

b. FDI is Foreign Direct Investment.

c. Includes errors and omissions.

Accounting the BOP

Table 1 shows (based on IMF data) the size and amount of change which took place in China's foreign exchange reserves and balance of payments (BOP) during the period 1998 to 2004. Foreign exchange reserves and alternative BOP figures have been discussed above. The balance of payments is a comprehensive picture of a country's international financial and commercial transactions. It has three parts: the current account balance, the capital account balance and the total for errors and omissions. The current account balance is the net sum of a country's exports and imports of goods and services plus its net income from foreign investment. The capital account balance is the net sum of all the monetary flows to or from a country — net foreign investments, loans made or received, transfers by individuals (remittances from migrant workers, for example) and other transactions needed to finance activity in the current account.

Conceptually, the current account and capital account balances should cancel each other out, one being positive and the other negative. Imports which are not paid for with current revenue, for example, would have to be financed directly or indirectly by capital from abroad. In fact, however, some financial and commercial transactions are not recorded and the current account or capital account is often larger than the other. To make the two parts of the BOP match, economists add a third figure, called "errors and omissions" (EandO), which acknowledges that for unexplained reasons more money is in one account or the other. This may reflect income from illegal trade, mis-measurement, or undisclosed movement of money by individuals ("capital flight") seeking to protect their assets from an expected change in the exchange rates or by speculators hoping to profit from that change.

Analyzing China's BOP

Table 1 breaks China's balance of payments figures into these three components. It also provides separate figures, in the capital account, for foreign direct investment. Prasad and Wei, the authors of the table, identified the annual changes in China's foreign exchange reserves and the amounts recorded for each element of China's balance of payments and they present the average annual amounts for each item for the first three and the last four years of the 1998 to 2004 period.[84] From that data, they derive the amount of change which occurred in each instance between the first and the last halves of that seven-year period.

On first inspection, looking only at the middle column, it seems that most of the growth in China's reserves was due to trade and investment. Between 2001 and 2004, Prasad and Wei note, China's net annual current account balance was $42.2 billion while the net inflow from FDI was $46.6 billion.[85] It appears, therefore, that the $88.8 billion from these two sources accounted for most of the $128 billion average annual increase in China's foreign exchange reserves during that period.

Prasad and Wei find, however, that other factors — particularly the inflow of "hot money" were more important. As *Table 1* also shows, comparing the first and second columns, that the average annual level of China's foreign exchange reserves grew by $8.5 billion from 1998 to 2000 and by $122.8 billion from 2001 to 2004. In column 3, Prasad and Wei found that the annual change in China's trade receipts ($18.5 billion) and FDI ($8.1 billion), shown in column three, were not sufficient to account for the average $114.3 billion in China's reserves. On the other hand, the swing in flows from non-FDI investment and EandO were substantial.

Between 1998 and 2000, they observe, capital flowed out of China openly (non-FDI) or covertly (EandO.) They speculate that initially Chinese firms and families moved money abroad to take advantage of favorable investment and exchange rate opportunities. After 2001, however, they suggest, Chinese firms and families and foreign speculators began moving money back into China in hopes of profiting from the expected increase in the value of the yuan. They observe that, as *Table 1* indicates, the net flow of funds from non-FDI investment and EandO between the two periods amounted to an average $87.7 billion a year, nearly 77% of total change in China's foreign exchange reserves during the 1998-2004 period.

Policy Implications

The policy prescriptions are different, depending on the source, if one wants to reduce the inflow of foreign currencies and to lessen the central bank's incentive to sell yuan in foreign exchange markets. If trade-related factors are the major reason why foreign exchange is flowing to China, then changes in the country's trade policies and exchange rate would help diminish the flow. China's government would need to take steps, in this scenario, to shift resources and employment from the export sector to the domestic economy.

On the other hand, if "hot money" is responsible for the buildup in reserves, then a gradual appreciation in the value of the yuan might encourage further inflows of speculative funds. In that case, the central bank might cool the inflow of "hot money" by holding the value of the yuan constant for a sustained period of time.

The *Economist* reported in late January 2006 that the delay and uncertainty of the new Chinese exchange rate system may have had this effect.[86] The flow of portfolio capital investment, one form of "hot money," declined to about $1 billion a month in late 2005, it reported, from the average level of $8 billion a month seen from late 2003 through mid-2005. It appears, the *Economist* suggests, that "the speculators who have been furiously pumping money into China for the past three years have at last given up and gone home." The magazine predicts that China's trade surplus may also start to fall and import growth may revive.

If the data for the last part of 2005 are correct and if the *Economist*'s predictions are right — and it is much too soon to know whether these are so — then the People's Bank of China may have an easier time managing monetary policy in the future. There would be less need, for example, for it to print yuan in order to keep down the value of the yuan by buying up the inflow of dollars. This would make it easier, if the PBC wishes to do so, for the central bank to relax its control and to allow market forces more influence on the yuan-dollar exchange rate.

WOULD REVALUATION HURT CHINA'S BANKS?

Many believe China needs to reform its financial system before the yuan can rise appreciably in value. If revaluation occurs first, they say, the banking system may not be able to cope and this might have negative effects on economic growth. Others believe, however, that — while more reform is needed — China's banking system should be able to accommodate more flexibility in the value of the yuan. Nevertheless, there is serious worry on the part of many that a floating exchange rate system could lead to destabilizing capital outflows.[87]

The IMF says that major steps have been taken to restructure the banking system (even though further action is required) and the condition of the banking system is no longer an obstacle to exchange rate reform. As a result of recapitalization, sales of nonperforming loans, and other reform efforts, the IMF staff reported, the capital strength, asset quality and operating results for China's banks have significantly improved. In the old days, state banks made loans to state industry with little expectation those loans would be repaid. Thus the savings of Chinese individuals were sunk into subsidizing these money-losing firms.

Most of these "legacy" loans have been transferred to four government-owned asset management corporations (AMCs), so the government budget rather than the banking system will bear the cost of those bad loans. Consequently, the IMF reports, bad loan ratios for the major commercial banks (the four largest state banks and 14 joint stock commercial banks) have fallen from about 24% of loans in 2002 to about 13% in September 2005.[88] These institutions account for about three-quarters of total bank assets. They say that efforts to tighten the banks' balance sheets and to strengthen their internal controls and risk management procedures are still needed.

The IMF does not report figures for the ratio of bad loans (non-performing loans) in the banking system as a whole because the procedures for reporting bad loans by small banks are different from those for large banks. Two IMF economists, Prasad and Wei, reported in their 2005 article that non-performing loans in the banking system amounted to 30% of GDP in 2003.[89] IMF staff indicates that this larger figure calculates the bad loan ratio for smaller banks in the same way that bad loans are calculated for the larger banks. Prasad and Wei suggest that a major share of China's foreign exchange reserves may need to clear up the accumulated bad debt.

Setser asserts that conditions in the Chinese banking system are grim and the costs of reform will be great.[90] He says the banking system is not ready yet for a more flexible currency. Bad debt in the banking system is equivalent to 20% or 30% of GDP, he says. Officials estimates reported that 40% of all loans in 2002 were non-performing, he indicates, and "legacy" bad loans (debt owed by state firms) totaled $400 billion. Other estimates put the figure at $650 billion, he says, or about 50% of China's 2002 GDP. The recent boom in bank lending may have reduced the level to 25% or so, he says. However, he suggests, the total volume of bad debt may be higher once the bad loans made since 2002 are included in the total.

Setser says that many analysts believe that the government will need to buy out the bad "legacy"debt if it wants to improve the soundness of the banking system. The IMF's statement (see above) that some bad loans were transferred out of the banking system seems to confirm this view. Setser says the government will also need to provide large amounts of money to stabilize its undercapitalized state banks. Some estimates report, he says, that the cost of cleaning up the financial system could equal 20% of national GDP (about $340 billion of China's 2004 GDP) and nearly all of it will be borne by the national government. This could push the national debt-to-GDP ratio, he says, from 33% in 2004 to perhaps 50% overall.

IMF experts say that China does not need to resolve the problem of bad debt in its banking system before its currency can be liberalized. They argue that — so long as capital controls continue — the yuan-dollar exchange rate could be more flexible without harming the Chinese banks. The Chinese banks know how to trade currencies and manage their foreign exchange exposure, the IMF staff reports. They already do this in their worldwide operations. Some economists believe that China cannot have a flexible currency until it ends capital controls.[91] IMF experts argue, however, that China's banks cannot handle full liberalization of the capital account at this juncture. If capital controls were removed, they assert, a substantial outflow of capital from the banks would likely occur and this would be very destabilizing.[92]

OPTIONS FOR THE UNITED STATES

There are several ways the United States might encourage China to move more quickly towards increasing the value of the yuan. These options or policy tools are not mutually exclusive, but it might be difficult or awkward for the United States to pursue some of them simultaneously. [93]

First, the U.S. Government might continue pressing China publicly for additional changes in its foreign exchange system in order to make the international value of the yuan better reflect market conditions and economic realities. This assumes either that China is reluctant to change or that reformers in China will be helped by external stimulus. Second, the U.S. Government might stop pressing China publicly for change. This option is predicated on the expectation that reformers will be able to move China more rapidly towards currency liberalization if China is not pressured from abroad.

Third. the United States could enact legislation restricting Chinese exports to the United States if the value of the yuan is not increased. This assumes that China will change its exchange rate policies only if forced to do so. Fourth, the U.S. Government might refer the question to the IMF, asking the international agency to determine whether China has been manipulating its currency in violation of IMF rules. This assumes that technical findings and persuasion by the IMF and its major member countries may have effect. Fifth, the U.S. Government might refer the issue to the World Trade Organization (WTO), alleging that the United States has been injured by unfair trade practices linked to the undervaluation of China's currency. If the WTO found that the U.S. petition had merit, it could authorize trade remedies to correct the allege abuse. This assumes that exchange rate issues and questions of general system-wide subsidy will fall within the purview of the WTO rules.

CONTINUE PUBLIC PRESSURE

Continued public pressure is one method the United States might use to encourage China to adopt further reforms in its foreign exchange procedures. This might include official findings by the Treasury Department that China is a manipulator or strong exhortations by high-level U.S. officials. Among other things, U.S. officials might press Chinese officials to provide them more information as to the ways they intend to link reform of their domestic economy to reform in their exchange rate regime and the criteria they might use for discerning progress.

In evaluating this option, it would be helpful to know whether Chinese officials really intend to move towards a market-based valuation of the yuan or whether they intend to drag the process out as long as possible. If China adopted the reforms announced to date mainly in response to foreign pressure, then it is possible that further pressure might persuade them to go faster. However, if Chinese officials adopted these reforms because they believe that market-based reform is in China's best interests, foreign pressure may complicate this process. China has a long tradition of not giving in to foreign pressure. Foreign pressure might strengthen the hand of the reformers, but it might also stiffen resistence by the opponents of reform and make it harder for the reformers to achieve their ends.

It also might be helpful if U.S. officials and legislators had more information about China's internal decision making process. How strong are the reformers? What key choices do Chinese officials believe they face as regards the economy and value of the yuan? How do they think China and other countries can best determine what the true international value of the yuan might be? What criteria do they believe are relevant for determining currency value and their timetable for change?

Given their most recent statements, other G-7 countries will likely support the United States if it continues to press China for more rapid action. However, they may also back away and leave the United States on its own if they believe U.S. efforts are potentially counterproductive.

PURSUE A POLICY OF RESTRAINT

Instead of pressing China publicly for reform, the United States might decide on a policy of restraint. This is not an option in favor of the status quo. Rather, it accepts the premise that Chinese officials want to proceed with their reform program as rapidly as economic conditions and the policy consensus in China permits. This option assumes that overt foreign pressure may be counterproductive if it slows the process and strengthens the hand of those in China who oppose reform. Arguably, the Treasury Department has shown restraint of this sort when it said, in its recent reports, that China was not manipulating the value of its currency.

Some might argued that the United States should view the trade and currency dispute within the context of its overall relationship with China. While economic issues are important, this view would suggest, it is also important not to raise tensions to the point where China becomes reluctant to cooperate with the United States on other issues, such as North Korea's policies on nuclear weapons. Pressing the yuan-dollar exchange rate issue to the exclusion of other important U.S. interests might be seen, from this perspective, as counterproductive. Others might respond, however, that China will cooperate with the United States in other areas when it believes that this serves its interests.

China may have strong reasons for wanting change in its foreign exchange system. As noted before, China faces the prospect of serious inflation if it does not slow or stop the growth in its foreign exchange reserves. An increase in the value of its currency would be a key way of accomplishing that goal.

Ironically, some kind of external encouragement may still be needed to help China accomplish its plans. Even if Chinese authorities want to move forward with their reform program, they may need some external pressure — if only in the form of agreed deadlines and benchmarks — to help them overcome inertia when they encounter difficult choices as they put their currency reform policies into effect.

RESTRICT EXPORTS TO THE UNITED STATES

Instead of exerting public and mostly verbal pressure, the United States could adopt legislation restricting China's access to the U.S. market until it raises the value of its currency. There are several ways this could be done. The English bill (H.R. 3282), Ryan-Hunter bill (H.R. 1498) and Schumer/Graham bill (S. 295), all both mentioned above, would have this effect. By raising the U.S. price of Chinese imports, they would presumably reduce the flow of Chinese exports to the United States, raise the prices paid by U.S. consumers (perhaps helping some U.S. producers) and stimulate the growth of export industries in other countries that would take China's place.

Similar effects would likely occur if the U.S. Government invoked the provisions of Section 301, authorizing the U.S. Trade Representative to respond to unreasonable or discriminatory practices that burden or restrict U.S. commerce. [94] Likewise, if the Treasury Department found in its semi-annual report that China was manipulating the value of its currency to the detriment of the United States, consultations with China and trade actions would also be required. Under the Section 301 mechanism, the United States could impose trade sanctions against Chinese goods if China does not change its trade or foreign exchange policies. The United States could also use other U.S. trade laws to impose special "safeguard" restrictions on Chinese goods if the growth in Chinese imports is found to have caused (or threatens to cause) market disruption to U.S. domestic produce.[95] Measures of this sort are allowable under WTO rules on a temporary or limited basis but it is less clear that they may be used across the board or for longer periods.

It is not clear how much the price of Chinese goods would need to increase, or the volume of Chinese exports to the United States would decrease, though, if the value of the yuan increased. Components purchased from other countries account for a major share of the value of exports bearing the label "Made in China." The cost of Malaysian or Thai inputs would not change for the producer in China if the value of the yuan increased. The price of the final product would only need to increase by an amount sufficient to recover the higher cost of the producer's that were denominated in yuan. Depending on the products and methods of production, it is possible that the overall increase in product costs would be modest and the volume of Chinese exports to the United States would be large even after the value of the yuan increased.

It is uncertain what the Chinese authorities and Chinese firms would do if faced with restrictive import legislation of this sort. They might cut prices and trim profits in order to keep unchanged their share of U.S. markets. They might retaliate against U.S. exports, setting off a trade war between the United States and China. They might also ask the WTO for authority to levy trade sanctions, on grounds that the United States was not complying with the WTO rules on international trade. Alternatively, they might raise the value of the yuan in hopes that this will eliminate the new U.S. tariffs on their goods.

The WTO trade rules allow countries to levy countervailing duties to offset any subsidies foreign exporters might receive from their home governments. WTO rules do not allow countries to impose tariffs or restrictions merely for the purpose of excluding foreign goods. If the United States hopes to persuade other countries that its special levies on Chinese imports are fair and compensatory, it will likely need to show that the size of the levies match the degree of subsidy which Chinese producers receive through the undervalued yuan. It might be helpful in this regard if there were more agreement among scholars and the affected countries as to whether and by how much China's currency is undervalued.

If the United States put special levies on Chinese goods, China might ask the WTO to rule that the United States acted in a manner inconsistent with its obligations.[96] The countervailing duties and anti-dumping penalties allowed under WTO rules are usually applied to specific goods rather than to all exports coming from a particular country. Exchange rate manipulation might be seen as a type of general across-the-board subsidy for a country's exports. Nevertheless, there is little precedent (but see below) at the WTO for considering exchange rates from this perspective. The WTO may be concerned that the rules governing world trade would be harder to enforce if countries were free to impose countervailing duties whenever they decided unilaterally that the currencies of other countries were undervalued.

If the WTO agreed with China's petition, it could authorize China to retaliate by withdrawing tariff concessions on U.S. goods. The WTO dispute settlement process is adjudicated with reference to the WTO rules and there seems little room for political pressure by the United States and other countries. Other countries could, however, submit briefs in support of the U.S. or the Chinese position. Countries likely will give some thought to the potential impact that a trade dispute between the United States and China might have more broadly on world trade negotiations.

If the volume of Chinese exports to the United States declines because of new trade legislation, the profits of foreign firms located in China which produce those goods will likely go down as well. Exporters could shift their production facilities further to the west in China, where labor costs are lower than on the coast. This might reduce costs enough for Chinese exporters to pay the new tariff and leave their prices unchanged. Alternatively, Chinese companies and international firms might shift production to other countries where the costs of production have become lower than those in China because of yuan revaluation. In that case, these countries might replace China as major suppliers of manufactured products to the United States.

If the United States wants to keep out foreign products (not just Chinese products) which undersell U.S. manufactures, then new legislation would be needed to penalize other countries as they ramp up to take China's place. This would violate WTO rules and the terms of international trade agreements to which the United States is a party. Because the U.S. economy needs to import foreign goods of similar value to the foreign capital it imports each year, it may be hard for the U.S. government to stop countries from expanding their exports to the United States. role. If the volume of imports declines, however, prices for manufactured products in the United States may increase, giving U.S. producers some relief. U.S. consumers would likely need to spend a larger portion of their income in this case to purchase the goods which were previously produced abroad.

TAKE IT TO THE IMF

The United States could also pursue the issue of China's exchange rate policy at the International Monetary Fund. The key issue is whether China is complying with the requirements of Article IV of the IMF Articles of Agreement and, if not, what steps it should take to comply. Though other countries seem to have preferred that the United States take the lead and break the ice for them, they are also affected by China's trade policies. Arguably, international meetings where representatives of the major countries may speak with Chinese officials at the same time will be more persuasive than scattered bilateral talks where the only strong public statements come from the United States.

There continues to be debate as to what, if anything, the outside world can do to accelerate the reform process in China. In late September 2005, Treasury Under Secretary Adams demanded that the IMF crack down on countries that violate the prohibition in Article IV against currency manipulation, though it is not clear what tools he thought the IMF should use.[97] The IMF was, he said, "asleep at the wheel" and it should confront China concerning the deficiencies in its exchange rate policies.

IMF Managing Director Rodrigo de Rato rejected that charge.[98] The IMF was addressing all aspects of the issue, he replied. The IMF had already investigated and rejected suggestions that China's currency policies warrant the use of "special consultations." Rather, he suggested, the United States should act more vigorously to straighten out its own budget and economic policies rather than blaming other countries for its problems.

According to IMF sources, special consultations between IMF management and a country have occurred twice previously in response to formal complaints by another country that it was manipulating its currency. In the 1990s, the United States made a complaint about Korea and Germany filed a complaint about Sweden. The two countries eventually adjusted their currency values, though they may have done this for their own reasons rather than in response to IMF consultations.

In January 2006, Adams maintained that the IMF should play a stronger role enforcing exchange rates and preventing currency manipulation.[99] The IMF should demonstrate strong leadership on multilateral exchange rate surveillance, he said. "A strong IMF role in exchange rate issues is central to the stability and health of the international economy," he remarked. The IMF's leaders "should endorse such an enhanced role for the IMF, restoring its central role on exchange rates." While Adams did not mention China by name, he said the IMF should identify countries "whose exchange rate policies might not be in accord with Fund principles" and it should "seek to identify problematic or inappropriate exchange rate behavior."

However, IMF Managing Director Rato told a session at the World Economic Forum in Davos, Switzerland that he does not consider China to be a currency manipulator. He rejected proposals that the Fund should put greater pressure on China. He said "there is a trade-off between our role as confidential adviser in our surveillance work and our role as a transparent judge."[100] He noted that the IMF had been the first international body to urge China to move from its fixed peg to a more flexible exchange rate process. Rato also said the IMF should not take a proactive role on exchange rates, in response to Adam's question what the IMF should do about countries "that are attempting to thwart balance of payments adjustments."

On February 9, 2006, Rato outlined his future plans for the IMF. He said the IMF should put more emphasis on surveillance but he raised several reservations about the Fund's taking the central policing role Adams had proposed.[101]

The IMF is a place where the views of affected countries can be presented to China and efforts can be made to press China to revalue its currency. The IMF cannot force countries to have exchange rate policies which mirror underlying economic conditions, even if they might be non-compliant with IMF rules. However, continuing discussion at the IMF and at other international meetings serves to focus attention on the issue. At the least, it puts Chinese officials in a situation where they need to explain or justify their policies and to respond in some way to international pressure. Arguably, it has caused them to take steps towards liberalization that they otherwise might be reluctant to take — or they might have taken more slowly — if these conversations had not taken place.

If the IMF were given the broader authority contemplated by Adams and others, the fundamental structure of the world exchange rate system would change and many countries, in addition to China, would have to seriously revise their domestic and international economic policies. China might not be willing to make fundamental changes in its foreign exchange and economic policies unless other major countries make fundamental changes in their policies as well.

REFER IT TO THE WTO

The United States could petition the World Trade Organization (WTO) that it believed China was subsidizing its exports by undervaluing its currency. It could argue that China gains unfair trade advantages because of the artificially low value of its currency and it could ask the WTO to settle this dispute. Normally, arguments about subsidy reference individual products. In this case, however, the U.S. could argue that the subsidy applies to all Chinese goods. By undervaluing its currency, the United States could argue, China is artificially reducing living standards and prices in its domestic economy in order to stimulate and facilitate growth in its export sector. Arguably, subsidies do not have to be paid by governments directly to exporters for them to affect output. In China's case, the United States could argue, the lower production costs caused by the reduction in the standard of living would be the means by which the subsidy were delivered to Chinese export firms.

WTO rules do not permit individuals or private groups to appeal trade controversies to it. Under Section 301 of the Trade Act of 1974, however, groups and individuals may petition the U.S. Trade Representative for action concerning harmful foreign trade practices. In 2004, the Bush Administration rejected two petitions — one by the China Currency Coalition and one by 30 members of Congress — which proposed that the United States should refer the yuan-dollar trade issue to the WTO. The Administration expressed doubt, at the time, that the United States could win a case of this sort in the WTO. It also said, in rejecting the petitions, that action of this sort might be "more damaging than helpful at this time."[102]

The WTO's dispute settlement process is a quasi-judicial process that is intended to resolve trade disputes between countries which cannot be resolved through conciliation or negotiation. A three member panel of experts is appointed by the WTO secretariat reviews the facts and arguments in the case and to render judgment based on principles embodied in WTO rules and international trade agreements. An appellate panel may review the initial panel's findings and, unless its findings are set aside by the WTO membership by consensus, the disputing parties are expected to implement the decision. If a country does not comply within a reasonable period of time, the WTO may authorize the complaining country to impose retaliatory duties on the non-compliant country's goods. Those duties or barriers remain in force until the country complies or until the disputing parties otherwise resolve the issue.[103]

The WTO has no authority to address exchange rate issues. However, the IMF and WTO have an agreement which requires the WTO to refer exchange rate disputes of this sort to the international monetary body and to accept the IMF's findings as conclusive.[104] By itself, a finding by the IMF that China is manipulating its currency would have no "teeth" that would require Chinese officials to change their procedures. However, in conjunction with a positive finding by the WTO, an IMF finding of this sort might have considerable affect. If a WTO dispute settlement panel found that China was gaining unfair trade advantage through a low valuation of its currency, it might authorize the United States to put special tariffs on Chinese products into effect until China raised the value of its currency.

It might be awkward for the United States to take a complaint of this sort to the WTO if it unilaterally imposed tariff restrictions on Chinese goods. Moreover, it would be risky for the United States to apply to the WTO for relief if it does not know how the IMF would rule on this. Support from the other major IMF member countries in the IMF would be critical. Unlike the dispute settlement in the WTO, decisions of this sort in the IMF are made by individuals representing member country governments. The G-7 countries and other members of the European Union comprise a majority of the voting power in the IMF. It might be helpful if the United States consulted with the other countries about their potential vote, if the issue were come to the IMF, before it approached the WTO with a complaint.

REFERENCES

[1]   For a comprehensive discussion of the China exchange rate issue, see CRS Report RS21625, China's Currency Peg: A Summary of the Economic Issues and CRS Report RL32165, China's Exchange Rate Peg: Economic Issues and Options for U.S. Trade Policy.See also CRS Issue Briefs IB91121, U.S.-China Trade Issues and CRS Report RS22338,China's Currency: A Brief overview of U.S. Options. The term "renminbi" means "people's currency" while "yuan" is the unit of account (one yuan, two yuan, etc.) In this report, for simplicity, China's currency will be called the "yuan" except in instances where the term "renminbi" is used in a quotation or official statement.

[2]   For a further discussion of the effects of the undervalued yuan on the U.S. economy, see CRS Report RS21625, China's Currency Peg , pp. 4-6 and CRS Report RL32165, China's Exchange Rate Peg, pp. 19-2, note 1.

[3]   See, for example, a report and data published by the China Currency Coalition. Chinese Currency Manipulation Fact Sheet, April 2005. The Coalition is a group of U.S. industrial, service, agricultural, and labor organizations seeking change in the yuan exchange rate. In addition to labor unions, most of its members appear to represent import-sensitive products. Available at [http://www/chinacurrencycoalition.com/factsheet.html].

[4]   Articles of Agreement of the International Monetary Fund. 60 Stat. 1401, TAIS 1501.

[5]   The Omnibus Trade and Competitiveness Act of 1988, P.L. 100-418, sec. 3004.

[6]   Triennial Central Bank Survey: Foreign Exchange and Derivatives Market Activity in 2004. Bank for International Settlements, March 2005, pp. 1-2. A copy of this report is

available at [http://www.bis.org/publ/rpfx05t.pdf]. The 2001 survey is : Central Bank Survey of Foreign Exchange and Derivatives Market Activity in April 2001: Preliminary Global Data. Bank for International Settlements, October 2001.

[7]   A currency is said to "rise" in value compared to the U.S. dollar when one dollar buys a smaller amount of that currency than before. By convention, it is said that the yuan or renminbi rose in value by a little over 2% (even though the number gets smaller) when it went from Rmb 8.28 to Rmb 8.11 to the dollar on July 21, 2005.

[8]   The new procedure was widely discussed in the press. See, for example, "2% Solution: China lets Yuan Rise vs. Dollar, Easing Trade Tensions Slightly." Wall Street Journal, July 22, 2005, p. 1; Richard McGregor et al. "China revalues the renminbi." Financial Times, July 22, 2005, p. 1; and Peter Goodman. "China Ends Fixed-Rate Currency." Washington Post, July 22, 2005, p. 1.

[9]   See, for example: "Richard McGregor. "Aim is to allow greater flexibility while still keeping firm control." and "Making sense of China's choice." Financial Times, July 22, 2005, pp. 2 and 4.

[10]   "Chinese bank reaffirms revaluation policy." BBC Monitoring Asia Pacific. September 21, 2005.

[11]   See, for example: Morris Goldstein and Nicholas Lardy. "China's revaluation shows size really matters." Financial Times, July 22, 2005, p. 13.

[12]   This argument is the author's synthesis of conversations he and other members of his group had with Chinese and U.S. officials and other persons in early January 2006 during a congressional staff visit to China and Hong Kong.

[13]   Patrick Higgins and Owen F. Humpage. "Nondeliverable forwards: can we tell where the renminbi is headed?" Economic Commentary. September 1, 2005. Federal Reserve Bank of Cleveland. Settlement on these contracts is in dollars, not in yuan. Keith Bradsher. "China Loosens Limits on Trading Against Other Currencies but Keeps Rein on Dollar." New York Times, September 24, 2005, p. C6.

[14]   These included five foreign banks (ABN Amro Holding NV, Bank of Montreal, Standard Chartered PLC, Citigroup Inc. and HSBC Holdings PLC) and eight Chinese banks (Bank of China, China Construction Bank, Industrial & Commercial Bank of China, Agricultural Bank of China, Bank of Communications Co., China Merchant's Bank Co., Citic Bank Co. and Industrial Bank Co.) Jane Lanhee Lee. "International Investor: China approves banks as renminbi market makers; Move is set to bring more-active trading of domestic currency." The Wall Street Journal Asia (Hong Kong), January 3, 2006, p. 32.

[15]   Prashant Rao. "Rates ease pressure on yuan to strengthen." International Herald Tribune (Paris), December 29, 29005, p. 17.

[16]   Shai Oster. "Beijing hints at a shift in its foreign holdings; Desire to diversify may hurt the dollar; Controls to be eased." The Wall Street Journal Asia (Hong Kong), January 6, 2006, p. 1.

[17]   Both cited in Steve Johnson, "Traders price in surging renminbi." Financial Times (London), January 6, 2006, p. 38.

[18]   EIU ViewsWire. New York, December 8, 2005.

[19]   Article IV of the IMF Articles of Agreement require it to meet annually with member countries to discuss their economic and foreign exchange policies.

[20] International Monetary Fund. IMF Concludes 2004 Article IV Consultation with the People's Republic of China, August 25, 2004. Public Information Notice 04/99. It appears from context that "greater flexibility" meant an upward valuation of the yuan. The statement by China is taken from the IMF's summary the board discussion.

[21] International Monetary Fund. IMF Concludes 2005 Article IV Consultation with the People's Republic of China. September 12, 2005. Public Information Notice 05/122. Available from the China page of the IMF website as well as in an annex (pp. 69-72) to the 2005 Article IV staff report. See IMF. People's Republic of China: Staff Report for the 2005 Article IV Consultation. July 8, 2005, p. 14. Available from the China page on the IMF website.

[22] Paul Brent. "Dodge's call to free the Chinese yuan has strong backing." National Post (Don Mills, Ontario), June 6, 2005, p. FP2.

[23] "Tanigaki says quick action on yuan needed." Economic Times of India., The Electronic Times Online, July 9, 2005. See the Economic Times of India's website at [http://economictimes.indiatimes.com/articleshow/1165902.cms]. By contrast, Japan previously had called for China to take immediate action. The Japanese Finance Minister told the G7 finance ministers in February 2003 meeting, that change was urgently needed and "Too much importation of China's cheap goods" was "the root-cause of the global economic depression." Yang Jian and Melinda Moore. "Renminbi" Eurobiz Magazine, July 2003, found at [http://www.sinomedia.net/eurobiz/v200307/rmb.html].

[24] Kervin Yao and Yoko Nishikawa. "Yuan Dominates Asia-Europe meeting." Reuters, June 26, 2005, reported at [http://news.yahoo.com/s/nm/economy_china_dc&printer].

[25] Cindi Sui. "Europe backs off on yuan value." The Australian, June 27, 2005, at [http://theaustralian.news.com.au/common/story_page/0,5744,15741709%255E31037,00.htm]. Cary Huang. "World clamours for Beijing to revalue yuan; But there is agreement that China should dictate timing of any currency reforms." South China Post (Hong Kong), June 27, 2005, p. 5.

[26] "G-7 Ministers Urge China to Make More Progress on Exchange Rate." Bloomberg News, September 26, 2005, available from Bloomberg News at [http://www.bloomberg.com/apps/news?pid=10000080&sid=a86iuRuMx.4g&refer=asia].   "G7 demands more flexible yuan regime." The Daily Yomiuri, Sept. 25, 2005, p. 1.

[27] Scott Hills. "China's Hu sidesteps yuan debate in G8 address." Reuters, July 1, 2005, at [http://today.reuters/PrinterFriendlyPopup.aspx?type=live8News&StoryiD-uri:2005-o.html].

[28] Simon Kennedy and Gonzalo Vina. "G-7 prods China to let yuan rise; Beijing is accused of "rigidity" as currency appreciates little." International Herald Tribune (Paris), December 6, 2005, p. 20.

[29] Jane Wardell. "Economic officials chide China." (Associated Press) Deseret News, December 4, 2005, p. A12; "G-7 prods..." ibid.

[30] Gonzolo Vena and Simon Kennedy. "G7 pushes China on the yuan; Rates 'should reflect' fundamentals, it says." International Herald Tribune, December 5, 2005, p. 15.

[31] White House. "President Discusses Job Training and the Economy in Ohio." January 21, 2004. See [http://www.whitehouse.gov/news/releases/2004/01/200401221-2.html].

[32] Snow Welcomes China's Currency Reforms, at [http://www.treas.gov/news/index1.html].

[33] Susie Gharib. "Secretary of State John Snow Sounds-off On China's Money Move."
      Nightly Business Review, July 21, 2005. Interview, available at [http://www.
      nightltybusiness.org/transcript.html].

[34] Bloomberg News. "Dickering at Davos: Which way yuan; Pace of China yuan reform
      takes center stage at World Economic Forum." January 25, 2006: 2:17 PM EST.
      Available at [http://207.25.71.61/2006/01/25/news/international/bc.davos.china.reut/
      index.htm].

[35] World Economic Forum Annual Meeting 2006, Fixing Up Fixed Exchange Rates,
      summary of discussion, January 1, 2006. Available by searching Google by title or at
      [http://www.weforum.org/site/knowledgenavigator.nsf/Content/_S15322?open&event_i
      d=].

[36] [U.S. Department of the Treasury.] Report to Congress on International Economic and
      Exchange Rate Policies, May 2005. Obtained from [http://www.treas/gov], the Treasury
      Department website. See especially pp. 11-14.

[37] See, for example Andrew Balls, "US sets out revaluation deadline for China," Financial
      Times, USA edition, May 18, 2005, p. 1. See also Edmund L. Andrews, "Bush's
      Choice: Anger China or Congress over Currency," The New York Times, May 17,
      2005, p. 1, and Andrew Balls, "FT.com site: China told to revalue by 10% by US,"
      Financial Times, May 24, 2005, p. 1.

[38] [U.S. Department of the Treasury.] Report to Congress on International Economic and
      Exchange Rate Policies, November 2005. Available from [http://www.treas/gov], the
      Treasury Department website. See especially pp. 17-21.

[39] The fiscal 2006 defense appropriations act, H.R. 1815, approved by Congress in
      December 2005 and signed into law (Public Law 109-163) on January 6, 2006. The
      relevant language is found in Section 1234 of that act.

[40] H.R. 3283, passed by the House (255 to 168) on July 27, 2005. Senator Susan Collins
      introduced a similar bill (S. 1421) in the Senate in July 2005 but no action has been
      taken.

[41] For more on the issue of countervailing duties and nonmarket economies, see CRS
      Issue Brief IB10148, Trade Remedy Legislation: Applying Countervailing Action to
      Nonmarket Economy Countries.

[42] H.R. 1498, the Chinese Currency Act of 2005, introduced April 9, 2005.

[43] Greg Hitt. "Senate Slams China's Currency Policy." Wall Street Journal. April 7, 2005,
      p. 1.

[44] International Monetary Fund. People's Republic of China: Staff Report for the 2004
      Article IV Consultation. July 6, 2004, p. 12. This report is available from the China
      page in the country section of the IMF website at [http://www.imf.org].

[45] IMF, 2005 Article IV Staff Report, note 21.

[46] See http://www.economist.com/markets/bigmac/displayStory.cfm?story_id=5389856].
      See also [http://www.stanford.edu/class/msande247s/bigmac02.htm] for a reference to
      the "light hearted" nature of the measure.

[47] For one thing, consumption patterns for this product varies from country to country.
      Also, while the hamburgers are the same worldwide, most of their inputs are supplied
      locally. Few hamburgers are exported from China to the United States. Labor, rent and
      paper products are cheaper in China, for instance, than in the United States. Other
      factors besides currency valuation can influence the cost of these local components.

[48] For a simple guide to the process of calculating equilibrium exchange rates, see Sergio Da Silva. Classroom Guide to the Equilibrium Exchange Rate Model. It is available at [http://ideas.repec.org/p/wpa/wuwpif/0405019.html].

[49] See Chinese Currency Manipulation Fact Sheet, cited in note 3.

[50] The full names and citations to sources were not provided. Many economists would argue that the World Bank data were misconstrued, as the Bank's figures are not measures of the extent to which currencies are over- or undervalued compared to the dollar but rather two ways that per capita income levels in poor countries may be compared internationally. question whether the World Bank's purchasing power parity index can be used to measure deviations in exchange rates is also discussed in CRS Report RL32165, China's Exchange Rate Peg, pp. 12-13, note 1.

[51] Steven Dunaway and Xiangming Li. Estimating China's "Equilibrium" Real Exchange Rate. IMF Working Paper WP/05/202, October 2005. Available from the China page in the country section of the IMF website: [http://www.imf.org]. The eight studies referenced in the IMF report were by Virginie Coudert and Cécile Couharde (2 studies), Tao Wang (3), Morris Goldstein, Jeffrey Frankel, and J. Lee. Full citations may be found in the report.

[52] Michael Funke and Jörg Rahn. "Just How Undervalued is the Chinese Renminbi?" The World Economy 28:4 (April 2005), pp. 465-489.

[53] Patrick Higgins and Owen Humpage. "The Chinese Renminbi: What's Real, What's Not." August 1, 2005, at [http://www.clevelandfed.org/Research/Com2005/0815.pdf].

[54] See, for example: Clifford Coonan. "Services sector plays major role in surging Chinese economy." Irish Times (Dublin), December 27, 2005, p. 16. The calculation that China could move from sixth to third place was made by the Congressional Research Service using data in this and other newspaper reports.

[55] Some prominent studies which argue that the yuan is substantially undervalued seem to have been based on back-of-the-envelope calculations rather than on systematic econometric analysis. Others use questionable assumptions or weak economic logic. For a discussion, see CRS Report RL32165, China's Exchange Rate Peg, pp. 8-13, note 1.

[56] These are published in the IMF's Selected Decisions and Selected Documents of the International Monetary Fund, 24th issue. Washington, D.C. June 30, 1999, pp.10-29. Reference here is to the General Principles, Principles for the Guidance of Members' Exchange Rate Policies, and Principles of Fund Surveillance over Exchange Rate Policies specified in the IMF board decision Surveillance over Exchange Rate Policies: Review,Decision No. 6026-(9/13), January 22, 1979, as amended, pp. 10-16.

[57] In addition to the four cited here, the other IMF criteria include numbers three (a prolonged reductions or incentives for BOP purposes affecting current transactions or the inflow or outflow of capital) and six (unsustainable flows of private capital.)

[58] IMF. Selected Decisions, note 55. See "Principles of Fund Surveillance over Exchange Rate Policies," pp. 12-15, section 2(i), (iv) and (v).

[59] See, for example, Morris Goldstein's argument to that effect. "China and the Renminbi Exchange Rate" in C. Fred Bergsten and John Williamson, eds. Dollar Adjustment: How Far" Against Whom? Washington, D.C.: Institute for International Economics, November 2004. Special Report 17.

[60] For discussion of Japan's efforts at currency manipulation, see CRS Report RL33178,Japan's Currency Intervention: Current Issues, updated January 12, 2006. See also J.T. Young. "Japan's subtle subsidy." The Washington Times, December 5, 2005, p. A19. Japan's foreign exchange reserves are larger than those of China and its exports have had a greater impact arguably on the U.S. manufacturing sector than have those of China.

[61] Ibid., p. 14.

[62] Raghuram Rajan. Remarks on Global Current Account Imbalances and Financial Sector — Reform with Examples from China. Address to the Cato Institute, November 3, 2005. Available from the China page on the IMF website.

[63] See, for example, the argument to this effect in Chinese Currency Manipulation, note 3.

[64] Brad Setser. The Chinese Conundrum: External financial strength, Domestic financial weakness. October 31, 2005. Available (with registration) from the RGEmonitor website at [http://www.rgemonitor.com/redir.php?sid=1&tgid=10000&cid=108028].

[65] Nouriel Roubini and Brad Setser. The sustainability of US external deficits and Chinese external surpluses. November 22, 2005. PowerPoint Slides. Available from the RGEMonitor website at [http://www.rgemonitor.com/redir.php?sid=1&tgid=10000&cid=108683].

[66] See the Chinese Currency Coalition factsheet cited in note 3.

[67] For a discussion of China trade data, see CRS Report RL31403, China's Trade with the United States and the World. Updated January 23, 2006. IMF figure cited on p. 9.

[68] IMF. Direction of Trade Statistics, 2005 yearbook, p. 2. The DOTS data are computed on a somewhat different basis than are those for individual countries. On this table, industrial countries are net exporters and developing countries are net importers. For purposes of this table, China has a net trade deficit of over $300 billion.

[69] China reported net exports of $80.29 billion to the United States for 2004 while the United States reported net imports of $176.8 billion from China. India reported a net trade surplus of $6.86 billion with the United States while the United States reported a net deficit of $10.56 billion with India. France reported a surplus of $6.28 billion while the U.S. figures show a $11.06 billion deficit. Malaysia reported a surplus of $8.49 billion while the United States reported a $18.15 billion deficit with Malaysia. . Senegal reported a deficit of $89 million while the United States reported a surplus of $86 million. Direction of Trade, 2005, pp. 133, 203, 252, 322, and 431.

[70] See IMF Article IV 2005 staff report, p. 73. See note 21 above.

[71] See, for example: Geoff Dyer and Andrew Balls. "Questions grow over China's forex strategy." FT.com. (London) January 6, 2006, p. 1.

[72] For a further discussion of the causes of the U.S. trade deficit, see CRS Report RL31032,The U.S. Trade Deficit: Causes, Consequences, and Cures, updated September 15, 2005.

[73] Not all would agree with this view. One manufacturer notes, for example, that labor and other Chinese content account for no more than 30% of total operating costs for Chinese exporters and — with most materials costs denominated in dollars — content priced in yuan accounts for only about 20% of total costs. If China's currency were to increase in value, the cost of the imported components would be unchanged and the price of China's exports would need to be increased only marginally to recover the higher local costs. See, for example, Kathrin Hille, "China's currency shift frays

nerves." Financial Times August 7, 2005, p. 1, available from its website at [http://www.FT.com].

[74] Cited in the IMF's staff report on the 2005 Article IV consultation, note 21 above.

[75] "Beijing officials signal support for higher yuan." The Wall Street Journal Asia (Hong Kong), December 13, 2005, p. 9.

[76] Ibid., pp. 14-16.

[77] "China's currency reserves hit $819bn." The Times (London), January 16, 2006, p. 39.

[78] "Revised growth figures send mixed signals." South China Morning Post (Hong Kong), December 27, 2005, p. 1.

[79] Brad Setser. The Chinese Conundrum, note 64

[80] IMF. Staff Report for the 2004 Article IV Consultation, note 44, p. 9.

[81] China keeps its books in yuan. The dollar value of the Chinese assets would not change but their value from the Chinese perspective would decline. Likewise the international value of assets denominated in yuan would increase.

[82] The Associated Press. "China might diversify investments: U.S. mortgage industry worried; Drop in Treasury purchases could hurt home buyers." Columbian (Vancouver, Washington), January 11, 2006. "Forex reserves could be used to set up national investment trust firms." South China Post (Hong Kong), January 16, 2006, p. 5.

[83] To dampen concern, the governor of the People's Bank of China personally met with press to affirm that China had no plans to reduce its dollar holdings or to use them to buy other assets, such as oil. See "Forex reserves could be used...." (note 82.) Many analyst predict that, if China reduces its rate of investment in the United States, U.S. interest rates will increase. A large sale of China's dollar assets could also drive down U.S. security prices.

[84] Eswar Prasad and Shang-Jin Wei. The Chinese Approach to Capital Inflows: Patterns and Possible Explanations. National Bureau of Economic Research. NBER Working Paper Series, Working Paper 11306, April 2005.

[85] The sources of FDI coming to China have changed over the years. In 2004, the major sources were Hong Kong (32%), Virgin Islands (12%), Korea (11%), Japan (9%), European Union (7%), United States (7%), Taiwan (5%), Western Samoa (2%) and Singapore (2%). The sources for the Virgin Islands and Western Samoa money are unknown. The five Asian countries accounted for 60% of the total. See Prasad and Wei, p.79.

[86] "Portfolio Investment in China: Cooling Down." The Economist, January 28, 2006, p. 73.

[87] As noted earlier, though (text and note 16 above), China has announced that it will soon relax its controls over capital outflows It is unclear if this is a precursor for greater future exchange flexibility or merely a means to limit growth in China's forex reserves.

[88] Author's interview with IMF staff, December 2005.

[89] Prasad and Wei, note 84, p. 13.

[90] See note 64.

[91] See, for example, comments by Gail Foster, chief economist for the Conference Board, in Peter Bartram, "Insight — Yuan weak link." Financial Director, September 30, 2005, p. 14.

[92] [92] See, for example: Edward Prasad, Thomas Rumbaugh, and Qing Wang. Putting the Cart Before the Horse? Capital Account Liberalization and Exchange Rate Flexibility in

China.IMF Policy Discussion Paper PDP/05/01, January 2005. Available from the IMF website.

[93] Some of these options are also discussed, with similar conclusions, in CRS Report RL32165, China's Exchange Rate Peg, pp. 28-30, note 1.

[94] Section 301 to 309 of the Trade Act of 1974, as amended. See also CRS Report 98-454,Section 301 of the Trade Act of 1974, as Amended: Its Operations and Issues Involving its Use by the United States. See, for example, China Currency Coalition factsheet, note 3.

[95] See CRS Report RS20570, Trade Remedies and the U.S.-China Bilateral WTO Accession Agreement, updated August 4, 2003.

[96] For a discussion of the WTO dispute resolution mechanism, see CRS Report RS20088, Dispute Settlement in the World Trade Organization., updated December 28, 2005.

[97] Paul Blustein. "IMF Chief Pressured on Trade Imbalances." The Washington Post, September 29, 2005, p. D1.

[98] Ibid.

[99] U.S. Department of the Treasury. "Remarks by Under Secretary for International Affairs Tim Adams at AEI Seminar Working with the IMF to Strengthen Exchange Rate Surveillance." February 2, 2006, JS-4002. Available from the Treasury Department website at [http://www.treas.gov/pres/releases/js4002.htm].

[100] Chris Giles and Krishna Guha. "Interview with Rodrigo de Rato." Financial Times (London), January 28, 2006, p. 8

[101] Rodrigo de Rato. The IMF's Mid-Term Strategy: New Priorities, New Directions.Remarks at the Aspen Institute, Rome Italy, February 9, 2006. Available from the IMFwebsite at [http://www.imf.org/external/np/speeches/2006/020906.htm]. Some analysts speculate that, if the IMF was given the power to police exchange rates and BOP policies, it would probably start with the industrial countries whose policies have the greatest impact on the world economy rather than middle-income countries such as China.

[102] U.S. Trade Representative. Statement from USTR Spokesperson Neena Moorjani Regarding a Section 301 Petition on China's Currency Regime. November 12, 2004 Available from the USTR website. Put quoted words in search box to locate text.

[103] For further information on the WTO's dispute settlement procedures, see CRS Report RS20088, Dispute Settlement in the World Trade Organization: An Overview, updated December 28, 2005.

[104] See Arrangement for Consultation and Cooperation with the Contracting Parties of GATT, September 9, 1948, and Guidelines/Framework for Fund Staff Collaboration with the World Trade Organization, April 21, 1995. Both are included in the IMF's Selected Decisions, note 56, pp. 546-9 and 552-9.

In: Economics and Foreign Investment in China
Editor: J.I. Cheng, pp. 151-161

ISBN 1-60021-238-7
© 2007 Nova Science Publishers, Inc.

Chapter 6

A COMPARATIVE STUDY OF CHINESE AND AMERICAN ADVERTISING APPEALS AND IMAGES

Carolyn A. Lin[1]

Department of Communication
Cleveland State University, Cleveland, OH USA

ABSTRACT

The recent success of transnational advertising campaigns starring Chinese NBA star Yao Ming—spokesman for Citibank and Apple--underscores the robust potential for international collaboration in advertising. Yet, aside from a few notable exceptions, American advertisers have yet to penetrate the Chinese consumer veneer in China. Observers suggest that difficulties in reaching the Chinese market stem from Westerners' poor understanding of how to engage consumers in a venerable Eastern culture. The present study content analyzed television commercials aired during prime time in these two countries to contrast the differential uses of advertising appeals and images conveyed in these commercials and to explicate these differences from a cultural perspective.

A COMPARATIVE STUDY OF CHINESE AND AMERICAN ADVERTISING APPEALS AND IMAGES

The recent success of transnational advertising campaigns starring Chinese NBA star Yao Ming--spokesman for Citibank and Apple--underscores the robust potential for international collaboration in advertising. As American brands like the NBA continue to expand their international markets, global advertisers are focusing on the biggest potential market in the world, China. Yet, aside from a few notable exceptions (e.g., the NBA, McDonalds), American advertisers have yet to penetrate the Chinese consumer veneer with traditional Western-style advertising in China.[2]

---

[1] 2121 Euclid Avenue,Cleveland, Ohio 44115,Fax: 216-687-5435,Voice: 216-687-4641,Email: c.a.lin@csuohio.edu
[2] Alexandra A. Seno, "8 Things You Didn't Know About Chinese Consumers," *Asia week*, 26 (April 28, 2000): 1-5.

Observers suggest that difficulties in reaching the Chinese market stem from Westerners' poor understanding of how to engage consumers in a venerable Eastern culture.[3] For instance, Seno concludes that Western style celebrity testimonials, consumerism appeals and "in your face" marketing approaches typically fail in China.[4] These marketing challenges auger in favor of a "specialization" approach in global advertising, even though such an approach may be fraught with unforeseen pitfalls.[5] The present study content analyzed television commercials aired during prime time in China and the U.S. to contrast the different uses of advertising appeals and images conveyed in these commercials and to explicate these differences from a cultural perspective.

BACKGROUND

When profiling American and Chinese cultures, Hsu notes that the Chinese way of life is based on a set of relationships defined by Confucian doctrine: ancestor worship, fidelity and virtue, women's chastity, benevolent fathers and filial sons, and submission to authority. [6] These themes have also emerged in the analyses of East Asia offered by other scholars.[7] Hsu further characterizes the U.S. way of life as "individual-centeredness" and as a variant of Western individualism (i.e., a greater emphasis on "self-reliance," equality, resentment of class-based distinctions, and rejection of the past).[8]

Pan and colleagues conclude that the traditional value system of cultural China flows from a value system rooted in Confucianism. For instance, when compared to American culture, Chinese culture emphasizes one's relationship with nature in the manner of "passive acceptance" instead of "active mastery" and one's place in society as centered around "duties to family, clan and state" rather than "individual personality."[9] According to Cheng, these values were reflected in Chinese advertising, as Chinese messages continued to honor "tradition" and "group consensus" in contrast with American advertising messages that focused on "individualism."[10] This emphasis on collectivism and tradition is characteristic of

---

[3] e.g., Lin, Carolyn A. and Michael B. Salwen, "Product Information Strategies of American and Japanese Television Advertisements," International Journal of Advertising, 14 (Spring 1995), 55-64.; Lohtia, Ritu, Wesley J. Johnston, and Linda Aab, "Creating an Effective Print Advertisement for the China Market: An Analysis and Advice," Journal of Global Marketing, 8 (Summer 1994), 7-29.

[4] Seno, "8 Things."

[5] Dentsu Incorporated, *Marketing Opportunities in Japan.* McGraw Hill Book Co., London (1978): 84-114.

[6] Francis L.K. Hsu, Americans and Chinese: Passage to Differences (Honolulu, HI: University Press of Hawaii, 1981).

[7] e.g., William B. Gudykunst, Stella Ting-Toomey, and Tsukasa Nishida, Communication in Personal Relationships Across Cultures (Thousand Oaks, CA: Sage Publications, 1996); Kang Zhang, Yueh-Ting Lee, Yanfang Liu, and Clark McCauley (1996), "Chinese-American Differences: A Chinese View," in Personality and Person Perception Across Cultures, Ed. Yueh-Ting Lee, Clark McCauley, and Juris.G. Draguns (Mawhah, NJ: Lawrence Erlbaum Associates, 1996): 127-138.

[8] Francis Hsu, Americans and Chinese: Passage to Differences.

[9] Zhondang Pan, Steven H. Chaffee, Godwin C. Chu, and Yanan Ju, To See Ourselves: Comparing Traditional Chinese and American Cultural Values (Boulder, CO: Westview Press, 1994).

[10] Hong Cheng, "Reflection of Cultural Values: A Content Analysis of Chinese Magazine Advertisements from 1982 and 1992," *International Journal of Advertising*, 13 (Summer 1994): 167-183.

Eastern cultural values.[11] Based on these observations, the following hypotheses are proposed:

H1. Chinese commercials are more likely to use traditional appeals than will their U.S. counterparts.

H2. Chinese commercials are more likely to use oneness with nature appeals than will their U.S. counterparts.

H3. Chinese commercials are more likely to use collectivism appeals than will their U.S. counterparts.

As the observance of "traditions" typically counters the core idea of "modernity," Cheng and Schweitzer found that "modernity" was also a prominent value displayed in Chinese television advertising, even more so than in the American sample.[12] The reason for this apparent contradiction is rooted in China's concurrent pursuit for modernity and preservation of tradition. Even so, Cheng notes that Western advertisers are more likely to emphasize product merit appeals that are grounded in a direct, rational and informational approach than Chinese advertisers.[13] This is similar to the findings showing that the more introverted and polite Japanese culture typically features a less direct-speech or emotional advertising style, while the more extroverted and aggressive American culture tends to forward a direct-speech or informational advertising style.[14]

H4. Chinese commercials are more likely to use modernity/youth appeals than will their U.S. Counterparts.

H5. U.S. commercials are more likely to use product merit appeals than their Chinese counterparts.

These distinctive national media dynamics can be further explained by Hall's concept of cultural context.[15] In essence, implicit appeals are characteristic of an older, "high context" culture such as China's, where communication is customarily indirect, modest and vague, as compared to the "low-context" American culture where direct, stalwart and explicit messages prevail.[16] For instance, Proctor and Gamble recently ran a campaign in China for a new shampoo that "barely revealed the product's name."[17] To wit, commercials in the U.S. typically focus less on soft-sell mood effect than Asian ads and include more hard-sell

---

[11] Ladd Wheeler, Harry T. Reis, and Michael Harris Bond (1997), "Collectivism-Individualism in Everyday Social Life: The Middle Kingdom and the Melting Pot," in *Sociocultural Perspectives in Social Psychology: Current Readings*, ed. Letitia Anne Peplau and Shelley E. Taylor (Upper Saddle River, NJ : Prentice Hall, 1997): 297.

[12] HONG CHENG AND JOHN C. SCHWEITZER, "CULTURAL VALUES REFLECTED IN CHINESE AND U.S. TELEVISION COMMERCIALS," *JOURNAL OF ADVERTISING RESEARCH*, 36 (FALL 1996): 27-45.

[13] Hong Cheng, "Reflection of Cultural Values: A Content Analysis of Chinese Magazine Advertisements from 1982 and 1992."

[14] Carolyn A. Lin, "Cultural Differences in Message Strategies: A Comparison Between American and Japanese TV Commercials," Journal of Advertising Research, 33 (Fall 1993): 40-48; Barbara Mueller, "Standardization vs. Specification: An Examination of Westernization in Japanese Advertising," Journal of Advertising Research, 32 (Spring 1992):15-24; Jyotika Ramaprasad and Kazumi Hasegawa, "Informational Content of American and Japanese Television Commercials," Journalism Quarterly 69 (Fall 1992): 612-622.

[15] Edward T. Hall, *Beyond Culture* (Garden City, NY: Anchor Books, 1976).

[16] Yueh-Ting Lee, Clark R. McCauley, and Juris G. Draguns (1999*), Personality and Person Perception Across Cultures* (Mahwah, NJ: Lawrence Earlbaum Associates, 1999).

[17] Seno, "8 Things you didn't know about Chinese consumers."

information in their messages.[18] Based on that distinction, as well as the earlier discussion, it is hypothesized that

> H6. Chinese commercials are more likely to use soft-sell appeals than their U.S. counterparts.

In line with the logic of cultural context idiosyncrasies between Western and Eastern cultures, the dimension of time is also conceived differently between these two traditions. According to Berry, Western cultures operationalize the unit of time in a monochronic manner, one that emphasizes discrete and standardized units for the purpose of formulating concrete schedule segments.[19] Eastern cultures, however, treat time as a polychronic concept that is not necessarily linear and remains interwoven with spontaneous and emergent events.[20] Industrialization or modernization of a country is also considered a key determinant for a society's perception of time, aside from cultural traditions.[21] In light of these countervailing influences, the following research question is posed:

> RQ1. Are U.S. commercials more likely to use time-oriented appeals than their Chinese counterparts?

While the image of modernity was found to be common in Chinese advertisements, the portrayals of "social status" in advertising messages could also help enhance such an image.[22] Just as the concept of "social status" is a measure of one's success in controlling their destiny in the West, status is also a significant indicator of achievement and upward mobility in a Confucian society such as China.[23] According to Mueller, Japanese print ads utilized the status appeal to a greater degree than American ads; such an appeal often featured the use of foreign words or models to confer status appeals of the products, as Western-looking product images could imply both higher prestige and greater luxury.[24] The following research question is thus posed:

> RQ2. Are Chinese commercials more likely to use status appeals than their American counterparts?

By the same token, to the extent that Japanese ads utilized Western models, words, languages or images to present a Westernized look for certain products, this may not be a unique phenomenon in Asian advertising. The use of Western models in Asian advertising, in

---

[18] Barbara Mueller, "Reflections of Culture: An Analysis of Japanese and American Advertising Appeals," Journal of Advertising Research, 27 (Fall, 1987): 51-59.

[19] Leonard Berry, "The Time-Buying Consumer," Journal of Retailing, 55 (winter 1979), 58-69.

[20] Edward T. Hall, The Dance of Life: The Other Dimension of Time (Garden City:Anchor Press/Doubleday, 1993).

[21] Tom Bruneau, "The Time Dimension in Intercultural Communication," in Communication Yearbook, Dan Nimmo, ed., New Brunswick, NJ: Transaction Books, 1979): 71-92.

[22] Cheng, "Reflection of Cultural Values"

[23] Nancy Y. Wong, and Aaron Ahubia C., "Personal Taste and Family Face: Luxury Consumption in Confucian and Eastern Societies," Psychology & Marketing, 15 September/October 1998): 423-441.

[24] Mueller, "Reflections of Culture.

particular, increased dramatically beginning in the late 1970s.[25] As Western media content--especially American movies, television programs and popular music--dominates global youth cultures, it is not surprising that Western products or Westernized advertising appeals are seen as symbols of modernity, wealth and quality. The Chinese have been more restrictive in their in-flow of Western media products than the Japanese. To further explore our national contrasts, the following question is proposed:

RQ3. What are the relative tendencies for Chinese and U.S. advertisers to use native or foreign elements when featuring product manufacturers, models, and languages as well as the ad's overall look and overall appeal?

METHODOLOGY

Sampling Method

This study was based on a comparative analysis of Chinese and U.S. networks, involving parallel program contents aired during primetime in the areas of news, sports, entertainment, arts and cultural programs. The two national Chinese networks owned and operated by the government at the time of this study--Channel One (CCTV1) and Channel Two (CCTV2) of China Central Television networks—were mandated to carry arts, educational and cultural programming in addition to news, sports, serials and entertainment programs. Beijing Television (BTV), a local station, was also selected for sampling because it delivered the third largest audience outside of the two national networks and mirrored a general purpose network.

A comparable set of U.S. broadcast and cable television networks was selected for this study, including NBC, ESPN, and AandE. In particular, NBC was randomly selected for its general news, sports and entertainment context, from among the four major full-fledge U.S. broadcast networks. AandE was selected for its focus on cultural and entertainment programming, while ESPN was picked for its sports programming.

Sampling Procedure

The sampling universe was comprised of television commercials aired during the fall sweeps on three Chinese and U.S. channels. For both national samples, one random week (last week of November) of primetime programming (8:00-11:00pm) was selected for videotaping during the sweeps period. With regard to the sampling procedure, first, the days of the week were randomized, as were the three networks from each country. The days of the week were then randomly assigned to each of the randomized sets of three networks from each country. These procedures produced a composite week containing two separate sets of randomly selected network/weekday recording schedules.

---

[25] Dentsu Incorporated, Marketing Opportunities in Japan (McGraw Hill Book Co., London, 1978): 84-114; Mueller, "Standardization vs. Specification; Sadafumi Nishina, Sadafumi (1990), "Japanese Consumers: Introducing Foreign Products in the Japanese Market," Journal of Advertising Research, 34 (35-45).

Unit of Analysis

The unit of analysis was defined as each complete television commercial. Promotional ads for the station, network, programs or duplicate commercials for a given brand (i.e., 78 American and 65 Chinese commercials) were excluded from the sample to prevent the skewing of the results. All told, the final sample was comprised of 401 commercials, of which 206 were American and 195 were Chinese.

Measurement

Television commercials were classified into ten product categories, based on Katz and Lee's categories.[26] These categories included clothing, food auto, beauty and personal care, clothing, food and drink, household appliances, medicine, service, travel, industrial products, and miscellaneous products. Each category was dummy coded (as "0" or "1").

Mueller's coding scheme[27] was selected as the starting point for this analysis, since it reflects the core differences that exist between Western and Far Eastern cultural traditions.[28] This index contains the following unique advertising appeal categories that are reflective of distinct cultural values: time orientation, collectivism, soft-sell appeal, veneration of elderly/tradition, modernity/youth, status, product merit, and oneness with nature.

Cultural values were coded on a three point scale, ranging from "weak"(coded as "1"), "medium"(coded as "2") to "strong"(coded as "3"). In that vein, a medicine commercial featuring a soft-sell appeal would be coded as "strong" if only soft imagery and no straightforward pitch were employed. By contrast, the spot would be coded as "moderate" if the soft imagery were balanced with a secondary straightforward pitch, such as a brief mention of the key selling point. In cases where the soft imagery was secondary to a straightforward pitch, the ad would be coded as "weak." When cultural value categories being coded were not present in a commercial, the ad was coded as "none" or "0." In the case of "soft sell," the ad would have been coded as "none" if only hard-sell strategy was used in the ad without any soft imagery element.

Coding Procedure

The coding scheme was derived from the conceptual and operational definitions discussed previously. A native English speaker and a native Mandarin speaker assisted in coding. After the researcher reviewed all operational and conceptual decisions with the coders, the two native speakers then respectively coded 25% of the U.S. and Chinese samples. The bilingual researcher also coded these identical sets of subsamples. Final intercoder reliabilities for these two sets of coding procedures, using Holsti's intercoder reliability

---

[26] Katz, Helen and Wei-Na Lee (1992). "Ocean Apart: An Initial Exploration of Social Communication Differences in U.S. and U.K. Prime-Time Television Advertising," International Journal of Advertising, 11 (1) 69-82.

[27] Mueller, "Reflections of Culture.

[28] e.g., Pan, Zhondang, Steven H. Chaffee, Godwin C. Chu, and Yanan Ju (1994), To See Ourselves: Comparing Traditional Chinese and American Cultural Values, Boulder,CO: Westview Press.; Gudykunst, William B., Stella Ting-Toomey, and Tsukasa Nishida, Communication in Personal Relationships Across Cultures, Thousand Oaks, CA: Sage Publications (1996); Peabody, Dean (1999), "Nationality Characteristics: Dimensions for Comparison," in Personality and Person Perception Across Cultures, ed. Yueh-Ting Lee, Clark McCauley, and Juris.G. Draguns (Mawhah, NJ: Lawrence Erlbaum Associates, 1999): 65-84.

coefficient calculation formula,[29] averaged 91% for the Chinese sample and 90% for the U.S. sample.

RESULTS

Discriminant analysis results for testing study hypotheses and research questions are presented in Table 1. The positive discriminant function (.479) indicates that Chinese ads were more likely to feature a veneration of elderly/traditional approach than their American counterparts, consistent with H1. The Chinese were also heavier users of appeals featuring oneness with nature (.148) and collectivism/group conceusus (.165), providing support for H2 and H3, respectively. However, the Chinese were no more likely to use modernity/youth appeals, leaving H4 without support. U.S. commercials, on the other hand, were more likely to use product merit appeals than their Chinese counterparts (-.118); this provided support for H5. Similarly, H6 was also supported, as the Chinese were more likely to use soft-sell appeals (.632).

Per research questions one and two, the findings show that U.S. advertisers were more likely to use time-oriented appeals (-.461) but the use of status appeals across both countries was not significantly differentiated (Table 1).

Table. 1 Discriminant Analysis of Sino-U.S. Cultural Values in Advertising Appeals

Structure Matrix

	Function 1	Wilks' Lambda	F	p
Soft-sell	.632	.658	207.278	.000
Traditional/Veneration elderly	.479	.770	119.481	.000
Time-Oriented	-.461	.783	110.267	.000
Collective/Group Consensus	.165	.966	14.189	.000
Oneness with Nature	.148	.972	11.441	.001
Product Merit	-.118	.982	7.290	.007
Social Status	-.039	.998	.793	.374
Modernity/Youth	.007	1.000	.029	.865

Eigenvalue = 1.864;   Canonical Correlation = .807;   Wilks' Lambda = .349
Chi-square = 414.575, $p \leq .000$; Box's M = 215.582, $p \leq .000$
88.8 of original grouped cases correctly classified.

Per research question three, Chi-square analyses comparing Sino-U.S. advertising issues are presented in Table 2. In cases where product categories had a cell size smaller than five, the correction for continuity procedure was executed to calculate chi-square values (Blalock, 1979). Results indicate that Chinese advertisers used more foreign images (χ^2 = 4.48, p ≤ .000) and featured more foreign product manufacturers (χ^2 = 39.39, p ≤ .000) than their American counterparts. Americans, on the other hand, were more likely to employ native

---

[29] Ole R. Holsti. "Content Analysis for the Social Sciences and Humanities, Reading, MA: Addison-Wesley Publishing (1969).

languages (χ^2 =13.81, p ≤ .000), while over 10% of Chinese ads were presented in a foreign tongue. The same is true of the "overall look" of product presenters (χ^2 =10.93, p ≤ .001), which were present in nearly an eighth of Chinese ads coded here. Americans were also more likely to feature an overall appeal that's native to their domestic culture (χ^2 =15.45, p ≤ .000), while just over 15% of Chinese ads featured a foreign appeal.

Table. 2 Comparative Analysis of Sino-U.S. Advertising Images

	U.S.		China		χ^2	Corrected χ^2
Product Manufacturer	%	n	%	n		
Native	97.5	199	76.6	147	39.49	37.61
Foreign	2.5	5	23.4	45		
p					.000	.000
Model						
Native	89.7	156	81.7	138	4.48	3.85
Foreign	10.3	18	18.3	31		
p					.034	.05
Language						
Native	98.5	198	89.7	166	13.81	12.23
Foreign	1.5	3	10.3	19		
p					.000	.000
Overall Look						
Native	96	192	86.7	169	10.93	9.78
Foreign	4	8	13.3	26		
p					.001	.002
Overall Appeal						
Native	96.1	198	84.6	165	15.45	14.14
Foreign	3.9	8	15.4	30		
p					.000	.000

DISCUSSION

Study results generally confirm and extend past work outlining the distinctive traditions in advertising appeals employed by Chinese and American advertisers.[30] Reviewing statistical contrasts between the Chinese and U.S. samples, the use of six of eight cultural values analyzed was significantly differentiated.

Product merit and time-oriented appeals represent conventional U.S.-style commercial appeals of particular interest here. Simply put, U.S. advertisers typically include more facts about products and suggestions from expert authorities. Chinese advertisers, on the other

---

[30] e.g., Katherine T. Frith, "Western Advertising and Eastern Culture: The Confrontation in Southeast Asia," in *Current Issues and Research in Advertising*, ed. James H. Leigh and Claude R. Martin, Jr.(Ann Arbor, MI: University of Michigan Graduate School of Business Division of Research, 1999): 63-73.; Yi-Hsun, Han, John C. Schweitzer, Benjamin J. Bates, and Tommy V. Smith (1992), "Reflections of Culture: An Analysis of Taiwanese and American Advertising Appeals," paper presented at the AEJMC Annual Convention, Montreal, Canada.992; Zhondang Pan Steven H. Chaffee, Godwin C. Chu, and Yanan Ju, *To See Ourselves: Comparing Traditional Chinese and American Cultural Values* (Boulder, CO: Westview Press, 1994).

hand, are more likely to build their marketing strategy on a product via images stressing emotional appeals (i.e., a "soft sell') that are freeof any supporting evidence.

This finding is consistent with past work comparing Eastern and Western advertising appeals.[31] As De Mooij reports, factually-based appeals are characteristic of low context (e.g., U.S.) culture, and may seem out of place in higher context Eastern contexts.[32] It should come as no surprise, then, that soft-sell appeals are more common in Chinese than in American advertising.

The finding that U.S. commercials feature more time-oriented appeals confirms past work, which shows that time perceptions are shaped by the industrialization level of a given culture.[33] Thus, insofar as American ads emphasize the "here and now" value in marketing their fast food and other "speed-oriented" services, Chinese ads still tend not to stress a fast-paced lifestyle that outpaces "nature." So even as China is undergoing rapid industrialization, its deep-seated value of keeping in harmony with nature stands in contrast to the Western notion of conquering nature.

Similarly, study results bear out that tradition and veneration for the elderly occupy a central position in Chinese ideology systems. Rather than being marginalized as in American ads, the elderly may be shown in Chinese ads as the experienced and respectable figures in society or the venerated product recipients. Stylistic distinctions are also borne out by the finding that, consistent with past work, Chinese advertisers employ group consensus appeals more than their U.S. counterparts.[34] For example, a commercial about a washing machine will show how the purchase may reflect a family (or even extended family) rather than individual preference. Nonetheless, group consensus appeals, relative to the findings of Cheng, were found to be less commonplace in Chinese magazine advertising.[35] This contradicts work suggesting that American identity is conceived of as individualized, relative to Asian identities.[36] The present study findings may indicate the increased individualism and independent spirit among a younger millennial generation in search of unique fashion symbols to express themselves.[37]

Yet the large number of significant differences across these culturally bound advertising appeals is truncated by Westernization trends in China that flow from more powerful indigenous factors. Specifically, the theoretical assumptions with regard to the differential use of "modernity/youth" and "status" appeals between the U.S. and Chinese commercials were not supported by the findings. These findings portend a convergence of marketing styles in the U.S. and China in certain areas, as evidenced by the comparatively larger percentages of Chinese ads that presented products with a foreign flavor—through the use of product (manufacturer) names, models, and language as well as overall look and appeal. This

---

[31] Lin, "Cultural Differences in Message Strategies

[32] D. Marieke De Mooij, Global Marketing and Advertising: Understanding Cultural Paradoxes, Thousand Oaks, CA: Sage Publications (1988).

[33] e.g., Leonard Berry, "The Time-Buying Consumer," Journal of Retailing, 55 (winter 1979), 58-69; Tom Bruneau, "The Time Dimension in Intercultural Communication," in
Communication Yearbook, ed. Dan Nimmo (New Brunswick, NJ: Transaction Books, 1979): 71-92.

[34] Pan, Chaffee, Chu, and Ju, To See Ourselves: Comparing Traditional Chinese and American Cultural Values.

[35] Hong, "Reflection of Cultural Values: A Content Analysis of Chinese Magazine Advertisements from 1982 and 1992."

[36] e.g., Gudykunst, Ting-Toomey, and Nishida, Communication in Personal Relationships Across Cultures.

[37] Yunxiang Yan (2000), "Of Hamburger and Social Space: Consuming McDonald's in Beijing," in The Consumer Revolution in Urban China, ed. Deborah S. Davis (Berkeley,CA: University of California Press, 2000): 201-225.

advertising trend is similar to what Mueller reported in her study, which reveals that products presented in Western sounding and looking products can bestow a certain type of desirable "social status" for some consumers.[38]

This is not a surprising development, as the Chinese advertisers have been adopting more youthful or Westernized appeals in recent years to target a large youth population. The Chinese youth market, characterized by the so-called "little emperor and empress" generation (the products of China's one-child policy), often craves Westernized goods and fashions to project a modern or even rebellious self-image that embodies a chic social status.[39] Since capitalist economies took root in China during the last decade, exhibiting material wealth has also been equated with a show of status—a behavior that is usually shunned in the Confucian tradition but common in the American society.[40]

This social modernization process occurs in tandem with the globalization process, which commentators see being driven by industrialized Western multinational corporations.[41] But these centrifugal forces have yet to homogenize global advertising appeals, because native cultures often localize western strains.[42] Thus, just as China has adopted a form of capitalism "with Chinese flavors," her advertisers can put a local face on such products of fast foods.[43]

In summarizing main themes, this study suggests that Chinese ads are able to supercede Western influences and remain true to such cultural traditions as veneration of the elderly, collectivism/group consensus, indirect sales tactics (via a soft-sell pitch) and oneness with nature. U.S. ads, on the other hand, reflect the Western penchant for a fast-paced, time-pressured and a positivistic emphasis on product merits (often delivered via a hard-sell pitch).

It should be noted that the current study sampled a composite week of data as opposed to a more longitudinal sample that may provide a trend analysis. The potential reliability concerns associated with a content analysis study—including the occasional small cell sizes and the coding scheme adopted—can only be allayed through study replication.

CONCLUSION

As present study findings demonstrate how Eastern and Western cultures can meet in lieu of the shared sphere of modern consumer values, this study underscores the open venues in which global advertising strategy can be constructed. Even though these modern consumer values may be similar in their psychological origin across national boundaries, they remain largely reflective of the traditions of their native culture. This includes the manner in which these consumer values are cognitively internalized as well as behaviorally manifested.

---

[38] Mueller, "Reflections of Culture: An Analysis of Japanese and American Advertising Appeals."

[39] Todd Crowell and David Hsieh (1995), "Little Emperors: Is China's One-Child Policy Creating a Society of Brats?" Asiaweek, 21 (1995): 44-50; . Deborah S. Davis and Julia S. Sensenbrenner (2000). "Commercializing Childhood: Parental Purchases for Shanghai's Only Child," in The Consumer Revolution in Urban China, ed. Deborah S. Davis (Berkeley, CA: University of California Press, 2000): 54-79.

[40] e.g., Wong and Ahubia C., "Personal Taste and Family Face: Luxury Consumption in Confucian and Eastern Societies."

[41] Pieterse, Jan Nederveen Pieterse, "Globalization as Hybridization," in The Globalization Reader, ed. Frank J. Lechner and John Boli (Malden, MA: Blackwell, 2000).

[42] Roland Robertson, "Globalization: Time-Space and Homogeneity-Heterogeneity," in Global Modernities, ed. Mike Featherstone, Scott Lash, and Roland Robertson (Thousand Oaks, CA: Sage Publications, 1995): 45-46.

[43] e.g., Yan, "Of Hamburger and Social Space: Consuming McDonald's in Beijing

Rather than focus on this strict dialectic, future work should conceptualize localism and globalizaton as part of a continuum. To wit, we might expect to see greater evidence of globalized appeals in more Westernized Asian societies like Japan, Hong Kong and Taiwan.[44] Even so, the present study finds that Chinese advertising is not as Western as Cheng had found, suggesting that they have returned to more traditional values over time.[45] Given that these advertising appeals do not remain static, it's essential to continue examining how continued industrialization in China influences her consumer and advertising culture, as compared to that of the United States.

[44] Yorgo Pasadeos and Mei-Chiung Chi, "Traditional vs. Western Appeals in Chinese Magazine Advertisements: Hong Kong and Taiwan," in *Proceedings of the 1992 Conference of the American Academy of Advertising* ed. Leonard N. Reid (Toronto, Canada: Nelson, 1992): 166-169; Alan Shao, Mary Ann Raymond and Charles Taylor, "Shifting Advertising Appeals in Taiwan," *Journal of Advertising Research*, 39 (November/December, 1999): 61-69; David K. Tse, Russell W. Belk, and Nan Zhou, "Becoming a Consumer Society: A Longitudinal and Cross-Cultural Content Analysis of Print Ads from Hong Kong, the People's Republic of China, and Taiwan," *Journal of Consumer Research*, 15 (Winter, 1989): 457-472.

[45] Cheng, "Reflection of Cultural Values: A Content Analysis of Chinese Magazine Advertisements from 1982 and 1992."

In: Economics and Foreign Investment in China
Editor: J.I. Cheng, pp. 163-179

ISBN 1-60021-238-7
© 2007 Nova Science Publishers, Inc.

Chapter 7

THE CHALLENGE OF REMOVEING ADMINISTRATIVE BARRIERS TO FDI IN CHINA

Yong Li[1] and Shukun Tang

School of Business, University of Science & Technology of China
Hefei, Anhui, 230026 P. R. of China

ABSTRACT

This paper presents a picture of administrative barriers to foreign direct investment (FDI) in China –its current situation, manifestations, causes, damaging effect and related measures to curb it. China is in a transition from a closed economy to an open market economy. Administrative barriers to FDI in China is reflected largely in investment restriction, non-transparent and inaccessible FDI rule and regulation, as well as bureaucratic interference in terms of the distortion of FDI operation behavior and the preclusion of market competition. They have become a pressing issue facing foreign investors in making decision to invest in china. China has made great effort to develop a regulation framework on incentive FDI, but this framework currently appears weak and powerless in the face of the administrative barriers. However, the construction of a complete legal framework for FDI and rebuild the government administrative system will be undoubtedly helpful in removing excessive administrative barriers.

INTRODUCTION

China has benefited from its foreign direct investment (FDI) boom in 1990s, which has been accompanied by high GDP growth. For a long-term prospect, it is indispensable that China has a sustainable growth of FDI inflows. Unfortunately, FDI inflows have declined in the last few years. More precisely, FDI went from a peak of 45.46 U.S. $billion in 1998, to 41.73 U.S. $billion in 2001, when foreign investors withdrew or reduced their investment in China. The most important factor for blocking inward FDI is its high administrative barriers.

---

[1] Current address: 86 Foster Street, New Haven, CT 06511, U.S.A.,Telephone: 1-203-772-4202,E-mail: yyililei@hotmail.com

What was enough for attracting FDI before 1998 will not be enough when the competition for FDI has increased, and most developing countries in Asia have already liberalized FDI regimes and economies at large, during the last years. The situation is aggravated by structural changes or economic recessions in some of the larger home countries of FDI, notably Japan, Korea and Hong Kong. Economic turmoil in these countries has decreased the supply of FDI in South East Asia. Removing excessive administrative barriers have become a pressing issue facing China in order to keep the trend of attracting FDI. The purpose of this paper is to present a picture of administrative barriers to FDI in China –its current situation, manifestations, causes, damaging effect and related measures to curb it. The main argument put forward, is that it is essential for China to remove excess administrative barriers in order to build a favorable investment climate for FDI, and any such remove will have to rely on some crucial factors, such as good legal institutions and an effective administrative mechanism.

BACKGROUND

1. China's FDI Regime Liberalization Program

Attitudes and policies toward FDI in China have undergone a marked change, from hostility and distrust in the 1960s to passive acceptance since the 1970s, and then to active encouragement since mid-1980s. Several considerations lie behind these changing perceptions. The first is the increasing preference for the non-debt-creating forms of capital finance over commercial bank borrowing due to the debt crisis of the early 1980s. The second is the growing awareness of FDI's benefits as exemplified by the positive role played by FDI in Chinese economy.

Although the promulgation of the 1979 "Law on Chinese-Foreign Equity Joint Ventures" together with the establishment of the four special economic zones formally signaled the adoption of the "open-door" policy by the central government, only in 1986 and 1987 was serious attention given to providing investment incentives. The "Provisions for the Encouragement of Foreign Investment" were promulgated in October 1986 and their implementing regulations announced over the next year. These measures addressed some of the problems, and improved the investment climate both by adding new incentives and by reducing past uncertainties.

In order to make foreign investment further meet the national industrial development direction and avoid blind investment, in June 1995, China formulated and published "Temporary Provisions for Direction of Foreign Investment" and "Master List for Foreign Investment Industries", announcing the industrial policies of attracting foreign investment in the form of regulations, and lightened the transparency of policies. The Provisions and List divide industrial items into four kinds including the encouraged, the permitted, the restricted, and the forbidden, making investors clear at first sight.

According to the development of China's economy, in December 1997, the government revised the "Master List for Foreign Investment Industries". The revised List encourages foreign investors to set up export enterprises and has put the permitted items 100 per cent of whose products are for export into the encouraged items. During period of "the Ninth Five-year-scheme" (1995-2000), Chinese government depresses customs in a large scope so as to further open the market. The average duty level has been depressed from 35.6% in 1995 down to the current 16.7%. The range of depressed tariff is 53%. The scope of import license management commodity was decreased from 53 classifications in 1992 down to the existing 35. In addition, the import commodity classifications checked and ratified used for management by government are further decreased to 13 at the moment.

The Chinese government promulgated new policy measures to encourage foreign investment in 1999, in order to get adapted to the new challenges imposed by scientific and technological breakthroughs and the rapid changes of knowledge economy and, to act in line with the overall arrangement for China's economic development strategic objective and industrial restructuring. The core of these new policies is: First, to further push forward the opening-up in the service sector gradually. Second, to encourage the establishment of RandD centers and investment in high-tech enterprises by foreign investors. Thirdly, to promote the technological innovation for existing enterprises with foreign investment. Fourthly, to encourage foreign investors to invest in central and western China. In order to achieve these goals, a series of new preferential treatments, which include the exemption or reduction of import duties, income tax holiday, decentralization of the approval power, improving of the legal system and so on, were unveiled to further perfect the investment environment and create even better conditions for foreign investment enterprises (FIEs) in their competitiveness improvement.

China's recent revisions to its regulatory regime governing foreign investment is the "Regulations Guiding the Direction of Foreign Investment" (Guiding Regulations) and the "Catalogue Guiding Foreign Investment in Industry" (Catalogue), both were enacted on April 1, 2002. They broaden the scope of foreign investment opportunities and ease approval requirements for a number of industries, particularly those in manufacturing. The new regime, brought about largely as a result of the country's December 2001 World Trader Organization (WTO) entry and national plans for economic development, outlines which foreign investment projects can be approved by local or central authorities, which projects enjoy preferential tax treatment, and which projects are off-limits to foreign investment. China has already put in place an FDI regulation framework that is relatively mature and liberal by international standards.

Over the last two decades China's FDI inflows has undergone fundamental changes. The main indicators of these changes are:

1. With the exception of those sectors relating to national security, scarce resources, natural resources, and a few others thought unsuited to competition (such as civil aviation, express mail service, electric publication and water processing), an attract FDI mechanism has been established in a majority of sectors, By the end of 2001, China has accumulatively approved the establishment of more than 411,495 foreign-invested enterprises with a total contractual foreign capital of US$69.76 billion and over US$41.73 billion of actually paid-in foreign investment, with a total output accounting for about 25% of GDP, tax takes account 19.01%, export 50.1%, and employees 23 million (China Daily, May 9, 2002). FDI has generated large and significant spillover effects in that it raises both the level and growth rate of productivity of non-recipient firms, and the domestic (previous state-owned) enterprises are the main beneficiaries (Liu 2000).

2. Using natural resources, a vast market potential, and a wide pool of cheap labor, and preferential policies, numerous foreign companies have achieved great economic benefit. As indicated in table 1, in 1999 the provinces in which foreign-funded industrial enterprises got highest efficiency in terms of productivity were Shanxi (116,553 Yuan/person-year), Jilin (108,825), and Hubei (102,992).

3. With the government's gradual open domestic market, FIEs have begun to acquire various autonomous rights in their business operations. Ownership restrictions, rate of return restrictions have been loosen since 1996, following China's admission to WTO, they will be further freed from administrative dependencies.

Table 1. Main Indicators on Economics Benefit of Foreign-Funded Industrial Enterprises by Region (1999)

Region	Ratio of Value Added to Gross Industrial Output Value (%)	Ratio of Total Assets to Industrial Output Value (%)	Assets-Liability Ratio (%)	Annual of Turnover Circulating Funds (times/year)	Ratio of Profits to Cost (%)	Productivity (yuan/ person-year)	Proportion of Products Sold (%)
National Total	25.59	7.93	57.73	1.69	4.39	61260.23	97.18
Beijing	27.88	7.87	61.41	1.50	3.91	85611.93	97.94
Tianjin	18.28	8.68	53.52	1.77	5.81	63351.14	99.85
Hebei	27.33	7.67	63.59	1.56	3.41	56360.63	96.87
Shanxi	30.22	3.89	63.02	1.19	-1.83	40804.65	92.35
Inner Mongolia	32.56	8.93	53.44	0.83	7.38	42001.01	106.87
Liaoning	25.18	7.30	54.10	1.72	4.25	62905.76	99.20
Jilin	32.23	12.06	61.42	1.78	6.27	108825.53	98.25
Heilongjiang	31.29	5.25	71.29	1.02	1.15	62524.18	94.81
Shanghai	25.73	9.31	51.52	1.52	6.12	96270.37	97.84
Jiangsu	24.50	7.95	58.53	1.97	3.91	69637.61	96.97
Zhejiang	23.83	9.24	57.85	1.73	5.40	49201.90	96.01
Anhui	26.82	7.53	60.37	1.69	2.07	54824.16	96.14
Fujian	27.34	7.48	55.01	1.87	4.16	51172.46	95.41
Jiangxi	23.21	7.80	63.56	1.46	3.64	37417.41	96.02
Shandong	26.60	9.00	63.14	2.00	4.91	49067.15	96.38
Henan	32.53	8.49	55.26	1.29	5.71	71095.91	96.45
Hubei	34.58	8.76	70.05	1.51	5.77	102992.86	98.05
Hunan	28.98	11.82	51.79	1.64	8.37	52172.28	95.79
Guangdong	24.87	6.76	59.97	1.79	3.34	51930.26	97.03
Guangxi	29.19	5.75	52.00	1.38	1.70	51536.85	94.98
Hainan	27.95	5.89	55.17	0.74	3.89	70980.18	95.52
Chongqing	27.50	6.55	48.43	1.29	1.45	76275.47	100.09
Sichuan	31.86	6.33	58.12	1.28	2.99	66943.48	94.81
Guizhou	27.81	0.90	61.63	0.73	-6.16	27617.45	96.26
Yunnan	34.61	8.22	49.08	1.23	10.37	85163.04	95.79
Tibet	39.28	0.31	13.45	0.70	2.19	4080.21	87.92
Shaanxi	28.09	12.39	56.49	1.37	12.26	116553.06	96.08
Gansu	26.61	7.55	62.71	1.15	4.32	42132.17	99.24
Qinghai	23.52	3.71	60.48	1.26	1.20	60286.65	92.97
Ningxia	33.47	8.11	58.86	0.95	3.21	44178.54	95.75
Xinjiang	32.39	8.20	61.39	1.21	7.83	72531.14	97.96

Data: http://www.allchinadata.com/english/industrial%20economy.htm (2002)

2. Chinese FDI Pattern

2.1 FDI's Time Trend

The most impressive feature of the time trend is the sharp FDI boom in 1990s in contrast with steady but small amount of inflows in the 1980s and slightly slow down in recent years (table 2). Literatures (Lardy 1995, Zhang 2001) attributed the FDI boom to a further liberalization of China's FDI regime and the explosive growth of domestic economy, along with the worldwide rise in FDI outflows in the first half of the 1990s and China's political stability. After its peak year 1998, Actual foreign investment in China in 1999 was US$40.32bn, 11.3 per cent less than the total in 1998, and contracted foreign investment was US$41.24bn, 18.9 per cent less. Investment from Hong Kong and Macau fell by 6.2 per cent, from the rest of Asia by 10.3 per cent, from the US by 10.2 per cent and from the EU by 33.4 per cent (China Economic Review, 2001, September). Although there is a little rise again (2.3% year to year increase) in 2001, China cannot expect a higher FDI growth unless further steps are taken to open more sectors and improve the climate for foreign investors. We argue that weaknesses in China's legislation and complex bureaucratic procedures are significant deterrents to FDI, according to our analysis below.

Table 2. FDI Flows to China, by Time Trend and Origin, 1979-2001

Year	FDI (US$ bn)	Percent change of flow from previous year (%)	FDI Distribution by Source (%)		
			Asia	Western	Others
1979-1982	1.17				
1983	0.64	81.9			
1984	1.26	98.3			
1985	1.66	32.2	67	27	6
1986	1.87	12.7	74	23	3
1987	2.31	23.4	84	14	3
1988	3.19	38.1	82	12	6
1989	3.39	6.2	77	14	9
1990	3.48	2.8	84	16	0
1991	4.37	25.3	82	13	5
1992	11.01	152.1	90	8	3
1993	27.52	150.3	87	11	3
1994	33.77	22.7	84	13	3
1995	37.52	11.0	82	15	4
1996	41.73	11.2	80	15	5
1997	45.26	8.9	68	16	16
1998	45.46	0.42	69	18	13
1999	40.32	-11.3	59	21	20
2000	40.77	1.1	57	22	21
2001	41.73	2.3	59	24	17

Data: Computed based on data from International Trade (various issues) by MOFTEC for 1992-2001, and from China Statistical Yearbook (various issues) by SSB for other years.

Note: All numbers of FDI flows and stock are realized investment in current values.

2.2 FDI's Origins

As table 2 shown, among all FDIs, Asian direct investment (ADI) was the dominant source of Chinese FDI activity, particularly Hong Kong direct investment (HKDI) constituted over one half of China's inward FDI in almost every single year since 1979, which are otherwise not significant international investors. Even after the government strengthened the project's examination and approval to enhance the FDI's quality from September, 1999, in 2001, HKDI still constituted 36%, While U.S. direct investment constituted 8.02%, Japan 8.2%, and European 7.9% (the US-China Business Council). A well accepted reason for this structure is ADI which primarily is export oriented, has been encouraged by China's cheap labor and incentive policies toward this type of FDI; the Western investors has been induced essentially by China's potentially huge market and trade barriers, the amount of Western FDI flows has been limited largely due to China's restrictive policy toward the market-oriented FDI. Table 3 suggests that relative to the Asian developing economies, industrial countries have places less emphasis on export-oriented light industries and textile projects in China. Though the share of ADI in these two groups is as high as 44%, that for the Western FDI is only 26%, the ADI is concentrated on labor-intensive and relatively low-technology goods (such as garments, toys, shoes, and consumer electronics) aimed at the international market. Their products tend to be undifferentiated and sold mainly on the basis of price rather than distinct design or performance characteristics. In contrast, FDI from developed countries (the US, Japan, and western Europe) aim their investments much more to china's domestic market in capital-intensive goods such as machinery, chemicals, health care products, and services.

Table 3. FDI Sector Distribution in China in 2000, by Sources of FDI, Scale and Projects

	Asian FDI			Western FDI			Total		
Sector	Number	%	Average scale(US$ Million)	Number	%	Average scale	Number	%	Average scale
Agriculture	36	1.82	1.30	71	6.72	1.38	107	3.53	1.35
Building materials	96	4.86	1.51	56	5.30	2.32	152	5.02	1.81
Chemicals	152	7.68	1.92	87	8.24	1.02	239	7.91	1.59
Electronics	145	7.33	1.35	119	11.3	1.47	264	8.71	1.41
Energy	4	0.20	2.66	29	2.74	2.57	33	1.08	2.58
Food	101	5.11	0.75	84	7.95	1.94	185	6.10	1.29
Heavy industry	131	6.63	2.14	108	10.2	2.42	239	7.90	2.27
Light industry	570	28.8	1.87	173	16.4	2.09	743	24.5	1.92
Medical	34	1.72	2.26	69	6.53	2.22	95	3.13	2.42
Packaging	66	3.34	0.89	17	1.61	2.17	83	2.73	1.15
Printing	14	0.71	0.81	12	1.14	1.77	26	0.88	1.25
Property development	61	3.09	2.38	27	2.56	2.97	86	2.85	2.62
Services	73	3.69	0.75	35	3.31	1.49	108	3.57	0.99
Textiles	358	19.5	0.79	101	9.56	1.34	459	15.2	0.95
Transportation	94	4.76	1.35	54	5.11	2.57	148	4.90	1.79
Miscellaneous	46	2.33	1.28	14	1.33	1.42	60	1.97	1.31
Total	1,977	100	1.48	1,056	100	2.26	3,033	100	1.62

Data: Special Report on Foreign Direct Investment in China by the China Industry-Business Council (2001).

Notes: Western FDI denotes FDI from all developed countries. Asian FDI is the FDI from all developing economies.

Another plausible explanation is cultural similarity. Hong Kong and Taiwan's ethnic with China is an unique ownership: both share the same language and culture, which enables investors to conduct negotiations and operations much easier. Western investors who have a tendency to make business practice hurry, impersonal, shallow, and focus on the short-term bottom line can not endure Chinese executives who view business deals too personal, too time wasting, and too inefficiency.

2.3 FDI's Sectoral Distribution

The sectoral distribution of FDI is complicated and varies greatly from sector to sector. Most FIEs are small scale, especially Asian FIEs, only average 1.48US$ million per project (table 3). Studies show that there is very little technological content in FDI investment, at least regarding hardware transfer. The level of technology transferred through FDI is only 2 years ahead of current Chinese technological capabilities. However, the gap between Chinese and foreign technology levels is approximately 20 years (Sheng 1999).

According to FDI theory, small firms do not invest abroad, due to the many costs involved in overseas transactions. But small project, not large project was favored by foreign investors in China, the possible explanation is small projects were less stringently regulated which reduced their investment cost more than what their overseas transaction could bring in. Large market-oriented projects took higher administrative barriers which increased their investment cost more than what their low wages could saved.

Despite their small size, most FIEs in certain sectors such as home appliances, automobiles, chemicals and machine building engage processing trade as shown in table 4, the net trade effect was persistently and substantially negative.

Table 4. 1986-1999 External Trade of FIEs (10 thousands US$ and %)

Year	Export		Imports		Export and import	
	Value	As percent of national total (%)	Value	As percent of national total (%)	Value	As percent of national total (%)
Average 1985-90	33.96	5.23	65.51	10.98	99.47	8.28
Average 1991-95	272.47	24.32	402.01	37.70	674.48	30.86
1996	615.06	40.71	756.04	54.45	1371.10	47.29
1997	749.00	41.00	777.20	54.59	1526.20	46.95
1998	809.62	44.06	767.17	54.73	1576.79	48.68
1999	886.28	45.47	858.84	51.83	1831.33	50.78
2000	1194.00	47.90	1591.56	70.70	2785.56	58.73
2001	1271.47	49.56	1789.27	71.09	3060.74	60.79
Average 1985-2001	651.48	29.69	745.48	42.41	1409.28	36.26

Data: calculated according to China statistical yearbook (2000) and various issues of Foreign Investment Statistics.

There are two undesirable consequences of this processing trade for FDI recipient country. First, low labor cost would no longer be an advantage for domestic firms to gain more profit, when exports and imports were both controlled by FIEs or their subsidiaries because they had special competence, and could run them better, or simply because they had cash and the locals did not. Domestic exporter had to depend on FIEs' R and D, product design, brand and international market network. This situation depressed the development of domestic firms. Second, the increased import substitute decreased the demand for domestic intermediate-product industries, which in turn reduced the pulling effect of export to economic growth. So, the export processing would lead to slow growth of total foreign trade, thus weakened the positive effect of foreign trade on the economy as a whole.

2.4 FDI's Regional Distribution

The unevenness of the distribution of FDI inflows by province is well known. As table 5 shows, inflows to the ten (eastern) provinces which each took more than 5 per cent of cumulated FDI inflows in 1985-2000, accounted for 86.35 per cent of the total inflows in the same period. These ten provinces (the three municipalities of Beijing, Tianjin, and Shanghai plus the six eastern provinces of Liaoning, Jiangsu, Zhejiang, Fujian, Shandong, Guangdong and the island of Hainan), moreover, accounted for only 42.46 per cent of China's population in 2000.

Table 5. Foreign Direct Investment Inflows by Region (Millions $)

Year	Eastern Provinces		Central Provinces		Western Provinces		Eastern-Western
	Value	% of total	Value	% of total	Value	% of total	
1985-89	10,417.9	87.78	823.1	6.93	627.9	5.29	9,790
1990	2,974.10	93.86	122.60	3.87	71.71	2.26	2,902.39
1991	3,888.49	94.28	168.46	4.08	67.61	1.64	3,820.88
1992	6,715.50	59.32	4,397.88	38.85	207.59	1.83	6,507.91
1993	23,887.99	87.37	2,427.99	8.88	1,025.76	3.75	22,862.23
1994	25,872.40	86.47	2,612.69	8.73	1,434.91	4.79	24,437.49
1995	31,669.39	87.38	3,429.36	9.46	1,144.74	3.16	30,524.65
1996	36,859.58	88.03	3,985.92	9.52	1,024.21	2.45	35,835.37
1997	34,782.30	84.58	4,787.65	11.64	1,554.14	3.78	33,228.16
1998	39,490.12	87.21	4,420.22	9.76	1,373.55	3.03	38,116.57
1999	35,049.74	87.77	3,747.41	9.38	1,137.67	2.85	33,912.07
2000	35,675.49	88.12	3,585.72	8.85	1,221.72	3.01	34,453.77
2001	36,397.56	87.22	4,189.31	10.04	1,145.13	2.74	35,252.43
1985-2001	287,283	86.35	34,509	10.37	10,891.5	3.27	276,391.5
Population (Million)	535.97	42.46	439.40	34.81	286.91	22.73	249.06

Data: Computed based on data from International Trade (various issues) by MOFTEC for 1992-2001, and from China Statistical Yearbook (various issues) by SSB for other years.
Note: All numbers of FDI flows and stock are realized investment in current values.

Even though the government deliberately introduced incentives to invest in west regions. For example, offer super-national treatment of foreign investors in a variety of ways (e.g., benefits of reduced or exempted taxes that are not available to other regions' FIEs). Both in terms of the overall shares and on the per capital basis, the inequality between the East and the West has been enlarged. Besides, we may also note that all the major recipient provinces/ cities of FDI are located in the East. In terms of the share in the total national cumulative actual investment, the four biggest recipient provinces/cities are Guangdong, Jiangsu, Fujian, and shanghai, in descending order.

The reason for this concentration are multiple. Provinces with much better industries and human capital bases as well as the infrastructure attract more multinational enterprises. The recent literature, e.g. Dollar, et, al (2001) also demonstrated that administrative procedures-and the costs and delays associated with them-can significantly influence the location of multinational firms and their resulting productivity. Compared with West province, the investment climate in east area generally have held a permanent dominant position as self-authorized operators and have easy market access to other firms. Their low administrative barriers, such as hardly suffering from work stoppages or other turbulences can reduce greatly investment cost and increase investment profit.

The distribution of the 500 largest foreign-funded enterprises (FIEs) (in terms of sales value in 1999) is even more skewed. The top 500 FIEs were mainly engaged in electronics; machine-making; food-processing; textiles and clothing and automobiles and more than half of them (257) were funded with capital from Hong Kong and Macau. Of the rest, Japan accounted for 66 and the USA for 50. The top 500 were distributed among 24 provinces and municipalities, 91 per cent of them along the coast (China Economic News, 2000, 12.9).

MANIFESTATIONS OF ADMINISTRATIVE BARRIERS

Administrative barriers exist in all countries. Indeed, it is legitimate for governments to control or even screen for some activities and investors who are going to install on their territory. Authorities have generally advanced arguments such as security, protection of the environment, health protection, and quality control. But the excessive administrative barriers which lie in fundamental factors such as the legal system, the political regime, trade and financial openness, and public wages hinder necessary FDI inflows. A country where it takes excessive time and costs to accomplish all the procedures necessary to establish and operate a business will see its potential investors lose money and decide to locate elsewhere or cancel their investment projects. The problem tends to be more serious in China because of the incomplete regulation framework and because of unnecessary bureaucratic interference. Major Chinese barriers of concern include:

3. Investment Restrictions

3.1 Ownership Restriction

Although the number of projects in the encouraged category has increased from 186 to 263 while the number of restricted projects has been reduced from 112 to 75. The new Catalogue brought no significant breakthrough other than the existing commitments contained in the WTO Protocol; moreover, while the total number of encouraged projects may have increased and the number of restricted areas is fewer, some of the key industries and big ticket items, such as construction and operation of power grids, and futures, are still off-limits to foreign investors. Here are percentages of permitted foreign ownership of businesses in several "restricted" sectors of China's economy:

1. Advertising agencies: Will rise from current 49 percent limit to 100 percent by 2005.
2. Banking and financial services: Local currency transactions with Chinese enterprises starting 2003. With Chinese individuals, starting 2006. Financial companies can offer auto financing.
3. Insurance: Non-life insurers, from less than 51 percent now to 100 percent by 2003. Life insurers, limit will remain at less than 50 percent, though AIA has offered life and non-life insurance through a wholly owned subsidiary since 1992. Brokerages, from less than 50 percent now to 100 percent by 2006.

4. Securities and mutual funds: Prohibited till 2004, when up to one-third or more will be permitted. Mutual fund companies, to 49 percent by 2004.

5. Telecom: Paging services, to 50 percent by 2003; mobile voice and data, 49 percent by 2004 and 100 percent by 2006; international and domestic long distance, 49 percent by 2007.

6. Wholesale and retail: 50 percent as of 2002, rising to 100 percent by 2004, except for chain retailers, which cannot be majority-owned by foreigners. Chains cannot have more than 30 stores (Source: Mike View partner-Asia business group, Ernst and Young LLP).

3.2 Rate of Return Restrictions

Although not officially documented, there is general agreement that beginning in 1993, the State planning Commission, which must approve all projects costing more than $30 million, stopped approving all FDI projects with projected rates of return in excess of a limit, for example, fifteen percent for power project, (World Electric Power Industry, 1996). Though regulations on rates of return to FDI in power sector are not uncommon in developing countries, the Chinese government's de facto cap was set at an unusually low level given the risks involved. In other Asian countries, rates of return in excess of twenty percent are the norm (Blackman 1997).

The de facto cap on rate of return had several impacts. First, many foreign investors lost interest completely. And second, a bias was created in favor of small-scale projects costing less than $30 million that do not need the approval of the state Planning Commission. It is not uncommon for foreign investors to split relatively large projects into several "phase" to by-pass the state regulatory agencies.

3.3 Operating Rights Restriction

Chinese officials pressure foreign investors to agree to contract provisions which stipulate technology transfers, exporting a certain share of production, and commitments on local content. China restricts the number and types of entities in China that are allowed to import products into China, and foreign companies are not permitted to directly engage in trade in China.

3.4 Distribution Rights Restriction

Most foreign companies are prohibited from selling their products directly to Chinese consumers.

4. Non-Transparent and Inaccessible FDI Rules and Regulations

While China has enacted legislation to facilitate foreign investment in general, the country lacks of an adequate rule-based legal and regulatory environment for investment FDI. Among problems disappointed foreign investors are:

1. There are too much uncertainty, as interpretation and enforcement of rules-from registering a new company, to acquiring land, to paying taxes-change rapidly and depend on which government official is doing the interpreting or enforcing.

2. The country lacks a specific law governing the specific sectors to serve as a basis for operating business. For example, the telecom sector is currently guided only by a few fragmented administrative rules and regulations. Several drafts of a telecom law have been prepared, but bureaucratic inertia and irreconcilable interests have stymied the process. Without a national law with an overarching set of regulations, procedures, and enforcement mechanism, the legality of foreign investment projects remain unclear, thus most foreign investors interested in China's post-WTO telecom market are wary of this lack of protection, and many are holding off on future investment until the investment environment improves.

3. It is not easy to get access to the content of the laws and regulations that apply to business operations. The dissemination of legal information in China is so underdeveloped, so unsystematic that it is often difficult simply to find the applicable law. Even when the relevant rule can be found, provisions are often so broad and sketchy that it is difficulty to be certain of correct interpretation. There is also no systematic compilation of case-law precedents that would aid in the interpretation of statutes and regulations. There is also the vexing problem of the so-called "neibu" or internal agency rules.

4. Until now, minority shareholders rights have not been understood by Chinese officials, or addressed fully and consistently in Chinese law.

5. Bureaucratic Interference

Most of the complaints by foreign-investors is unnecessary bureaucratic interference on their firm's decision-making process, and subordinates' appointment and dismiss, unexpected labor, health and safety inspections, etc. The party's pervasive influence is in every branch of government. According to a survey of firms around the world by the world bank (1997), on a 1-7 scale where 7 indicating the highest level of regulatory burden, China received a rating of 4.58 (In comparison, Singapore's bureaucratic burden received a score of 2.08). The viability of foreign firms in China depends critically on their ability to enforce business contracts in an environment in which contract law is still in its infancy. Though legal uncertainties affect operating contracts for production, input and sale, they are perhaps most daunting for so-called "power purchase contracts". The mechanism that foreign private investors seem to have relied upon in lieu of improvement in the investment environment is to create incentives for various level governments to uphold their contracts by including them as partner in joint ventures. But this strategy promotes rent seeking and vertical integration that limits competition.

Given the advantage of teaming up with strategically chosen Chinese partners to mitigate financial and operational risk, the joint corporations (JCs) has been a main vehicle for FDI, it has been reported recently that more than half of JCs in China are failing to make a profit (Henley et. al. 1999). Of the three main kinds of foreign direct investment, table 6 shows the number of JC decreased considerably during 1990s, declining from 72.9 percent of the total value of projects signed in 1992 to 60 percent in 2000. The decreasing popularity of this form of foreign direct investment testifies, inter alia, to a losing confidence which investors feel about establishing a presence in China.

Table 6. FDI by Type of Investment, 1992 and 2000

	1992			2000		
	No of Projects	Value ($m)	% of total	No of Projects	Value ($m)	% of total
Joint venture	34,354	29,128.5	50.1	7,050	15,827.3	39.9
Co-operative venture	5,711	13,255.5	22.8	1,656	8,233.7	20.8
WFO	8,692	15,696.2	27.0	8,201	15,544.8	39.3
Total	48,764	58,123.5	100	16,907	39,605.8	100

Data: From China Statistical Yearbook by SSB, 1994 and 2001

High administrative barriers made the other vehicles of foreign investment, such as Joint stock companies and limited-liability companies, are less prevalent. Wei (1999) offered a striking sample calculation: if China is able to reduce red tape and corruption to a level comparable to Singapore, a double FDI increase could be expected.

5. Foreign Exchange Control

After the January 1994 reform prohibited the settling of transactions in foreign currency and eliminated the swap centers,, now foreign firms must use a network of foreign exchange banks. These provide foreign exchange subject to the annual approval of the State Administration of Exchange Control (SAEC). FDI firms are no longer guaranteed by the government that sufficient foreign exchange will be available to them. Because the Chinese currency is not yet fully convertible, foreign joint ventures have to take a risk that their foreign exchange needs cannot be met by purchasing it at banks.

CAUSES OF EXCESSIVE ADMINISTRATIVE BARRIERS

As already noted, administrative barriers in China mainly arises from incomplete regulation framework and bureaucratic interference. China's economy remains an unbalanced mixture of imperfect markets with noncompetitive enterprises and markets where market systems and the forces of competition are gradually emerging. Its administrative system remains politics. China's major problem in achieving perfect investment climate is the immaturity of government policy, mainly reflected in the following ways:

1. Current Chinese FDI policy is vague regarding the administrative of foreign investor's entry and operation, the project's examination and approval are implemented by government politics, and obtaining a operation licence to some extend depends on officials' willingness not on clear criteria. They held monopoly status when their

authority cannot be supervised, and once they became profit-oriented, tended to seek profits far higher than normal.

2. Unequal treatment, due to unfavorable policy reasons, makes it impossible for some FIEs to compete with an equality of opportunity to succeed. Export-oriented FDI policy made Western investors who are aim at China's potential vast market frustrated in 1990s, but current hi-tech-oriented FDI policy ignoring local capabilities and economic fundamentals also let them disappointed.

3. In the process of transition and without a sound supervisory system, officials of various level governments tend to take a short-term view and pursue local protectionism policy against foreign investors.

An absence of institutional independence from political control and the uniform enforcement of national regulations present a serious obstacle to the establishment of an good investment climate. For example:

1. The government's multiple roles as social and economic manager, owner of state assets, and business operator, have remained basically unchanged.

2. Government regulatory bodies do not have enough control over local level sectors. Control, if any, stays at the administrative levels, without legislative and regulatory support.

3. For the administrative mechanism to play its role in securing the FDI entry and operation, the competitive process must be allowed, and encouraged, to work. Problems arising in the transition of the open market in China have to be addressed through the reform of FDI regime. The unique situation in China is a problem of the institution, not one caused by the institution. Distortions of administrative mechanisms caused by the administrative economy over the years can be observed everywhere. It will take time to remove them, and to build up a universal appreciation in China of the sound institution structure.

THE DAMAGING EFFECTS OF EXCESSIVE ADMINISTRATIVE BARRIERS

Excessive administrative barriers represent an abuse of power by government, driven by the vested interests of a department or a locality, and manifested in local blockades, departmental barriers, sector monopolies, and collaboration between the bureaucracy and businesses. FDI can damage indigenous industries' development are deeply rooted in some aspects of China's economic life, are extremely powerful, and directly affect the development of an open, competitive economy and hinder it integrate into international market. Among the damaging effects are:

1. Harm to the enthusiasm of foreign-investors. Excessive administrative barriers discourage foreign investors show no current signs of abatement. Most foreign companies are hesitant to say the least, regarding the formation of new venture. For example, two of the largest chemical multinational corporations, E.I. du Pout de

Numours and Co. and the Dow Chemical Co. have tended to adopt a more cautious approach, no more investment in China in 2002 because of concern about profitability and administrative risk. Disillusioned from their idealism and tired of the bureaucratic red tape and regulatory hassles involved in investing in China, many investors who are developing an Internet business have exited the Chinese market (Gigalaw.com).

2. Lead to inadequate investment. This, together with declining employment and depressed consumer demand, are major issues facing China's economy. Take the power sector as an example, according to China's Ministry of Electric Power, between 1995-2010, China's power sector need an average investment of 15.8 billion $ per year in order to meet the growing demand for electricity. Of the funding needed between 1995-2000 China expected to be able to finance 30 percent (about 4,740 million per year) with foreign resources. Only one third was realized in 1998, the most ideal FDI inflows year for power industry. As for construction industry, during 1999 the value of contracted (as opposed to realized) FDI fell by 124 per cent; it fell by another 120 per cent, to $916.9 million in 2000 (China Statistical yearbook, 2001).

3. Reduce FDI's leading effect on economic growth. Although development experiences in many industrial and developing countries indicate that FDI can lead to desirable outcomes such as positive spillovers for the local economy in terms of growth and productivity. Li (2002) demonstrate the experience of China suggests that Policies biased against FDI in an attempt to protect national industrial and export-orientation have undermined FDI's contribution to national economic development, according to the analysis in this paper. On one hand, domestic enterprises (DEs)-FIEs segmentation made it impossible for economy to benefit from productivity improvement via technology transfer and spillover, which can be obtained through the introduction of capital-intensive technology that can be emulated by domestic firms, the training of workers and managers who may transfer their skills elsewhere. On the other hand, export oriented FDI, which has been encouraged by China's cheap labor and incentive policies toward this type of FDI, concentrated on labor-intensive and some simple capital-intensive manufacturing activities. Processing trade has been taken as its first choice. The increased import has lead to a reduction in China's favorable balance of trade, thus weaken the pulling effect of foreign trade on the economy as a whole.

4. Breed corruption. State propaganda decries corruption, yet China has been called one of, if not the most corrupt nations in Asia. With a few officials abusing their power in public administration to get money, FDI has become a hotbed of corruption, from high-level officials who demand "partnership" in companies that look like they will be profitable ventures-to the lowest level customs or expertise official. The problem in China is that besides published regulations agencies often issue internal (neibu) unpublished rules, which are inaccessible to outsiders and which at times are the real rules under which the agency operates. To find out the content of these rules would require many visits to an agency and even then would often not result in disclosure. This practice leaves too much power in the hands of agency bureaucrats, forms a main source breeding corruption. There is a sentence "relative connection is very important to do business in China". Jeffrey McChesney, vice president of process

excellence for corporate services with Atlas Air Inc., the world's third-largest air cargo carrier based in White Plains (Harrison), acknowledged Atlas Air has spent the past five years developing relationships with Chinese officials in hopes of tapping into China's air cargo market, especially as it looks to grow through foreign investment in the next few years. Corruption not only causes reduced inward foreign direct investment due to higher sales expenses in the invested country, but also reduces incentives for the foreign-invested company to re-invest in the host country. This can result in the flight of the foreign-invested company to another country for their investments.

CONCLUSIONS AND FUTURE MEASURES TO CURB EXCESSIVE ADMINISTRATIVE BARRIERS

China is in a transition from a closed economy to an open market economy. Administrative Barriers to foreign direct investment in China is reflected largely in investment restriction, non-transparent and inaccessible FDI rule and regulation, as well as bureaucratic interference in terms of the distortion of FDI operation behavior and the preclusion of market competition. They have become a pressing issue facing foreign investors in making decision to invest in china. China has made great effort to develop a regulation framework on incentive FDI, but this framework currently appears weak and powerless in the face of the administrative barriers. In order to maintain China's inward FDI trend, the aims of the measures to be taken against excessive administrative barriers are:

1. To complete a legal framework on FDI entry and operation. Reform and liberalizing of the FDI regime should be carried out within this legal framework. With China's accession to the WTO and the need for international integration, it is all the more important and urgent to develop legislation governing FDI entry and operation. The purpose of the existing laws relating to FDI (such as Guiding Regulations and Catalogue) is to ensure the safety of national industries rather than regulating the behavior of FIEs in these sectors. It is necessary to review, revise and improve the existing laws and regulations which are helpful to form excessive administrative barriers and the introduction of effective competition, and to speed up the formulation of a systematic compilation of case-law precedents that would aid in the interpretation of statutes and regulations.

2. To rebuild the government administrative system and exercise effective supervision. Removing excessive administrative barriers should be carried out simultaneously with a change in the role of the government. An effective government supervisory institution and system should be established, so as to ensure the development of rationalizing administrative procedures: to reduce bureaucratic red tape, simplify approval procedures, eliminating unnecessary forms, signatures, and documents. Establishing virtual network or on-line registration linking together agencies and, thus, facilitating the relations not only between investors and government's officials but also within the public administration.

3. To develop institutional mechanisms that limit default contracts. In its current state, Chinese contract law may not be sufficient to eliminate default risk. But it might be possible to structure rules that would at least provide some certainty about the legal process that would ensue upon default and about what remedies could reasonably be expected.

4. To deepen state-owned enterprise reform and the adjustment of ownership structures and to improve competition within sectors. Existing monopolistic sectors should carry out reforms and get ready for competition. The discriminatory policy against FIEs needs to be changed. Competition among state, private and foreign investors should be encouraged through the promotion of foreign investment, breaking up monopolies, and the establishment of a modern corporate system.

5. Last but not least, administrative barriers reflect more profound characteristics of a country. Administrative reforms must be incorporated in broader reforms, such as trade and financial liberalization, corruption and public sector reforms. the reform of the devolved and localized character of the investment regime, especially in the realm of taxation and the foreign exchange regime. Smash the high degree of local government autonomy, develop a united open market in China. Build a good operation environment for FDI enterprises. Reduce interference by party and local government officials in FDI's operation.

REFERENCES

Blackman, A., and X. Wu, (1997) "Climate Impacts of Foreign Direct Investment in the Chinese Power Sector: Barriers and Opportunities" *http://www.rff.org/reports/1997.htm*

Anonymous, (2001) "The institutional and policy environment for investment in Russia" *Financial Market Trends*, Paris, Issue 79, Page 137.

D. Dollar et al., (2002) "Investment Climate and Firm Productivity: India 2000-01 " *World Bank, mimeo. http://econ.worldbank.org/staff/mhallward*

Djankov, S. La Porta, F. Lopez De Silanes, A. Shleifer, (2002) "The Regulation of Entry" *Quarterly Journal of Economics*, February, Volume 9, Page 19.

Epstein, G. (1996) "Economic beat: Risk measures prove to be excellent forecasters of the rise and fall of markets abroad" *Barron's*, Chicopee, Mar 11, Volume 76, Issue 11, Page 48.

Henley, J., C. Kirkpatrick and G. Wilde. (1999) "Foreign Direct Investment (FDI) in China: Recent Trends and Current Policy Issues" *Public Policy and management Working Paper No. 7. http://idpm.man.ac.uk/wp/ppm/ppm_wp07abs.htm.*

Lardy, N. (1995) "The Role of Foreign Trade and Investment in China's Economic Transformation" *China Quarterly*, 144, 1065-82.

Li, Y. (forthcoming) "How Beneficial is Foreign Direct Investment for China's Economic Growth?" *Open Economic Review.*

Lui, Z. (2000) "Foreign Direct Investment and Technology Spillover: Some Evidence from China" *http://faculty.Washington.edu/karyiu/confer.*

Wei, S. J. (1999) "Can China and India Double Their Inward Foreign Direct Investment? " *NBER Working Paper*, No. 2399.

Y. Huang, (2000) "Why is Foreign Direct Investment Too Much of a Good Thing for China? " *http://www.fas.harvard.edu/~asiactr/mas/summaries/MAS_021100.html.*

Zhang, K. H. (2001) "What Attracts Foreign Multinational Corporations to China? " *Contemporary Economic Policy*, Vol. 19, No. 3, July, P336-346.

In: Economics and Foreign Investment in China
Editor: J.I. Cheng, pp. 181-215

ISBN 1-60021-238-7
© 2007 Nova Science Publishers, Inc.

Chapter 8

U.S.-China Trade Eliminating Nonmarket Economy Methodology Would Lower Antidumping Duties for Some Chinese Companies[*]

Government Accounting Office

ACCOUNTABILITY INTEGRITY RELIABILITY

Highlights

Why GAO Did This Study U.S. companies adversely affected by unfair imports may seek a number of relief measures, including antidumping (AD) duties.

The Department of Commerce (Commerce) classifies China as a nonmarket economy (NME) and uses a special methodology that is commonly believed to produce AD duty rates that are higher than those applied to market economies.

Commerce may stop applying its NME methodology if it finds that China warrants designation as a market economy.

In light of increased concern about China's trade practices, the conference report on fiscal year 2004 appropriations requested that GAO review efforts by U.S. government agencies responsible for ensuring free and fair trade with that country. In this report, the last in a series, GAO (1) explains the NME methodology, (2) analyzes AD duties applied to China and compares them with duties applied to market economies, and (3) explains circumstances in which the United States would stop applying its NME methodology to China and evaluates the potential impact of such a step.

Commerce agreed with our findings, commenting that our report provides timely and helpful information on the NME methodology and its application to China.

---

[*] Excerpted from GAO Report 06-231 dated Janueary 2006.

What GAO Found

Commerce's methodology for calculating AD duties on nonmarket economy products differs from its market economy approach in that (1) since NME prices are unreliable, it uses price information from surrogate countries, like India, to construct the value of the imported products and (2) it limits eligibility for individual rates to companies that show their export activities are not subject to government control. Companies that do not meet the criteria or do not participate in Commerce investigations receive "countrywide" rates.

China has been the most frequent target of U.S. AD actions. On 25 occasions, Commerce has applied duties to the same product from both China and one or more market economy. China (NME) duties were over 20 percentage points higher than those applied to market economies, on average. This is because average China country-wide rates were over 60 points higher than comparable market economy rates. Individual China company rates were similar to those assigned to market economy companies, on average.

COMPARISON OF CHINA AND MARKET ECONOMY ANTIDUMPING RATES FOR 25 PRODUCTS (1985-2004)

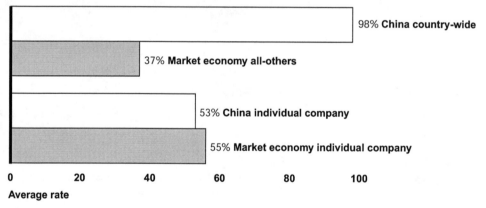

Source: GAO AD database.

Commerce can declare China a market economy if the country meets certain criteria, thus ending the use of surrogate price information and country-wide rates in China AD actions. These changes would have a mixed impact. Duties would likely decline for Chinese companies not assigned individual rates. Individual company rates would likely diverge, with those that do not cooperate with Commerce receiving rates that are substantially higher than those that do cooperate. In any case, it appears that the actual trade impact of the NME methodology will decline as the portion of total export trade conducted by Chinese companies assigned individual rates increases and as the country-wide rates that largely account for the comparatively high average rates applied to China decline in importance.

ABBREVIATIONS

AD-antidumping
HT-SHarmonized Tariff ScheduleI
TCU.S.- International Trade Commission
NME-nonmarket economy
WTO-World Trade Organization

Imports from China have grown rapidly over the last decade, from a total value of about $42 billion in 1995 to over $196 billion in 2004.[1] While the prices of these Chinese goods are often lower than U.S. prices and, therefore, benefit consumers, this growth has presented a major challenge for U.S. producers that compete with Chinese products in the U.S. market. Some U.S. companies adversely affected by this growth have alleged that Chinese success in the U.S. market has come partly as a result of unfair trade practices.

U.S. companies that are adversely affected by unfair imports from China (or other countries) may avail themselves of a number of relief measures, including antidumping (AD) duties. The United States has classified China as a "nonmarket economy" (NME) country since 1981[2] and employs a special NME methodology to calculate AD duties on unfairly traded products from that country. This methodology is commonly believed to result in duty rates that are significantly higher than those applied to market economy countries.

In light of increased concern about China's trade practices, the conference report on fiscal year 2004 appropriations legislation requested that GAO monitor the efforts of U.S. government agencies responsible for ensuring free and fair trade with that country.[3] In subsequent discussions with staff from the House Appropriations Committee's Subcommittee on Science, State, Justice, and Commerce and Related Agencies, we agreed to provide a number of reports on import relief mechanisms and the manner in which these mechanisms have been applied to China. To date, we have issued three such reports, focusing on textile safeguards, safeguards applicable to other products, and countervailing duties.[4]

This fourth and final report on China import relief mechanisms focuses on AD duties. In this report, we

- explain the special methodology that the United States employs to calculate AD duties on products from China and other NME countries,
- • analyze the application of AD duties to China over the last 25 years and compare the duty rates applied to Chinese products with the duty rates applied to products from market economy countries, and
- • explain the circumstances in which the United States would stop using its NME methodology to calculate AD duties on Chinese products and evaluate the potential impact of this step.

To conduct our review, we examined applicable U.S. laws and regulations and World Trade Organization (WTO) agreements, including relevant portions of the agreement through which China acceded to WTO membership in 2001. We reviewed scholarly literature and consulted with trade and legal policy experts from the U.S. government, private sector trade associations, consulting and law firms, and academic institutions, as well as representatives of the WTO, the government of China, and other governments. In order to analyze U.S. application of AD duties to China and compare the duties applied to China with those applied to market economy countries, we used information from the Department of Commerce (Commerce) and the U.S. International Trade Commission (ITC), including notices of Commerce determinations appearing in the *Federal Register*, to construct a database on all U.S. antidumping investigations from 1980 through 2004. We verified this database to the official sources. Our analyses focused on the 68 AD duty orders that Commerce issued against Chinese products during this period and especially on the 25 cases in which Commerce also imposed duties on the same products from market economy countries.[5] We performed additional (multivariate regression) analyses to determine the extent to which duty rate variations could be attributed to differences between China and these other countries, or to other factors, such as the type of product involved. Appendix I contains a detailed description of our scope and methodology.

We conducted our work from June 2005 through December 2005 in accordance with generally accepted government auditing standards.

RESULTS IN BRIEF

Commerce's special methodology for calculating the AD duties that it applies to China and other NME countries differs from its usual (market economy) approach in two key respects. First, since prices in NME countries do not reliably reflect the fair value of the merchandise, Commerce uses price information from surrogate countries (like India) to construct the value of NME products—and thus provide an appropriate basis for calculating AD duty rates—rather than relying entirely on information from the exporting country itself. Second, Commerce requires NME companies to demonstrate that their export activities are not subject to government control in order to be considered eligible for individually determined duty rates, rather than considering all companies eligible for such rates, as it does in market economy cases. NME companies that do not meet these criteria, or do not participate in Commerce's investigations receive "country-wide" rates.

Over the last 25 years, the United States has applied AD duties against China more often than against any other country. On 25 occasions, Commerce applied duties to the same products from both China and at least one market economy country. The duty rates assigned in these cases varied greatly. On average, however, the rates applied to China were over 20 percentage points higher than those applied to market economy countries. This difference is attributable primarily to the comparatively high country-wide duty rates applied to Chinese companies not eligible for individual rates. These country-wide rates averaged about 98 percent—over 60 percentage points higher than the average duty rates assigned to market economy companies not receiving individual rates. In contrast, when Commerce calculated individual rates for Chinese companies, these rates were not substantially different, on average, from those assigned to individual market economy companies.

Commerce has administrative authority to declare China a market economy, or find individual Chinese industries to be "market-oriented" in character—provided that China overall or individual Chinese industries meet certain criteria. Such a declaration would end application of the NME methodology to China, in whole or in part. This would (1) eliminate country-wide duty rates against China and (2) eliminate use of surrogate country information to calculate AD duty rates on Chinese products. These changes would have a mixed impact. Eliminating country-wide rates would likely reduce duty rates applied to companies not receiving individual rates. Individually determined rates would likely diverge into two distinct groups, with companies that do not cooperate in Commerce investigations receiving rates that are substantially higher than those that do cooperate. The impact of applying Chinese price information would likely vary by industry, and AD rates applied against China would continue to vary widely, both within and among cases. However, it appears that the significance of the NME country-wide rates is declining as more Chinese companies receive individual rates, although data that would permit quantification of the potential trade impact of these changes is not available. This suggests that the trade significance of the NME methodology now applied to China will likewise decline over time.

Commerce provided written comments on a draft of this report, which are reprinted in appendix IV. Overall, Commerce agreed with our findings. In addition, Commerce, the Department of Homeland Security, and the Office of the U.S. Trade Representative, provided technical comments. We took these comments into consideration and made revisions throughout the report as appropriate to make it more accurate and clear.

BACKGROUND

Dumping refers to a type of international price discrimination wherein a foreign company sells merchandise in a given export market (for example, the United States) at prices that are lower than the prices that the company charges in its home market or other export markets. When this occurs, and when the imports have been found to materially injure, or threaten to materially injure, U.S. producers, U.S. law permits application of antidumping duties to offset the price advantage enjoyed by the imported product.[6]

Any domestic industry that believes it is suffering material injury, or is threatened with material injury, as a result of dumping by foreign companies may file a petition requesting imposition of AD duties. Interested domestic industries file petitions simultaneously with Commerce and ITC. If Commerce determines that the petitioning parties meet certain eligibility requirements,[7] ITC determines whether the domestic industry has suffered material injury as a result of the alleged dumping (or is threatened with material injury).[8] While ITC is completing its work, Commerce conducts an investigation to establish the duty rates, if any, that should be applied.

To determine the duty rates to apply in an antidumping investigation, Commerce identifies (1) the foreign product's export price entering the U.S. market and (2) its "normal value." Commerce then compares these prices to determine whether—and by how much—the product's export price is less than its normal value. AD duty rates are based on these differences, which are called dumping margins.[9]

To establish a product's export price, Commerce generally refers to the prices charged in actual sales of that product to purchasers in the United States.[10] To establish its normal value, Commerce generally refers to the prices charged for the product in the exporting company's home market. In the event that the product is not sold in the exporter's home market, Commerce may refer to prices charged for the product in another export market or construct a normal value based on costs of production in the exporting country, together with selling, general and administrative expenses, and profit.[11] The two agencies make preliminary and, after additional investigation, final determinations as to whether injury has occurred (ITC) and the size of the duty, if any, that should be imposed (Commerce). When warranted, Commerce issues "duty orders" instructing Customs and Border Protection to apply duties against imported products from the countries under investigation. Both ITC and Commerce publish their decisions in the *Federal Register*.

Since AD duties address unfair pricing practices, and pricing decisions are generally made by individual companies, Commerce generally calculates and assigns AD duty rates on an individual company basis. As a result, AD investigations generally produce a number of individually determined, company-specific rates, reflecting differences in the extent to which companies have dumped their products—that is, exported them at less than their normal value.[12] In addition, AD duty orders also generally specify a duty rate for other companies that have not been assigned an individually determined rate.

In principle, Commerce bases its AD duty determinations on information obtained from interested parties—including foreign producers and exporters. Commerce obtains needed information from foreign companies by sending them questionnaires and following up with additional questions, as needed, and with on-site visits.[13]

However, both U.S. law and WTO rules recognize that, in some cases, officials charged with completing these investigations will be unable to obtain sufficient information. In such cases, Commerce officials apply facts available to complete their duty determinations.[14] This may include secondary information, subject to corroboration from independent sources.

Moreover, if Commerce finds that an interested party, such as a foreign company under investigation, "has failed to cooperate by not acting to the best of its ability to comply with a request for information" then, in selecting among the facts available, Commerce may apply an inference that is adverse to the interests of that party. In applying adverse inferences, Commerce can use (among other things) information contained in the petition filed by the domestic industry seeking imposition of AD duties, the results of a prior review or determination in the case, or any other information placed on the record.[15]

This authority provides an incentive for foreign companies to provide the information that Commerce needs to complete its work. For example, in a 1993 case that involved two Brazilian companies, one company attempted to cooperate in the investigation but nonetheless was unable to provide the information that Commerce needed, while the other declined to provide any information at all. Commerce used facts available to determine that the first company should be subject to a duty rate of 42 percent. For the second company, Commerce selected adverse inferences from among the facts available and applied these to calculate a duty rate of 109 percent.[16]

COMMERCE EMPLOYS A SPECIAL
METHODOLOGY TO CALCULATE CHINA AD DUTIES

The methodology that Commerce employs in NME cases differs from Commerce's usual (market economy) approach in two key ways. First, rather than rely entirely on information from the exporting country itself to establish a product's normal value, Commerce uses price information from surrogate countries to construct these values. Second, rather than consider all companies eligible for individually determined duty rates, Commerce requires NME companies to meet certain criteria to be considered eligible for such rates. Commerce generally employs different approaches to calculate duty rates for companies that do and do not meet these criteria.

AD CALCULATIONS FOR NME PRODUCTS EMPLOY THIRD COUNTRY INFORMATION

In AD investigations involving products from NME countries, U.S. law requires Commerce to use a special methodology to calculate duty rates in view of the absence of meaningful home market prices and information on production costs. When a product from China or another NME country is the target of an AD investigation, Commerce officials use price information and financial data from an appropriate market economy country to construct a normal value for the product under investigation.[17] India is the most commonly used surrogate for China.

To apply this methodology, Commerce (1) identifies and quantifies the factors of production (e.g., various raw materials) used by the NME producers, (2) identifies market prices for each factor in a surrogate country; (3) multiplies volume times cost for each factor; and (4) adds the results, together with a reasonable margin for selling, general and administrative expenses, and profit (based on surrogate country financial data), to produce a constructed normal value.[18] The dumping margin—and consequently the AD duty rate—is then determined by comparing this normal value with the NME company's export price to the United States.

NME COMPANIES MUST MEET CERTAIN CRITERIA TO BE CONSIDERED ELIGIBLE FOR INDIVIDUAL DUTY RATES

While all companies from market economy countries are eligible for individually determined or weighted average AD duty rates, companies from China and other NME countries must pass a separate rates test to be eligible for such rates. This test requires NME companies to meet two closely related criteria: they must demonstrate that their export activities are free from government control both in law and in fact.[19] To provide a basis for deciding whether companies meet these criteria, Commerce requires these companies to submit information regarding

- whether there are restrictive stipulations associated with an individual exporter's business and export licenses,
- any legislative enactments decentralizing control of companies,
- any other formal measures decentralizing government control of companies,
- whether export prices are set by or subject to approval by the government,
- whether the company has authority to negotiate and sign contracts,
- whether the company has autonomy in selecting its management, and

whether the company retains the proceeds of its export sales and makes independent decisions regarding disposition of profits or financing of losses.[20]

COMMERCE EMPLOYS DIFFERENT APPROACHES TO DETERMINE DUTY RATES FOR ELIGIBLE AND INELIGIBLE NME COMPANIES

As shown in figure 1, Commerce uses fundamentally different approaches to calculate duty rates to be applied against companies that do and do not pass the separate rates test.

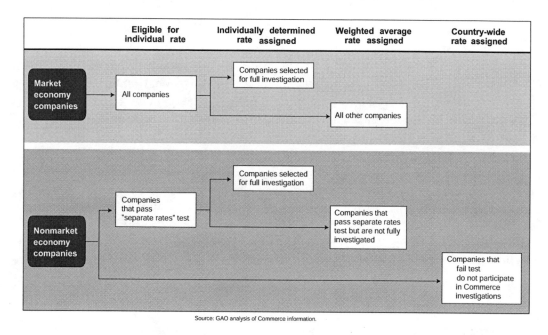

Source: GAO analysis of Commerce information.

Figure 1. Different Approaches to Determining AD Duty Rates.

ELIGIBLE NME COMPANIES RECEIVE INDIVIDUALLY DETERMINED OR WEIGHTED AVERAGE DUTY RATES

As shown in figure 1, Commerce treats companies from China and other NME countries that pass Commerce's separate rates test like market economy countries when assigning duty rates. When practical, Commerce fully investigates and establishes individually determined duty rates for each eligible NME company, just as it does for each market economy company. To the extent that fully investigated NME companies cooperate with Commerce, they receive rates based on the information that they provide. As explained in the background section of this report, Commerce uses facts available, and may use adverse inferences, to calculate duty rates when the companies under investigation cannot or will not provide the information that Commerce needs.

In both NME and market economy cases, Commerce may limit the number of companies it fully investigates when it is faced with a large number of companies. In such situations,

Commerce generally calculates individual rates for the companies that account for the largest volume of the subject merchandise.[21] In market economy cases, Commerce then calculates a weighted average of these rates and applies the resulting "all others" rate to companies that it has not fully investigated.[22] Commerce does not routinely calculate weighted average duty rates in NME cases. However, when the number of NME companies eligible for individually determined rates exceeds the number that Commerce can fully investigate, Commerce calculates a weighted average rate and informs Customs of the companies entitled to this rate.[23]

OTHER NME COMPANIES RECEIVE COUNTRY-WIDE DUTY RATES

In cases involving China or other NME countries, Commerce calculates a country-wide duty rate for companies that could not (or did not attempt to) pass Commerce's separate rates test. In NME cases, Commerce assumes that all exporters and producers of a given product are subject to common government control and that all of these companies should, therefore, be subject to a single country-wide duty rate. Commerce begins its NME antidumping investigations by requesting information from the government of the country in question and from known producers and exporters. If Commerce cannot identify all relevant producers and exporters, or if one or more of the identified companies refuses to cooperate in the investigation, Commerce relies on adverse inferences to calculate a country-wide rate. Commerce then instructs Customs to apply the countrywide rate against shipments from any company other than those specifically listed as eligible for an individually determined or weighted average rate.[24]

COMMERCE HAS APPLIED AD DUTIES TO
CHINA FREQUENTLY AT VARIED RATES

Over the last 25 years, the United States has applied AD duties against Chinese products more often than against products from any other country. While AD duty rates have varied widely, on average the rates assigned to Chinese products have been higher than the rates assigned to the same products from market economy countries. We found that this is attributable primarily to the comparatively high country-wide rates applied to Chinese companies not eligible for individually determined or weighted average rates. When Commerce has calculated rates for individual Chinese companies, the average rates assigned to these companies have not been substantially different from those assigned to market economy companies.

CHINA HAS BEEN THE MOST FREQUENT
TARGET OF U.S. ANTIDUMPING ORDERS

Over the last 25 years, Commerce has both considered and actually applied AD duties against China more often than against any other country. From 1980 through 2004,

Commerce processed 1,046 AD petitions and issued 455 AD duty orders. One hundred and ten of these petitions (11 percent) and 68 of these orders (15 percent) focused on China—both are the largest number against any U.S. trade partner.[25]

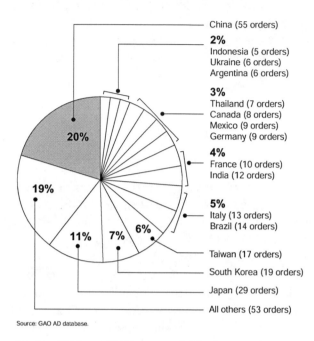

Source: GAO AD database.

Note: From 1980 through 2004 Commerce applied 68 orders against China. Thirteen of these were revoked, leaving 55 in place as of the end of 2004.

Figure 2: U.S. AD Orders in Place by Country as of December 31, 2004

Table 1. Products Affected by AD Duty Orders against China, 1980–2004

Type of product	Examples of affected products	Number of orders
Chemicals, plastics, pharmaceuticals	Barium chloride Polyethylene retail carrier bags Bulk aspirin	26
Steel, other metals	Carbon steel butt-weld pipe fittings Chrome-plated lug nuts Pure magnesium	20
Agricultural products	Crawfish Garlic Honey	5
Other products	Brake rotors Hand tools Cotton shop towels Automotive replacement glass windshields Folding gift boxes	17

Source: GAO AD database.

Note: Product categories based on the Harmonized Tariff Schedule of the United States, Annotated. See appendix I for more information.

The number of orders applied to China varied from year to year. For example, Commerce issued no AD duty orders against China in 1998 but issued 9 in 2003. Commerce had 272 orders in place as of December 31, 2004. Fifty-five of these (20 percent) apply to China. As figure 2 shows, this is also the highest percentage of any country. As shown in table 1, these duty orders have targeted a wide variety of products but have been concentrated in chemicals and plastics, metal products, and agricultural products.

Moreover, petitions for AD duties against China have resulted in application of duties more often than those against other countries. As shown in figure 3, 62 percent of the petitions filed against China over the last 25 years resulted in duty orders, while the equivalent figure for all countries was about 43 percent.[26]

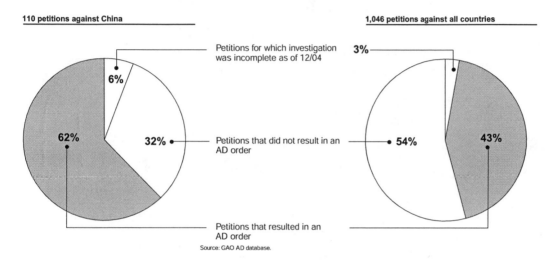

Source: GAO AD database.

Note: Petitions may not result in an AD order for several reasons. For example, if ITC does not find the domestic industry to be materially injured, or threatened with material injury, or if Commerce does not find that dumping has occurred, then the case is terminated. Also, Commerce may suspend a case if the United States reaches an agreement with the foreign government that would eliminate the impact of dumping (e.g., restrictions on exports). In addition, the petitioners may decide to withdraw their petition before ITC and Commerce have completed their work.

Figure 3. Results of AD Petitions, 1980-2004.

CHINA, MARKET ECONOMY RATES VARIED WIDELY

Over this 25 year period, Commerce issued duty orders against the same products from China and at least one market economy country on 25 occasions.[27] In 18 of these cases, Commerce calculated individual rates for companies from China and at least one market economy country. Fifteen of these cases involved more than one market economy country. In all, the orders applying to these 25 products contained a total of 243 individual, weighted average, and country-wide duty rates. Appendix II provides detailed information on the rates applied in each of these cases, as well as another 43 cases that we identified wherein Commerce applied duty rates to China but not to any market economy country.

These rates varied a great deal—both among the orders applied to different products and within the orders applied to the same products. Overall, these duty rates varied from zero to 218 percent for China and from zero to about 244 percent for market economy countries.

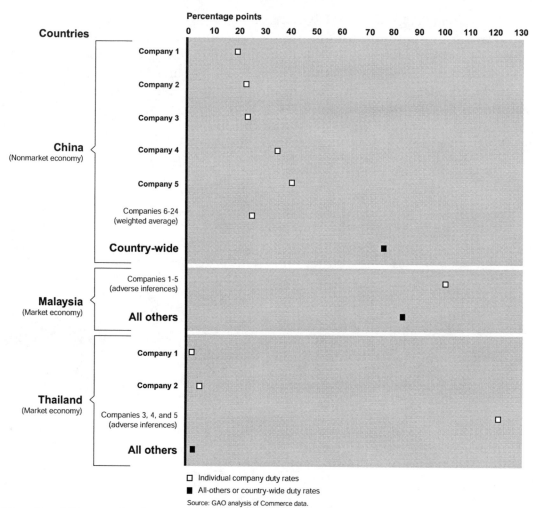

Note: In addition to the five individual Chinese companies shown above, two Chinese companies received de minimus rates and were excluded from the order.

Figure. 4 shows the extent to which duty rates applied to a single product can vary. [28]

OVERALL, CHINA RATES WERE
HIGHER THAN MARKET ECONOMY RATES

The average AD duty rates imposed on Chinese (NME) exporters over the last 25 years have been significantly higher than those imposed on market economy exporters of the same products. Taking all rates into consideration (including those calculated for individual companies, weighted averages of these rates, and country-wide rates applied to China) the average rate applied to Chinese companies in the 25 cases we examined was about 67 percent—over 20 percentage points higher than the average rate of 44 percent applied to market economy companies. As figure 5 shows, the overall average rates applied against China were higher for 18 of the 25 products in which there were AD orders against both China and at least one market economy.

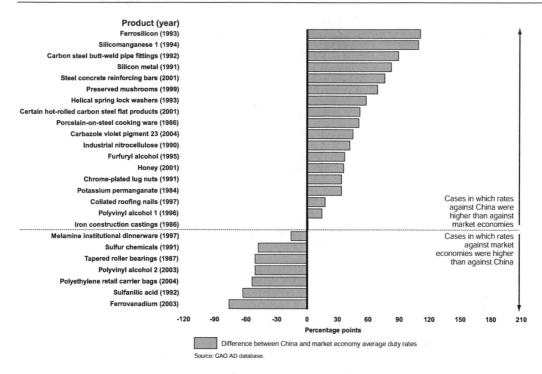

Figure 5. Differences between Overall Average Duty Rates—China and Market Economies, 1980–2004.

DIFFERENCE IN AVERAGE RATES DUE PRIMARILY TO HIGH CHINA COUNTRY-WIDE RATES

The difference between average China and average market economy duty rates was due primarily to the fact that the NME country-wide duty rates applied to China were substantially higher than the comparable all-others duty rates applied against market economy countries. In contrast, the individually determined duty rates assigned to Chinese companies in these cases were not substantially different, on average, from the individually determined rates assigned to market economy companies.

COUNTRY-WIDE DUTY RATES SUBSTANTIALLY HIGHER THAN MARKET ECONOMY ALL-OTHERS RATES

On average, the country-wide rates applied to China in these 25 cases were substantially higher than the comparable all-others rates applied to market economy countries. The country-wide duty rates applied against China averaged about 98 percent—over 60 percentage points higher than the average 37 percent all-others duty rate applied to market economy exporters of the same products. Figure 6 shows that the China countrywide rate was higher than the market economy all-others rate in 21 of 25 cases. As explained below, this difference was due largely to the use of different methodologies to calculate country-wide and all-others rates.

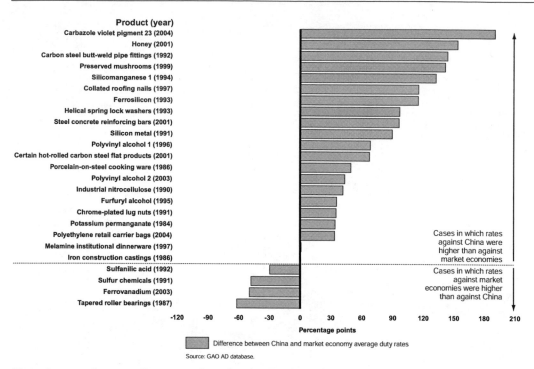

Figure 6. Differences between China Country-Wide and Market Economy All-Others Duty Rates, 1980–2004.

Note: In several cases, Commerce issued orders against several market economy countries, and we calculated an average all-others rate for all of the affected market economy countries.

Country-wide rates were nearly always equal to or higher than the highest individually determined rate applied to any Chinese company, due to application of adverse inferences.[29] According to Commerce, NME country governments themselves have never provided the information that Commerce needs to establish an appropriate country-wide duty rate. In addition, Commerce officials stated that, in most cases, participating NME companies have accounted for only a portion of known exports to the U.S. market from their country, indicating that others had not come forward. In most cases, therefore, Commerce has used adverse inferences to determine country-wide rates. For example, in its investigation of carbazole violet pigment, Commerce assigned three fully investigated Chinese companies individually determined rates of about 6, 27, and 45 percent. However, since other known Chinese producers did not respond to Commerce's request for information, Commerce used adverse inferences to determine that all other Chinese producers should be subject to an NME country-wide rate of about 218 percent.[30]

In contrast, the comparable market economy all-others rates were lower than the highest individual company rates assigned in any given case (if more than one other individual rate was assigned).[31] This is because, as discussed earlier, Commerce generally calculates all-others rates by averaging individually determined rates—excluding those derived entirely through application of facts available and those that are de minimis or zero.

With regard to carbazole violet pigment, for example, Commerce investigated not only China but also India. Commerce assigned two fully investigated Indian companies rates of about 10 and 50 percent and weight-averaged these rates to determine that shipments from all other Indian producers should be subject to a duty rate of about 27 percent.

INDIVIDUAL COMPANY RATES IN CHINA AND MARKET ECONOMY COUNTRIES NOT SUBSTANTIALLY DIFFERENT ON AVERAGE

On average, there was little difference between the individually determined rates applied to companies from China and those applied to market economy companies. The average individually determined rate applied to Chinese companies in these cases was 53 percent—a little less than the average rate of 55 percent applied to market economy companies.[32] The median rate for Chinese companies was 42 percent—the same as the median rate for market economy companies. Figure 7 displays the average individual company rates assigned to Chinese and market economy companies in the 18 cases in which Commerce assigned individual rates to both. As the figure shows, the rates assigned to Chinese companies were higher than the market economy rates in ten of these cases and lower in the other eight.

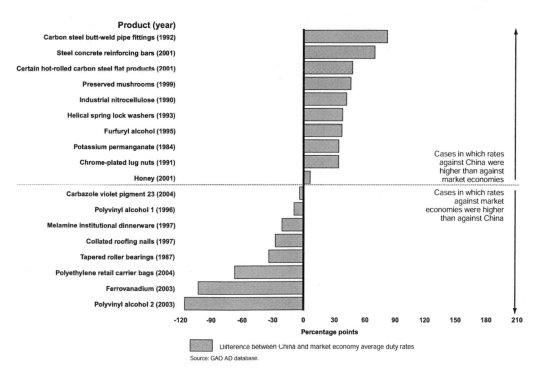

Figure 7. Differences between Average Individual Company Duty Rates—China and Market Economy Countries, 1980–2004.

Our statistical analyses provided additional support for the importance of the country-wide rates in accounting for the overall difference between the duty rates applied to China and to market economy countries. Using multivariate regression analysis, we found that a number of variables, such as the type of product involved, accounted for some of the overall variation in duty rates. However, after accounting for the China country-wide rates there was no statistically significant difference between the duty rates applied to China and those applied to market economy countries. As explained in more detail in appendix III, we found essentially the same results when we expanded our analyses to include data on AD actions against NMEs other than China.[33]

CEASING TO APPLY NME METHODOLOGY WOULD HAVE MIXED RESULTS

In certain circumstances, Commerce may stop using its NME methodology in China cases—and thus begin applying its market economy methodology to determine AD duty rates against that country. Such a step would lead to important changes in the methods that Commerce employs to determine China AD duty rates and in the duty orders resulting from these proceedings. These changes would have mixed results. Eliminating country-wide duty rates would likely reduce duty levels for Chinese companies that are not assigned individually determined rates. Individually determined rates would likely diverge into two distinct groups, with companies that do not cooperate in Commerce investigations receiving rates that are substantially higher than those assigned to companies that do cooperate. The impact of applying Chinese price information to calculate the normal value of Chinese products would likely vary by industry. In any case, rates would continue to vary widely based on the circumstances of each case. While trade data that would permit analysis of the potential trade impact of these changes is not available, it appears that the trade significance of country-wide duty rates is declining.

COMMERCE MAY STOP APPLYING NME METHODOLOGY TO CHINA IN CERTAIN CIRCUMSTANCES

Commerce has administrative authority to reclassify China and other NME countries as market economies or individual NME country industries as market-oriented in character. Such reclassifications would end Commerce's authority to apply its NME methodology to such countries or industries. Also, China's WTO accession agreement specifies that members may apply third-country information to calculate AD duty rates against that country, but this provision expires in 2016.

COMMERCE HAS ADMINISTRATIVE AUTHORITY TO CHANGE CHINA'S NME STATUS

Commerce has the authority to reclassify China as a market economy country, in whole or in part. As we explained in more detail in a prior report,[34] U.S. trade law authorizes Commerce to determine whether countries should be accorded NME or market economy status and specifies a number of criteria for Commerce to apply in making such determinations.[35] Countries classified as NMEs may ask for a review of their status at any time.[36] China has actively sought market economy status among its trading partners, and a number of them have designated China as a market economy. However, Commerce informed us that Chinese officials have not yet officially requested a determination as to whether their country merits reclassification under the criteria specified in U.S. law. In April 2004, the United States and China established a Structural Issues Working Group under the auspices of the U.S.-China Joint Commission on Commerce and Trade. This group is examining structural and operational issues related to China's economy that may give rise to bilateral trade frictions, including issues related to China's desire to be classified as a market economy.[37]

Commerce also has the authority to designate individual NME industries as market oriented in character, but has denied all such requests to date. Commerce determined in a 1992 case against China that, short of finding that an entire country merits designation as a market economy, it could find specific industries within such countries to be market oriented in character.[38] Commerce officials noted that on several occasions Chinese industries responding to antidumping duty petitions have requested designation as market-oriented industries. To date, Commerce has denied such requests—primarily on the grounds that the Chinese companies in question submitted information that was insufficient or was provided too late in Commerce's process to allow an informed decision.

CHINA'S WTO COMMITMENT ALLOWING THE USE OF THIRD-COUNTRY INFORMATION EXPIRES IN 2016

When joining the WTO, China agreed that other WTO members could use third-country information to calculate normal values in antidumping actions against Chinese companies. Specifically, China's WTO accession agreement provides that in determining price comparability in antidumping investigations WTO members may use "a methodology that is not based on a strict comparison with domestic prices or costs in China."[39] However, the accession agreement also specifies that this provision will expire 15 years after the date of the agreement—that is, by the end of 2016.[40]

After 2016, the ability of WTO members to continue using third-country information in AD calculations involving China would be governed by generally applicable WTO rules, according to officials at the Office of the U.S. Trade Representative. These rules recognize that when dumping investigations involve products from a country that "has a complete or substantially complete monopoly of its trade and where all domestic prices are fixed by the state," importing country authorities may have difficulty making the price comparisons through which AD duty rates are normally established. In such situations, importing countries may "find it necessary to take into account the possibility that a strict comparison with domestic prices in such a country may not always be appropriate."[41] WTO rules do not provide any specific guidance about how this provision should be implemented; such decisions appear to be left up to individual members.

TRANSITION TO MARKET ECONOMY METHODOLOGY WOULD BRING SIGNIFICANT PROCEDURAL CHANGES

Ending application of the NME methodology to China would bring two significant procedural changes in AD duty investigations against Chinese products. First, such a step would eliminate NME country-wide duty rates from China AD orders. Commerce would instead assign an individually determined rate to every relevant Chinese producer or exporter. If the number of companies involved were too great to allow full investigation of all relevant companies, Commerce would apply an all-others rate—a weighted average of the individually determined rates to all other Chinese companies (excluding those rates based entirely on facts available or that are de minimis or zero). However, Commerce would retain its authority to use facts available to determine the rates that it applies to individual Chinese companies. Second, transition to the market economy methodology would end Commerce's use of surrogate country information to calculate the normal value of Chinese products. Application of the market economy methodology would generally require Commerce to set the normal value of Chinese products equal to their sales price in China. If the product were not sold in China, Commerce could refer to prices charged for the product in another export market or construct the product's normal value, or it could continue to construct the product's normal value—using factor prices from the Chinese companies under investigation rather than from surrogate countries.

ELIMINATING COUNTRY-WIDE RATES WOULD LIKELY REDUCE DUTY LEVELS FOR COMPANIES NOT ASSIGNED INDIVIDUALLY DETERMINED RATES

The elimination of country-wide duty rates against China would likely reduce the duty rates applied to some Chinese companies. If Commerce applied its market economy approach to China, duty rates for companies not receiving individually determined rates would, in most cases, no longer be determined by applying facts available. Rather, Commerce would, for the most part, determine these rates by averaging the rates applied to fully investigated Chinese companies, with some exclusions. The default rate for uninvestigated Chinese companies would move, in most cases, from being the highest rate found to the average rate found among companies that cooperate in Commerce investigations.

Though not predictive, available evidence suggests that the all-others rates that Commerce would apply to China under the market economy methodology would be significantly lower than the country-wide rates currently applied to that country. As already shown, China country-wide rates have generally been significantly higher than the all-others rates that Commerce has assigned to market economy sources of the same products. As shown in table 2, the average country-wide rate for the 25 cases in which Commerce assigned duties to both China and one or more market economies was 98 percent, while the average market economy all-others rate was 37 percent. The average rate assigned to individual Chinese companies was 53 percent, and Commerce calculates all-others rates by weight averaging individually determined rates, excluding those that are derived entirely through application of facts available and those that are de minimis or zero.

Table 2. Comparison of China, Market Economy AD Duty Rates, Methodological Changes, and Potential Effects

	Overall [a]	Group [a]	Individual rates [b]		
			All	Cooperative	Adverse inferences
Average China (NME) rates	67%	98% (Country-wide)	53%	51%	(Rarely applied)[c]
Average market economy rates	44%	37% (All others)	55%	16%	77%
Change from NME to market economy methodology for China companies	Chinese price information replaces surrogate price information	Country-wide rates eliminated, uninvestigated companies receive all others rate	Separate rates test eliminated		
Potential effect on average China rates	Effect unknown but likely to vary by industry	Rates likely to be significantly lower	Rates likely to fall into two distinct groups	Rates likely to be relatively low for cooperative companies	Rates likely to be relatively high for uncooperative companies

Source: GAO analysis of Commerce data.

[a]Averages based on 25 products with comparable China and market economy cases (1985-2004).

[b]Averages based on subset of 18 products with comparable China and market economy cases in which individual rates were applied. However, averages are nearly identical for full group of 25 products.

[c]Commerce applied adverse inferences only three times, for an average rate of 78 percent.

INDIVIDUALLY DETERMINED RATES WOULD VARY, DEPENDING UPON COOPERATION

A simple comparison of the average individually determined duty rates calculated under the NME and market economy methodologies suggests that a change in methodology would not result in any significant overall change in duty rates applied to individual Chinese companies. For the comparable cases, individual AD duty rates for Chinese companies averaged 53 percent and were not substantially different from individual market economy company rates, which averaged 55 percent.

However, a more detailed examination of the data indicates that the impact of a change in methodology on individual Chinese company duty rates would depend on the extent to which Commerce applies adverse inferences to calculate these rates. The rates assigned to individual companies under the market economy methodology fell into two distinct groups, depending on whether the companies cooperated with Commerce investigations. In the 25 cases that we examined in detail, about half of the fully investigated market economy companies cooperated with Commerce. On average, Commerce assigned a duty rate of about 17 percent to these companies.[42] Commerce found the other half of the fully investigated companies uncooperative and, therefore, applied adverse inferences to determine the duty rates to be applied to these companies. On average, Commerce assigned a duty rate of about 77 percent to these uncooperative market economy companies.[43]

Though not predictive, this suggests that a change from the NME methodology for China would result in a significant number of (cooperative) companies receiving relatively low rates, while another significant group of (uncooperative) companies would receive relatively high rates.[44] Our regression analysis confirmed the importance of adverse inferences as a determinant of variation in duty rates. As explained in appendix III, we found that application of adverse inferences tends to increase duty rates by a large margin.

IMPACT OF APPLYING CHINESE PRICE INFORMATION WOULD VARY BY INDUSTRY AND IS LIKELY TO DECLINE OVER TIME

The impact of using Chinese price information on China AD duty rates would likely vary from one industry to another under the market economy methodology. Chinese prices are widely viewed as distorted to varying degrees. Where prices for key inputs are artificially low, relying on Chinese price information would produce an artificially low normal value. The result would be an AD duty that is lower than would be obtained by applying surrogate country input prices. Conversely, where Chinese prices are artificially high, AD duty rates may be higher if based on Chinese prices. To the extent that Chinese economic reforms bring Chinese prices more into line with world markets, the impact of abandoning the use of surrogate country information can be expected to decline. At any point in time, however, the probable effect of such a methodological change in an individual industry investigation would depend on the particular facts applying to that industry. The net impact of changing the source of price information on overall China duty rates cannot be estimated with confidence.

DUTY RATES WILL CONTINUE TO DISPLAY GREAT VARIATION

Our multivariate regression analyses suggest that, regardless of changes in methodology, there will continue to be a great deal of variation among the AD duty rates applied to products from China and other countries. Our analyses showed that application of country-wide duty rates to China largely explained the difference between the overall average duty rates applied to China and to market economy countries. Eliminating these rates would likely have a substantial overall reducing effect on China rates. However, a number of other factors, such as the type of product involved, also helped to account for differences among rates overall, and these factors will continue to have an impact on duty rates, regardless of whether Commerce applies country-wide rates to China. Furthermore, even after taking these factors into account, our analyses still explained only about half of the total variation in duty rates.[45] This means that about half of the variation in duty rates is attributable either to idiosyncratic factors or to systematic factors that we did not capture in any of our variables.[46]

TRADE SIGNIFICANCE OF COUNTRY-WIDE RATES APPEARS TO BE DECLINING

Available evidence suggests that the volume of trade affected by countrywide rates is declining and that, consequently, the trade impact of China duty orders will in the future depend increasingly on the magnitude of the individually determined rates. Commerce officials observed that in the early 1980s it was not unusual for China AD duty investigations to produce only a country-wide rate. However, as the Chinese economy has evolved, individual Chinese companies have become more likely to request—and receive— individually determined or weighted average rates. Since 1980, Commerce has applied country-wide rates alone in only 15 of 68 Chinese AD orders, and the last of these occasions was in 1995. The majority of all Chinese AD orders (about 78 percent), and all such orders issued over the last 10 years, have included at least one individual company rate.

Neither Commerce nor Customs and Border Protection maintain trade data that would permit analysis of changes over time in the relative volume or value of products imported into the United States under the country-wide or various individual duty rates listed in AD duty orders. However, as figure 8 shows, the average number of Chinese companies assigned individually determined rates (or assigned a weighted average rate) has been growing, though there continues to be variation from year to year. For example, in 2004 Commerce placed duties on six Chinese products and in doing so assigned individually determined or weighted average rates to 53 Chinese companies. Anecdotal evidence suggests that along with this rise in company interest in obtaining individual rates has come an increase in the volume of trade covered by these rates. For example, in one recent case Commerce fully investigated and assigned individually determined rates to four companies accounting for more than 90 percent of Chinese exports to the U.S. market. Commerce then assigned a weighted average of these rates to 9 additional companies, leaving only a very small portion of all Chinese exports to be covered by the country-wide rate.[47]

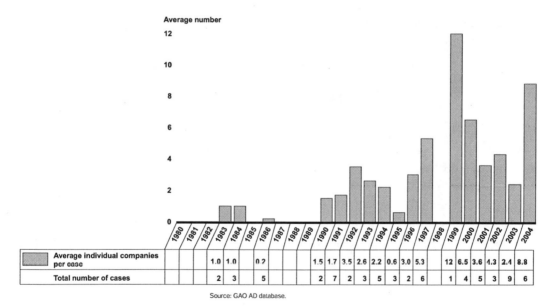

Source: GAO AD database.

Figure 8. Average Number of Individual Rates per Case per Year, All Orders against China, 1980–2004.

Notes: This table includes only the companies assigned individually determined or weighted average rates in initial AD duty orders. Other companies may be assigned such rates in subsequent reviews of these orders. The annual figures are the number of individual companies granted such rates divided by the number of AD duty orders. Commerce did not issue any individual company duty orders against China in 1980, 1981, 1982, 1985, 1987, 1988, 1989, or 1998. In the tapered roller bearings cases, Commerce originally put an order in place in 1987, but amended it in 1990. We use the information from the 1990 amendment in the above graphic.

CONCLUDING OBSERVATIONS

On average, Commerce's application of its NME methodology has produced AD duties on Chinese products that are substantially higher than those applied to the same products from market economy countries. Changing China's NME status—and thus eliminating the application of this methodology—would have a variety of impacts. The duty rates applied to companies that do not receive individual rates would likely decline. Chinese companies that cooperate in Commerce investigations may also receive comparatively low rates. However, the impact of these lower rates on overall China averages may be offset, to some extent, by application of adverse inferences to assign relatively high rates to individual Chinese companies that do not cooperate in Commerce investigations.

The net effect of these changes cannot be predicted. Such a prediction would require knowledge of price distortions in diverse Chinese industries, changes in these distortions over time, pricing decisions by Chinese companies in reaction to these changes, and decisions by U.S. companies about whether they should seek relief. Nonetheless, while the NME methodology is applied, it appears that the actual trade impact of using this methodology will decline as the portion of total export trade conducted by Chinese companies assigned individual rates increases, and as the countrywide rates that largely account for the comparatively high average rates applied to China decline in importance.

AGENCY COMMENTS AND OUR EVALUATION

The Department of Commerce provided written comments on a draft of this report. These comments are reprinted in appendix IV. Overall, Commerce agreed with our findings, observing that the report provided timely and helpful information on the NME methodology and its application to China.

Commerce identified a small number of apparent errors in our database. We re-examined our data, making corrections when necessary, and updated our analyses; these corrections did not have any significant impact on our findings. Commerce also made a number of technical comments, focusing primarily on our description of its NME methodology. We took these comments into consideration and made changes throughout the report to insure its clarity and accuracy. We also made a number of technical corrections suggested by the Department of Homeland Security and the Office of the U.S. Trade Representative.

APPENDIX I.

Scope and Methodology

To address our objectives, we examined and summarized applicable U.S. laws and regulations, as well as relevant World Trade Organization (WTO) agreements. These included the *Agreement on Implementation of Article VI of the General Agreement on Tariffs and Trade 1994*—commonly known as the "antidumping agreement"—and China's WTO accession agreement. We conducted a literature search and reviewed relevant scholarly and legal analyses and Department of Commerce (Commerce) determinations.[1] In order to corroborate and broaden our understanding, we consulted with trade and legal policy experts from the U.S. government, private sector trade associations, consulting firms, academic institutions, law firms with broad experience in trade actions involving China, as well as representatives of the WTO, the government of China, and other governments concerned about Chinese trade practices, including the European Union and Canada.

In order to analyze the application of antidumping (AD) duties to China and compare duty rates applied to China with those applied to market economy countries (our second objective) and to evaluate the potential impact of ceasing to apply the nonmarket economy (NME) methodology to China (our third objective), we collected information from the Department of Commerce and the International Trade Commission, including notices of Commerce determinations appearing in the *Federal Register*. We used this information to construct a database on all U.S. AD investigations from 1980 through 2004. In addition to information on the countries and products involved and the status of each investigation, our database included the duty rates applied upon completion of each new antidumping investigation against China during this period, as well as the duty rates applied against any producers of the same products from other countries. We verified this database to the official sources and found the data to be sufficiently reliable for the purposes of this report.

Our analyses focused on the 68 cases during this time period wherein Commerce imposed AD duties on Chinese products, and especially on the subset of 25 cases in which Commerce imposed duties against a similar product from one or more market economy countries.[2] Specifically, the 25 cases included all market economy cases that had the same product name and were initiated within 1 year of an AD investigation against China. In all, we assembled data on 303 company-specific, weighted average, and country-wide duty rate determinations on Chinese products, and an additional 168 duty rate determinations on market economy products. Appendix II provides additional analyses of this data.

As part of our examination, we also performed multivariate regression analyses to determine the extent to which duty rate variations could be attributed to differences between China and these other countries, or to other factors, such as the type of product involved. Appendix III provides more information on these analyses and their results.

In addition to comparing China and market economies, we also collected information on duty rates that Commerce applied to products from other NME countries at the same time as it applied them to similar products from either China or a market economy. Appendix III provides information on the results of our analyses of this data.

We did not collect or analyze information on duty rates applied against market economy countries in cases where no parallel action was taken against China or any other NME country. Therefore, our analyses of market economy duty rates are specific to the sample of market economy orders in which a corresponding NME order was also in effect. Inclusion of other market economy product duty rates may have produced different results. However, we determined that the appropriate comparison between China and market economy countries was between the 25 similar products. We found through our regression analyses (discussed in app. III) that the product being investigated does help explain the variation among rates and it is, therefore, important to make an appropriate comparison. In addition, duty rates for the 43 remaining orders against China alone followed a similar pattern as those contained in the 25 cases where we drew comparisons with market economy duty rates. The average country-wide rate for these 43 orders against China was higher than the country-wide rate for the 25 orders (118 percent compared to 98 percent), and the average individual rate was lower (41 percent compared to 53 percent) for the 18 orders with individual rates. These results were consistent with our findings that the country-wide rates tend to be significantly higher than individual rates.

In order to group specific products subject to AD orders into groups of similar products, we used the Harmonized Tariff Schedule (HTS) classifications for each product, as reported in the *Federal Register* announcement of the order. The HTS is the official U.S. classification of goods imported into the United States and includes 99 chapters covering all goods imports. In addition, the HTS chapters are grouped into larger sections that cover broad types of related products. The categories we used in this report are based on these HTS sections and chapters. Specifically, the category "Chemicals, plastics, pharmaceuticals" comprises HTS chapters 28 through 40 (which includes all chapters under the section "Chemical or allied industries"). The category "Steel, other metals" comprises HTS chapters 72 through 81 (which includes most chapters under the section "Base metals and articles of base metals" except those chapters covering articles of base metals). The category "Agricultural products" comprises HTS chapters 1 through 24 (which includes all chapters under the sections "Live animals; animal products," "Vegetable products," "Animal or vegetable fats, etc.," and "Prepared foodstuffs, beverages, spirits, and vinegar; tobacco and manufactured tobacco substitutes"). The category "Other products" comprises all other HTS chapters.

We conducted our work from June 2005 through December 2005 in accordance with generally accepted government auditing standards.

APPENDIX II.

Additional Information on Duty Rates Applied to China and Market Economy Countries

This appendix provides additional information on the antidumping (AD) duty rate data that we assembled for this report and provides some additional analytical information, including brief discussions of variation in the duty rates applied to China over time, Department of Commerce (Commerce) determinations on whether Chinese companies should be considered eligible for individual rates, and duty rates applied to selected market economy countries.

DUTY RATES IMPOSED ON CHINA

The overall average duty rate for all 68 orders against China from 1980 through 2004 was 65 percent. This was the result of 72 country-wide rates (on 68 products) with an average duty of 111 percent and 158 individual company rates with an average duty of 44 percent.[1] These rates ranged from zero to about 384 percent (see table 3). In our analysis, we identified 25 orders against China in which there was also an order against a market economy country on the same product put in place within 1 year from the order against China. Table 3 shows overall average duty rates from the 25 orders against China that were matched to market economy cases and the 43 orders in which no market economy order was identified. Table 4 at the end of this appendix provides information on each of the 68 orders against China, and table 5 provides comparative information for each of the 25 cases in which duties were also applied against market economy producers.

Table 3. Summary Data on China AD Duty Orders, 1980–2004

	Type of rate	Number of rates	Mean (%)	Minimum (%)	Maximum (%)
25 orders matched to similar market economy orders	Individual company rates	50	52	0	162
	Country-wide rate	25	98	3	218
	Total	**75**	**67**	**0**	**218**
43 orders not matched to similar market economy orders	Individual company rates	108	41	0	292
	Country-wide rate	47	118	1	384
	Total	**155**	**64**	**0**	**384**
All 68 orders	Individual company rates	158	44	0	292
	Country-wide rate	72	111	1	384
	Grand total	**230**	**65**	**0**	**384**

Source: GAO AD database.
Note: The overall average individual duty rates listed in this table for the "matching" orders are for the 25 products with both China and market economy orders. However, only 18 of these products had individual rates imposed on both China and at least one other market economy. We use these 18 products for our comparison of individual company duty rates imposed on China and market economies, rather than the 25 products, in the rest of the report. The average individual company duty rate imposed on China for these 18 products is 53 percent, rather than 52 percent.

About 78 percent (53 AD orders) of the 68 AD orders included not only country-wide rates but also individually calculated rates for at least one Chinese company. Of these, about 54 percent (37 orders) included company-specific rates that were lower than the country-wide rates imposed in the same cases. With regard to nonmalleable cast iron pipe fittings, for example, two Chinese companies submitted detailed information and met Commerce's criteria for assignment of individually determined rates. Other Chinese pipe fitting companies, however, did not provide any information. Commerce assigned the two cooperating companies duty rates of between 6 and 8 percent—a fraction of the 76 percent country-wide duty rate applied in this case.[2]

Only 15 orders issued against China during this period included just a country-wide rate. Most of these orders date from the period before 1991 when Commerce had not yet begun applying its separate rates test. However, from 1991 through 1995 Commerce issued six orders that contained only a country-wide rate. In most of these cases, Chinese companies failed to respond to Commerce requests for information. For example, in one case Commerce solicited information through both the Chinese government and the relevant Chinese industry association. However, the industry association responded that no Chinese producer or exporter wanted to participate in Commerce's investigation. Commerce, therefore, used facts available to establish a country-wide duty rate of about 156 percent.[3]

In 12 of the 68 orders, all the individual rates issued were equal to the country-wide rate. In some cases, Commerce specified an individual rate for one company and then used this rate as "facts available" to establish a country-wide duty rate at the same level.[4] For example, in its investigation of refined brown aluminum oxide from China, Commerce requested information from the government of China and more than 20 Chinese companies. Only one of these companies responded. Commerce found that this company qualified for its own duty rate and determined that this rate should be about 135 percent. Commerce determined that the failure of the other companies to provide requested information justified application of an adverse inference to determine the country-wide rate. Since the rate established for the lone cooperating company was higher than any of the rates suggested in the petition requesting imposition of duties on this product, Commerce set the country-wide rate equal to the rate applied to the one cooperating company—135 percent.[5]

DUTY RATES AGAINST CHINA HAVE FLUCTUATED OVER TIME

We found that there was a slight tendency for duty rates applied against Chinese products to rise over the period of our analysis, as well as to fluctuate over time. As figure 9 shows, individual company and countrywide duty rates tended to be larger from 1992-2004 than from 1980-1991. In addition, the individual company rates demonstrate a cyclical pattern over time. In our regression analysis, we found that there was a small positive trend in AD duty rates against China over time that was statistically significant. This result is consistent with research that has shown that overall U.S. AD margins have increased over time.[6]

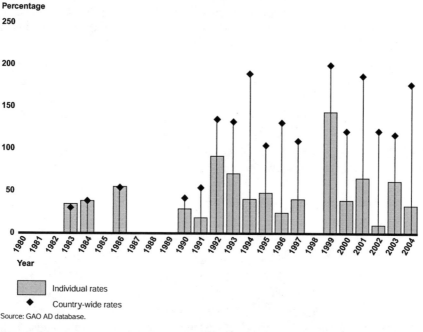

Source: GAO AD database.

[6]See Bruce Blonigen, "Evolving Discretionary Practices of U.S. Antidumping Activity" National Bureau of Economic Research, Working Paper #9625 (April 2003).

Note: Commerce did not issue any new AD duty orders against China in 1980, 1981, 1982, 1985, 1987, 1988, 1989, or 1998. In the tapered roller bearings cases, Commerce put an order in place in 1987 but amended it in 1990. We use 1990 information in the above graphic.

Figure 9. Average Country-Wide and Individual Rates, All Orders against China, 1980-2004.

AVERAGE DUTY RATES ON 68 ORDERS AGAINST CHINA AND SUBSET OF 25 ORDERS MATCHED TO MARKET ECONOMY ORDERS

Table 4 shows the duty rates on the 68 orders imposed on China between 1980 and 2004. Table 5 then shows the duty rates on the 25 orders imposed on China in which we also found matching orders imposed on market economies.

Table 4. Average Duty Rates for 68 Orders against China, 1980–2004

| Year and product | Average (all rates) (%) | Average country-wide rate (%) | Number of rates | Individual company rates | | |
				Average (%)	Minimum (%)	Maximum (%)
(1983) Cotton shop towels	35	36	2	34	30	37
(1983) Greig polyester cotton print cloth	22	22				
(1984) Barium chloride	15	15	1	15	15	15
(1984) Chloropicrin	58	58	1	58	58	58
(1984) Potassium permanganate	40	40	1	40	40	40
(1986) Iron construction castings	12	12				
(1986) Paint brushes	127	127				
(1986) Porcelain-on-steel cookware	67	67				
(1986) Steel wire nails	6	6				
(1986) Wax candles	54	54	1	54	54	54
(1990) Industrial nitrocellulose	78	78	1	78	78	78
(1990) Tapered roller bearings	3	3	2	3	1	5
(1991) Chrome-plated lug nuts	42	42	1	42	42	42
(1991) Hand tools	36	36				
(1991) Oscillating fans and ceiling fans	1	1	8	1	0	2
(1991) Silicon metal	139	139				
(1991) Sparklers	59	76	3	54	2	94
(1991) Sulfur chemicals	28	28				
(1991) Tungsten ore concentrates	151	151				
(1992) Carbon steel butt-weld pipe fittings	114	183	6	102	35	155
(1992) Sulfanilic acid	52	85	1	19	19	19
(1993) Compact ductile iron waterworks	127	127				
(1993) Ferrosilicon	138	138				
(1993) Helical spring lock washers	89	129	2	70	70	70
(1994) Cased pencils	14	45	4	6	0	17
(1994) Garlic	377	377				
(1994) Paper clips	73	127	3	55	46	61
(1994) Sebacic acid	98	243	4	61	44	85
(1994) Silicomanganese	150	150				
(1995) Furfuryl alcohol	46	45	2	47	44	50
(1995) Glycine	156	156				
(1995) Pure magnesium 1	108	108				
(1996) Manganese metal	33	143	4	6	1	12
(1996) Polyvinyl alcohol 1	78	117	2	58	0	117
(1997) Brake rotors	10	43	6	5	0	16
(1997) Collated roofing nails	39	118	2	0	0	0
(1997) Coumarin	87	161	2	51	31	70
(1997) Crawfish	133	202	5	120	92	157

Table 4. (Continued)

Year and product	Average (all rates) (%)	Average country-wide rate (%)	Individual company rates			
			Number of rates	Average (%)	Minimum (%)	Maximum (%)
(1997) Melamine dinnerware	2	7	4	1	0	3
(1997) Persulfates	55	119	3	34	32	35
(1999) Mushrooms	155	199	4	144	121	162
(2000) Apple juice	19	52	7	14	0	28
(2000) Bulk aspirin	57	144	2	14	11	17
(2000) Creatine	47	154	6	30	0	58
(2000) Synthetic indigo	96	130	2	80	80	80
(2001) Certain hot-rolled carbon steel flat products	76	91	4	73	64	91
(2001) Foundry coke products	109	215	4	83	49	106
(2001) Honey	72	184	4	45	26	57
(2001) Pure magnesium 2	165	306	1	25	25	25
(2001) Steel concrete reinforcing bars	133	133	1	133	133	133
(2002) Automotive replacement glass windshields	37	125	3	8	4	12
(2002) Certain folding gift boxes	58	165	2	5	2	9
(2002) Folding metal tables and folding metal chairs	28	71	2	7	0	14
(2003) Barium carbonate	58	81	1	34	34	34
(2003) Certain malleable iron pipe fittings	31	111	4	11	7	16
(2003) Cut to length carbon steel plate	62	129	5	49	17	129
(2003) Ferrovanadium	40	67	1	13	13	13
(2003) Lawn and garden steel fence posts	6	16	3	2	0	7
(2003) Non-malleable cast iron pipe fittings	30	76	2	7	6	7
(2003) Polyvinyl alcohol 2	52	98	1	7	7	7
(2003) Refined brown aluminum oxide	135	135	1	135	135	135
(2003) Saccharin	288	330	3	274	249	292
(2004) Carbazole violet pigment 23	74	218	3	26	6	45
(2004) Certain color television receivers	27	78	5	17	5	26
(2004) Hand trucks	105	384	4	35	26	46
(2004) Ironing tables	99	158	3	80	9	158
(2004) Polyethylene retail carrier bags	27	78	8	21	0	41
(2004) Tetrahydrofurfuryl alcohol	137	137	1	137	137	137
Total	**65**	**111**	**158**	**44**	**0**	**292**

Source: GAO AD database.

Note: The average (all rates) is calculated as the average of the country-wide rate and each of the individual company rates that Commerce issued in its order.

Table 5. Average Duty Rates for 25 Products with Orders against both China and Market Economies, 1980–2004

Product and year	Country and number of orders	Average (all rates) (%)	Average country-wide or all- others rate (%)	Individual company rates			
				Number of rates	Average (%)	Minimum (%)	Maximum (%)
Carbazole violet pigment 23 (2004)	China	74	218	3	26	6	45
	Market economies (1)	29	27	2	30	10	50
Carbon steel butt-weld pipe fittings (1992)	China	114	183	6	102	35	155
	Market economies (1)	25	39	3	21	0	51
Certain hot-rolled carbon steel flat products (2001)	China	76	91	4	73	64	91
	Market economies (7)	24	23	11	25	3	48
Chrome-plated lug nuts (1991)	China	42	42	1	42	42	42
	Market economies (1)	8	7	2	9	6	11
Collated roofing nails (1997)	China	39	118	2	0	0	0
	Market economies (1)	22	3	3	28	3	40
Ferrosilicon (1993)	China	138	138	0			
	Market economies (2)	27	23	4	29	3	89
Ferrovanadium (2003)	China	40	67	1	13	13	13
	Market economies (1)	116	116	2	116	116	116
Furfuryl alcohol (1995)	China	46	45	2	47	44	50
	Market economies (2)	10	10	2	10	8	12
Helical spring lock washers (1993)	China	89	129	2	70	70	70
	Market economies (1)	32	32	3	32	32	32
Honey (2001)	China	72	184	4	45	26	57
	Market economies (1)	36	30	3	38	27	55
Industrial nitrocellulose (1990)	China	78	78	1	78	78	78
	Market economies (6)	37	37	6	37	4	66
Iron construction castings (1986)	China	12	12	0			
	Market economies (3)	11	12	10	11	0	59
Melamine institutional dinnerware (1997)	China	2	7	4	1	0	3
	Market economies (2)	18	6	6	22	0	53
Polyethylene retail carrier bags (2004)	China	27	78	8	21	0	41
	Market economies (2)	81	44	10	88	2	123
Polyvinyl alcohol 1 (1996)	China	78	117	2	58	0	117
	Market economies (2)	63	48	6	68	19	77

Table 5. (Continued)

| Product and year | Country and number of orders | Average (all rates) (%) | Average country-wide or all- others rate (%) | Individual company rates | | |
				Number of rates	Average (%)	Minimum (%)	Maximum (%)
Polyvinyl alcohol 2 (2003)	China	52	98	1	7	7	7
	Market economies (2)	103	54	5	123	39	144
Porcelain-on-steel cooking ware (1986)	China	67	67	0			
	Market economies (2)	15	17	8	15	2	57
Potassium permanganate (1984)	China	40	40	1	40	40	40
	Market economies (1)	5	5	1	5	5	5
Preserved mush-rooms (1999)	China	155	199	4	144	121	162
	Market economies (3)	86	57	7	98	6	244
Silicomanganese 1 (1994)	China	150	150	0			
	Market economies (1)	41	18	1	65	65	65
Silicon metal (1991)	China	139	139	0			
	Market economies (2)	58	50	3	63	9	93
Steel concrete reinforcing bars (2001)	China	133	133	1	133	133	133
	Market economies (4)	57	37	12	64	17	102
Sulfanilic acid (1992)	China	52	85	1	19	19	19
	Market economies (1)	115	115	0			
Sulfur chemicals (1991)	China	28	28	0			
	Market economies (2)	75	75	2	75	50	100
Tapered roller bearings (1987)	China	3	3	2	3	1	5
	Market economies (3)	54	65	2	36	36	37
Total	**China**	67	98	50	52	0	162
	Market economies (54)	44	37	114	48	0	244

Source: GAO AD database.
Notes:

The average (all rates) is calculated as the average of the country-wide rate and each of the individual company rates that Commerce issued in its order.

The overall average individual duty rates listed in this table are for the 25 products with both China and market economy orders. However, only 18 of these products had individual rates imposed on both China and at least one other market economy. We use these 18 products for our comparison of individual company duty rates imposed on China and market economies, rather than the 25 products, in the rest of the report. The average individual company duty rate imposed on China for these 18 products is 53 percent and for market economies it is 55 percent.

APPENDIX III.

Regression Analysis Results

In order to examine the difference between duty rates applied to China and those applied to market economy countries, we performed multivariate regression analyses on the cases in which the Department of Commerce (Commerce) applied duties to both China and at least one market economy country. These involved 25 different products, affected by 25 duty orders against China, and 54 duty orders against market economies. Multivariate regression analysis makes it possible to examine the simultaneous effect of several different factors on the duty rates and to determine the extent to which these factors, taken together, explain variation in these rates. To determine whether our analytical results for China held true for all nonmarket economy (NME) countries, we also identified six instances in which Commerce applied duties to a nonmarket economy other than China, and at least one market economy country, and reran our analyses using data for all 31 products.

Table 6 shows the results of our multivariate regression analysis of variation in the dependent variable (the antidumping [AD] duty rate) attributable to the following independent variables:

- China (a variable indicating whether the AD duty rate is for China or not)
- the country-wide rate (a variable indicating whether the AD duty rate is a country-wide rate), and
- year (a variable indicating the year in which the duty went into affect).

We also included a constant term. The regression involved 25 products covered by 25 orders against China and 54 orders against market economies and included a total of 243 duty rates (the dependent variable) from these 79 orders.

The results show that the variable for China as the target country had a coefficient of 3.002 percent, indicating that duty rates against China tended to be about 3 percentage points higher than those against market economies, on average. However, this coefficient is not statistically significant, meaning that there was no statistically significant difference between the rates assigned to China and market economy countries, when the other factors in the regression are included. The coefficient for the country-wide rate, on the other hand, shows that there is a 52 percentage point difference between country-wide rates against China and other rates. This result is statistically significant at above the 99 percent level. The variable for the year of the order is also statistically significant, but it has a small coefficient.[1] The adjusted R-square measure shows that about 15 percent of the overall variation in duty rates is explained by the independent variables included here.

We then included additional variables for product groups, such as agriculture and steel, and, in separate regressions, individual product variables for each type of product. The additional variables generally improved the overall "fit" of the regression; the adjusted R-square measure with the individual product variables included showed that the regression explained between 24 and 31 percent of the overall variation in duty rates across the sample compared with 15 percent in the regression above. Also, certain types of products, such as agriculture products, tended to have higher duty rates relative to other types.

Table 6. Results of Multivariate Regression Analysis of Duty Rates on Explanatory

Variables for China, Country-Wide Rates, and Year

Dependent variable = AD duty rate

Independent variables	Unstandardized coefficients (B)	Standard error	Standardized coefficients (Beta)	t-statistic	Significance of t-statistic
China	3.002	7.511	.028	.400	.690
Year	2.095	.497	.252	4.218	.000
Country-wide rate	52.050	11.398	.316	4.567	.000

Source: GAO analysis of Commerce data.

Note: R-square = 0.164; Adjusted R-square = 0.154; Observations = 243.

Table 7. Results of Multivariate Regression Analysis of Duty Rates on Explanatory Variables for China, Country-Wide Rates, and Individual Products

Dependent variable = AD duty rate

Independent variables	Unstandardized coefficients (B)	Standard error	Standardized coefficients (Beta)	t-statistic	Significance of t-statistic
China	2.055	7.302	.019	.281	.779
Year	-6.022	20.636	-.726	-.292	.771
Country-wide rate	50.928	10.609	.309	4.801	.000
Carbazole violet pigment 23 (2004)	113.617	269.338	.380	.422	.674
Carbon steel butt-weld pipe fittings (1992)	70.893	30.579	.294	2.318	.021
Certain hot-rolled carbon steel flat products (2001)	82.479	207.275	.482	.398	.691
Collated roofing nails (1997)	46.480	126.162	.155	.368	.713
Ferrosilicon (1993)	40.090	58.403	.134	.686	.493
Ferrovanadium (2003)	136.023	249.034	.386	.546	.585
Furfuryl alcohol (1995)	30.585	86.044	.102	.355	.723
Helical spring lock washers (1993)	49.701	47.927	.166	1.037	.301
Honey (2001)	98.896	207.608	.373	.476	.634
Industrial nitrocellulose (1990)	21.805	30.079	.101	.725	.469
Iron construction castings (1986)	-33.870	105.554	-.158	-.321	.749
Melamine institutional dinnerware (1997)	32.449	125.663	.146	.258	.796
Polyethylene retail carrier bags (2004)	122.291	268.962	.686	.455	.650
Polyvinyl alcohol 1 (1996)	81.135	105.532	.337	.769	.443
Polyvinyl alcohol 2 (2003)	147.492	248.661	.556	.593	.554
Porcelain-on-steel cooking ware (1986)	-25.756	105.698	-.107	-.244	.808
Potassium permanganate (1984)	-44.131	147.104	-.112	-.300	.764
Preserved mushrooms (1999)	141.530	163.666	.680	.865	.388
Silicomanganese 1 (1994)	67.142	69.110	.148	.972	.332
Silicon metal (1991)	51.868	25.308	.161	2.049	.042
Steel concrete reinforcing bars (2001)	111.738	207.339	.584	.539	.591
Sulfanilic acid (1992)	51.956	41.151	.115	1.263	.208
Sulfur chemicals (1991)	44.355	26.424	.126	1.679	.095
Tapered roller bearings (1987)	-7.471	85.958	-.027	-.087	.931

Source: GAO analysis of Commerce data.

Note: R-square = 0.386; Adjusted R-square = 0.309; Observations = 243.

Table 7 shows the regression results when individual product variables are included. Once again the coefficient for China is insignificant, while the coefficient for the country-wide rate is significant at the 99 percent level. Some coefficients for individual products are significant (e.g., carbon steel butt-weld pipe fittings), but many are not. The overall adjusted R-square measure shows that this regression model explains about 31 percent of total variation in the duty rates.

In order to examine the effect of applying adverse inferences and facts available (other than adverse inferences) on the duty rates, we added additional variables indicating when Commerce used these approaches. The results show that application of adverse inferences is a significant variable and has a large effect on the duty rates, but that application of facts available (other than adverse inferences) is not. When adverse inferences are introduced, this results in the country-wide rate variable becoming insignificant (see table 8). However, this is likely due to the fact that the adverse inferences variable is highly correlated with the countrywide rate. Therefore, it is not surprising that the country-wide rate is no longer significant since the adverse inferences variable is already accounting for much of the variation. In addition, the variable for China once again becomes significant. As we discuss in the body of this report, Commerce uses adverse inferences in very few determinations for Chinese companies granted their own rates. Adverse inferences were applied in making only 3 out of the 50 individual determinations used in this analysis. However, Commerce used adverse inferences in nearly half of its determinations against individual market economy companies.

Since adverse inferences are already factored into this model, as is the country-wide rate, the remaining differences accounted for by the China variable in table 3 are between individual (noncountry-wide) Chinese rates and individual market economy rates in which adverse inferences are not used. Table 8 shows that there is a statistically significant 27 percentage point difference between these rates. However, because there are methodological differences between the NME and market economy methodologies for individual companies, it is not clear how often adverse inferences would be used against individual Chinese companies should they move to a market economy methodology. In other words, we cannot predict the extent to which, under a market economy methodology, individual Chinese companies would cooperate with Commerce or Commerce would find it necessary to use adverse inferences in its determinations against Chinese companies. It is possible that some Chinese companies that currently have an individually determined rate under the NME methodology would face adverse inferences under a market economy methodology, whereas others would not. This could produce a result similar to the market economy cases we have examined in which the overall average (for example, 55 percent) is the result of some companies receiving comparatively high duty rates (e.g., 77 percent) when adverse inferences are used and others receiving comparatively low rates (e.g., 16 percent) when adverse inferences are not used (see table 2). In any case, these results show that there is a remaining difference between these two groups after accounting for the use of adverse inferences and the country-wide rate.

In order to examine whether the above results hold for all NMEs, we ran the same regressions for a larger set of 31 products (compared with the 25 products above) in which we found matching cases between nonmarket economies other than China and market economies. The data set on these 31 products included rates from 128 orders (26 on China, 82 on market economies, and 20 on NMEs other than China) that contained 355 duty rates (dependent variable).

Table 8. Results of Multivariate Regression Analysis of Duty Rates on Explanatory Variables for China, Country-Wide Rates Adverse Inferences, Other Facts Available, and Individual Products

Dependent variable = AD duty rate

Independent variables	Unstandardized coefficients (B)	Standard error	Standardized coefficients (Beta)	t-statistic	Significance of t-statistic
China	27.342	6.856	.252	3.988	.000
Year	4.831	17.572	.582	.275	.784
Country-wide rate	9.910	10.064	.060	.985	.326
Adverse inferences	60.196	6.845	.587	8.794	.000
Facts available	10.135	8.495	.069	1.193	.234
Carbazole violet pigment 23 (2004)	-40.728	229.493	-.136	-.177	.859
Carbon steel butt-weld pipe fittings (1992)	39.749	26.189	.165	1.518	.131
Certain hot-rolled carbon steel flat products (2001)	-57.704	176.678	-.337	-.327	.744
Collated roofing nails (1997)	-45.478	107.679	-.152	-.422	.673
Ferrosilicon (1993)	-3.176	49.788	-.011	-.064	.949
Ferrovanadium (2003)	-40.348	212.436	-.114	-.190	.850
Furfuryl alcohol (1995)	-13.868	73.344	-.046	-.189	.850
Helical spring lock washers (1993)	-18.938	41.354	-.063	-.458	.647
Honey (2001)	-31.946	176.875	-.121	-.181	.857
Industrial nitrocellulose (1990)	8.668	25.589	.040	.339	.735
Iron construction castings (1986)	25.459	89.838	.118	.283	.777
Melamine institutional dinnerware (1997)	-53.825	107.215	-.242	-.502	.616
Polyethylene retail carrier bags (2004)	-55.280	229.336	-.310	-.241	.810
Polyvinyl alcohol 1 (1996)	-5.196	90.169	-.022	-.058	.954
Polyvinyl alcohol 2 (2003)	-22.256	211.996	-.084	-.105	.916
Porcelain-on-steel cooking ware (1986)	32.037	89.998	.133	.356	.722
Potassium permanganate (1984)	33.392	125.194	.085	.267	.790
Preserved mushrooms (1999)	32.301	139.519	.155	.232	.817
Silicomanganese 1 (1994)	3.633	59.124	.008	.061	.951
Silicon metal (1991)	39.950	22.201	.124	1.799	.073
Steel concrete reinforcing bars (2001)	-41.334	176.900	-.216	-.234	.815
Sulfanilic acid (1992)	-1.893	35.427	-.004	-.053	.957
Sulfur chemicals (1991)	-8.757	23.151	-.025	-.378	.706
Tapered roller bearings (1987)	12.952	73.025	.046	.177	.859

Source: GAO analysis of Commerce data.

Note: R-square = 0.562; Adjusted R-square = 0.502; Observations = 243.

These analyses confirmed our China-market economy only analyses but also showed that other NME countries tend to have duty rates that are statistically higher than market economy rates for this sample of matching cases. (Note that the number of additional products—six—is relatively small.) Controlling for both the NME designation and the country-wide rate, the NME designation itself is a significant variable at the 97 percent level of confidence with a coefficient of 23 percent (the coefficient for China is not statistically significant). The country-wide variable is also significant (99 percent level) and larger with a coefficient of 48 percent. As additional variables are added for individual products, the NME designation continued to be significant along with the country-wide rate variable.

There may be other systematic factors not accounted for in this regression model that would explain some of the variability not accounted for by the variables we included. As shown in table 7, our model accounted for about 50 percent (half) of the variation in rates. Some of this variation may be idiosyncratic and related to differences in individual companies' practices, other may relate to how Commerce has implemented its analysis. However, these unexplained factors do not appear to be systematically related to whether the case involved China or a market economy since the regression analysis already controls for that difference.

APPENDIX IV.

Comments from the Department of Commerce

Note: GAO comments supplementing those in the report text appear at the end of this appendix.

See comment 1.

The following are GAO's comments on the Department of Commerce's letter dated December 8, 2005.

GAO COMMENTS

1. We re-examined our data, making corrections as appropriate, and updated our analyses. The report reflects these corrections, though they did not have a significant impact on any of our findings.
2. As discussed in the report, the overall difference between the duty rates applied to China and those applied to market economy countries is largely explained by the application of comparatively high countrywide rates to China. Therefore, the model allows us to conclude that elimination of the NME methodology—and thus these country-wide rates—would result in lower duties for some Chinese companies. Nevertheless, there would still be variation in duty rates among companies and products due to a range of other factors.

INDEX

C

D

E

J

K

L

M

N

O

T

U

V